# MURDER

## *in*

# MONTE CARLO

# MURDER
## *in*
# MONTE CARLO

## MICHAEL SHERIDAN

POOLBEG

Published 2011
by Poolbeg Books Ltd
123 Grange Hill, Baldoyle
Dublin 13, Ireland
E-mail: poolbeg@poolbeg.com
www.poolbeg.com

1

A catalogue record for this book is available from the British Library.

ISBN 978-1-84223-471-6

Typeset by Patricia Hope in Sabon 11/15.5
Printed and bound by CPI Group (UK) Ltd, Croydon, CR0 4YY

www.poolbeg.com

## ABOUT THE AUTHOR

Michael Sheridan is the bestselling true crime author of *Death in December*, an investigation into the murder of French film producer Sophie Toscan du Plantier; *Frozen Blood: Serial Killers in Ireland; A Letter to Veronica; Tears of Blood* and *Bloody Evidence*. He is co-author and ghostwriter of *Don't Ever Tell: Kathy's Story*, an account of Kathy O'Beirne's traumatic childhood, which spent 22 weeks in the UK top ten and was a *Sunday Times* bestseller.

In 2010 his bestselling *Murder at Shandy Hall (The Coachford Poisoning Case)* was published by Poolbeg.

Michael previously worked for the *Irish Press* and the *Sunday Independent* as a freelance journalist.

# ACKNOWLEDGEMENTS

Gaye Shortland, the editor from heaven, always punctilious with her unerring eye, and most of all encouraging. Every writer should have a Gaye Shortland.

The team at Poolbeg: Paula, Kieran, Sarah, Dave and all the rest of the staff.

My agent Christine, always able to deal with a howl and a moan.

The staff of Higgins in Clonskeagh: Debbie, Niall, John, Dave, Ronan.

The staff of the National Library, always helpful though undergoing the unmerciful cuts of an uncaring government whose denizens seem to suffer nothing themselves.

Alain Spilliaert, advocate of Paris, who has been always ready to inform about the French system of law.

My family: Ger, Cian and Fionn, Sarah and Marty and mother Patsy for putting up with the usual obsession.

To Aoife,

*light in my heart of darkness*

# CONTENTS

# INTRODUCTION

At the time of the murder chronicled in this book, the French investigative and judicial process was then, as now, inquisitorial. This differed from the adversarial system used in Britain and Ireland. In an adversarial system, the investigation is conducted by the police, the court later acting as impartial referee between prosecution and defence. In an inquisitorial system the court is actively involved in investigating the facts of the case from the start. The police get on with the investigation but under the instruction of a public prosecutor and an examining magistrate.

Thus, when the facts of the case in question were established at an early stage by the police investigation, a court process was begun by the examining magistrate, leading over a lengthy period to the actual trial – a process that very much suited the purposes of newspapers, as anything aired in court was in the public domain. The sensational details of such a case as this could be ventilated in public, generally speaking, without fear of legal retribution. There was nothing to prevent the Fourth Estate from engaging in the matter of concurrent investigation, to satisfy the public interest. This they did with great enthusiasm – their reportage, in fact, delivered with more enthusiasm than accuracy.

At a time when French criminologists and forensic experts were pre-eminent in their field, the matter of the background and psychology of the perpetrators of crime was considered important, as the ultimate punishment for murder was the guillotine. Extenuating circumstances could save a killer from death, commuting the sentence to life imprisonment. That could result in a benefit to the convicted – but not always, as the murder under consideration will prove.

In all ages there was and is an uneasy relationship between crime and punishment. Without giving too much away, there existed then in the French system, and for many decades later, penal colonies which were in essence death camps, with no redeeming features for the condemned, whatever the nature of their crimes. It was an issue that, in the light of the outcome of this murder, I felt worth examining.

From this and other issues of reconstruction, there arose the question of how best, in style and construction, to deal with them. A murder that occurs in an enclosed space with no witnesses is by its nature subject to reconstruction by police and judicial authorities, none of whom, it can be said, were there at the time. It requires, therefore, a nexus between facts gathered and an exercise of informed imagination. When two people are involved in the commission of a murder, it may well serve one or another to supply a different version of the event. This proved to be the fact in the two interrelated cases dealt with in this book. Hence, while an author usually wants to shun the border between what are conventionally described as fact and fiction, that borderline was the terrain I felt appropriate to explore in this case.

My aim was, I hesitate to say, to give life to the characters, or to bring to life the people involved at both the centre and periphery of the case, all now consigned to their respective graves. The vast majority of them have their real names. To the Marseilles police investigation team, undoubtedly crucial to the outcome but not mentioned in dispatches, I have taken the liberty to assign names. As to some at the Monte Carlo end.

Apart from the exigencies of the subject matter, I would like to mention the encouragement – not the possible blame – of a reviewer of my last book *Murder at Shandy Hall*. That is, if she does not mind my mentioning her name – Alannah Hopkin who writing for the *Examiner* said that I should let my imagination run more. I have done so and in an unlikely scenario between writer and critic, but well appreciated, have taken her advice.

# PROLOGUE

Nothing in his life had prepared him for this. His mind was a whirlpool of conflicting thoughts and emotions. Outside and inside the villa complex there was sunshine, laughter, enjoyment, eating, drinking, gambling, wealth, debauchery and all the other things that constitute the pursuits of human existence and expectation. Inside their apartment nothing but sheer fright and horror.

The dwindling of money, the panic that ensues when wondering where the next franc would come from, now seemed more a pleasure than a painful experience. There must have been a better alternative, a more civilised way of dealing with the onset of poverty. They could have promised, could have begged, stolen – anything but this with its terrible outcome that had for some reason previously escaped his drunken imagination.

Why had he agreed to his wife's plan? Because he was a weak, drunken, foolish man paralysed by his inadequacies. It had made no sense at the time and even less now.

The waft of cooking emanated from a neighbouring apartment, making him feel sick. But he knew he could not move to the bathroom.

He had carried out his part of the plan while his wife engaged the female visitor in conversation. A woman who was perceived to be the cause of their problems but was not. All their misfortunes were of their own making. He had downed another whisky while in the kitchen and then had taken the pestle in his hand. His hand was shaking, so he downed another drink.

Violence had never been part of his flawed nature. The only object he had ever hit with great intent and determination was a tennis ball in the great flush of his youth. The only person he had wanted to put away was an opponent on the court, and even that with the grace of skill rather than any aggression.

And now he was to hit an innocent woman over the head to stun her and to rob her of her much-vaunted jewellery and any cash she possessed. It made no sense. Even in their desperation. But his wife insisted and she had always got her way. He would have rather died in poverty, but she had other ideas and told him that he was responsible for the awful position they found themselves in. He had tried to argue. It was no good – he had lost all the arguments before, a long time ago.

It was no use. He staggered from the kitchen and quickly brought the pestle down as hard as he could on the back of the woman's head. The visitor fell to the floor, gurgling with shock, and then let out a scream. She was alive and tried to get up. He dropped the pestle on the floor. His wife was screaming at him but it was as if he heard nothing.

It was all happening a distance from him or, rather, he was distanced from it. He could and would do no more. He saw his wife as in a nightmare pounce on the unfortunate woman. They struggled and there were more screams.

"The dagger, the dagger!"

He walked in a waking dream to the sideboard, picked up the dagger and handed it to his wife who was punching the squealing victim and being scratched in return. He saw the flash of it as it was plunged into the chest of the struggling woman. He heard the slowly descending gurgle and saw the blood streaming from her nose. He ran to the bathroom and vomited the undigested contents of the whisky bottle.

"Come back here, come back!" His wife's order reverberated around the bathroom.

He rushed back to the living room. She handed him the knife. "Push it in, push it in!"

The woman was lying face to the ground. He shoved the bloodstained dagger into her back. It went through to the hilt.

"Pull it out!"

He did and, with a final gurgle and a tremor all over her body, the woman lay still.

He knew in that instant his life was over. The blood all over the carpet and seeping across the living room floor was evidence enough. He trembled from head to toe, ran back to the kitchen and put the whisky bottle to his mouth. He could hardly breathe with the shock of it all.

Tears rolled down his drunken face. What had his dissolute life been all about? Anything but this. The woman had done him no wrong. He wanted to join her in death right now. He was awoken from his instant remorse by a clunk on the kitchen sink. When he wiped away his tears a large knife and a saw came into focus.

"Now remember what comes next. She will be home soon. You know what we must do."

He did not want to go back to the sitting room. But now there was no choice. He did not want to look into those dead staring eyes that would haunt him for the rest of his life. But his wife said he must overcome such scruples. *There is nothing either good or bad, but thinking makes it so.* They would remove the body to the bathroom first, do the necessary and then plan the next move.

What did she mean by necessary? What next move? There would be blood everywhere and how could they get rid of those damned spots? Not to mind that damned guilt. He had no idea. All their time together, living on the edge, she had the ideas – as she would now. Maybe there was a way forward. He would listen to her suggestions and agree as he always had done.

As always there was no choice, no alternative. That had been the path of their lives. There was only one way forward, or backward. But he felt utterly sick in his heart and that had been the case for a very long time.

The rest was a blur of hacking, cutting and cleaning of a now inanimate thing that had once been a living human being. Blood provides the greatest challenge to erase after spilling in a variety of spots, splatters and formations from the body. Not to mind the soul which is beyond the constraints of the visible.

⁓

The sea was a dark shade of purple and blue under the scimitar moon. He looked furtively behind him and almost jumped at the small flat whale-like shape of Cap Martin. His nerves were shredded and he nearly let the bag slide out of his hand. From the white sand of the beach of Larvotto, the lights of Monte Carlo twinkled. From the direction of the seafront the warm wind carried sounds of gaiety. Their comforting timbre served only to mock him as he scuttled like a crab along the beach, fearful of encountering a human form.

He looked for an outlet that would carry the contents of his bag as far out to sea as possible. His glazed eyes were drawn to the moon from the shimmering reflection of its light on the calm surface of the sea. It watched him, unmoved, immutable. He trembled and trudged on, the sand tugging quietly at his feet.

The light reminded him of the streams of gold that flowed from the croupier's hands, and he could hear the dull thud of scattered coins on the table. It sent a shiver right down his spine. The cloying sense of greed that the image evoked was now a source of repulsion, for it was not a bag of coins he was carrying. The contents slid around as he stumbled on a mound of flotsam. Was it for this that he had stood around the tables, transfixed with trepidation? Always searching for something, a sign, a play, calculating, taking notes of the roll of the ball, the expression of the players, anything – even a hint of superstition – to lead to a reversal of fortune? But nothing turned in his favour and he was beset by more feverish thoughts and sudden false expectation that tomorrow would provide the break, and if not the following morrow. His chances were as good as being born all over again or rising from the grave given him by the dead hand of fate.

Of course he played the hand – it was his nature and nothing had ever changed that. It was copper-fastened by his companion in life, whose nature was the same if not worse. Without a check on that dual nature, nothing had even the remotest chance of improving their circumstances. Tomorrow it would all be ended. But now there was no tomorrow but certain ruin.

He slid across a number of small rocks beyond a turn in the beach. There in a modest gulf was a fast-flowing outlet. He opened the top of the bag, averted his eyes and slid the slippery stinking contents into the water. He heard a sickening plop and a gurgle. He dropped the bag in too and the current bore it away. He turned quickly away and made his way to the seashore and immersed his hands into the soft waves to wash them.

He gazed towards the moonlit horizon. If he walked towards that horizon it would be all over in a matter of minutes. But he lacked, as he always had, the courage of any conviction. Unlike his ancient ancestor, the crusader who had fought with distinction in Damietta. Unlike his domineering father, the resolute magistrate in Waterford who unflinchingly opposed the Fenian rebels.

The silent beauty of this place put the horror that he had left behind in the Villa Menesini into perspective. He shed some cowardly tears, for nothing or no one in particular, not for himself or the victim. He dreaded the return, and the dreadful aftermath of the awful act. He dragged himself to his feet and retraced his passage along the beach and onwards in the direction of Boulevard des Moulins.

The steps afterwards he did not dare to contemplate.

# PART ONE

# 1

## LA BELLE ÉPOQUE

La Belle Époque ('The Beautiful Era') was a period in European social history between the Great Depression of the 1870-1880's and the advent of World War I. It was so named in retrospect, when it began to seem like a lost 'golden age'. It roughly corresponded to the 'Gilded Age' in the United States (the boom period circa 1870–98) and the late Victorian Age in Britain. Like any boom that follows a bust, it encompassed the realities of expansion, care-free attitudes, faith in progress and an affluence spreading down through society. The approach of a new century signalled notable developments in fashion, art, literature, feats of engineering, technological progress and general economic wellbeing. These characteristics were common to boom times past and no doubt future, the good aspects and the bad.

There was a mood of optimism about the future, thanks in part to what at the time were considered extraordinary innovations in technology which created an aura of excitement and new belief in the fruits of human endeavour. This was manifest on the streets of Europe, in cafés, cabarets, art galleries, concert halls and salons, places frequented by the new middle

13

classes who benefited most in new status and income from economic stability and progress.

## POLITICS

This prosperity was aided and abetted by a new-found political stability with the establishment of the Third Republic in 1870 after the collapse of the Second French Empire of Louis-Napoléon III following defeat in the Franco-Prussian War. The new Republican Government survived the acute polarisation of the left, heir to the tenets of the French Revolution, and the right, rooted in rural areas, the Church and the army, wary of progress unless it was controlled by the traditional elite, including the remnants of the aristocratic classes.

It would become the longest-serving government in the country since the collapse of the ancien régime in the revolution of 1789. A series of parliamentary acts established the constitutional laws of the new republic. At its head was a 'President of the Republic' and a two-chamber parliament composed of a directly elected 'Chamber of Deputies' and an indirectly elected Senate. There was also a ministry under a 'President of the Council' answerable to the President of the Republic and the Parliament.

Governments during the Third Republic collapsed with regularity, many lasting only a few months as a result of radicals, socialists, liberals, conservatives and monarchists all vying for control. But the net result was that this often simply resulted in a formation of new alliances and ministerial shuffles and the government continued to function.

Despite a number of scandals, including the collapse of the Panama Canal project (1893) causing huge losses to investors, the Dreyfus Affair (1894-1906) and the separation of Church and State (1905), the government proved it was more than capable of weathering storms. As the first president of the Third Republic, Adolphe Thiers remarked: "Republicanism is the form of government that divides France least."

The Third Republic, in line with the imperialistic ethos sweeping Europe, developed a worldwide network of colonies, the largest in North Africa and Vietnam.

## TECHNOLOGY

After the depression years, the economy of France entered a period of sustained growth in what was termed the second industrial revolution. The rail network was largely extended with the ensuing growth of services in locations along the routes. And there was a succession of inventions that fundamentally altered people's lives for the better, including the harnessing and introduction of electricity, the combustion engine, photographs, film, the telephone and the bicycle.

These technological advances, and there were more to come, made life easier at all levels of society. The growing command of engineering in steel was dramatically expressed by the Eiffel Tower, the Viaduc de Garabit and the Grand Palais in Paris. All this progress impacted on the population with a sense of pride, optimism and the feeling that anything was possible.

The World Fair of 1889, when the Eiffel Tower was opened to the public, and the Universal Exhibition of 1900 put Paris and France on the European and world map as a lively and expanding place in international society. For the Universal Exhibition many new buildings were erected, often with the then-novel electric lighting. One of the main attractions was the Palais de l'Electricité, illuminated by 5,000 multicoloured lights at night and an electronic-powered triple-decker moving footpath. Paris became known as the City of Lights.

The Universal Exhibition attracted 50 million visitors from all parts of the world and France became a hugely popular destination for tourists. A person could travel throughout Europe without a passport. The English from different social groups came to France in great numbers during this period. The winter was a popular season for visiting, to escape the bleak northern weather. People of more limited means as well as the idle rich targeted France, the former because of low prices and the good weather. The latter disported themselves on the Mediterranean coast and in particular the Côte d'Azur. There were so many English people staying in Nice that the main road along the seafront was named La Promenade des Anglais.

Cheap coal and labour contributed to the cult of the orchid and the perfection of fruits gown under glass. And that French essential, champagne, was also perfected at the time.

## THE ARTS

Theatre adopted new forms of presentation and shocked contemporary audiences with frank depictions of ordinary daily life and sexuality.

Cabaret theatre was popular along with 'salon music', usually for solo piano and violin in the romantic style, and performed by composers at events known as salons. Operettas drew huge crowds and European literature went through a transformation with literary realism and naturalism to the fore, typified by Émile Zola and Guy de Maupassant.

Since the 18th century, Paris had been leading the way in fashion in all the courts of Europe but it was during the Belle Époque that 'haute couture' was 'invented' there and fashion began to move in a yearly cycle. Interestingly, it is an English *couturier* based in Paris from the late 1840's, Charles Frederick Worth, who is considered the father of *haute couture*, being the first to promote the concept of dressmaker as artist – as 'fashion designer'.

The vogue was heavy silks and satins with wide hats festooned with flowers and feathers. Lace was applied liberally to add even more heavy-handed femininity to the S-bend corset, contorting the bosom forward and thrusting the hips back. It was no time for revealing cleavage and necklines were very high.

At the Exhibition of 1889 Herminie Cadolle showed her new invention, the forerunner of the bra. As a simple ingenious idea for women's comfort, she cut in two the traditional corset, initially calling it a '*corselet gorge*'. She was the first to encourage the spinners of Troye to incorporate rubber into the threads of fabric and elastic thread would soon take over from whalebones and lacing.

By the end of the 19th century the horizons of fashion had broadened, partly due to the more stable and independent lifestyle of many well-off women who were getting the practical clothes they demanded. As yet, no fashionable lady would or could dress or undress herself without the help of a third party. The outfits of the couturiers of the time were incredibly extravagant, elaborate and labour-intensive.

The Maison Redfern, the highly prestigious Paris fashion house – opened by yet another Englishman, *couturier* John Redfern in 1881 – was the first fashion establishment to offer women a tailored suit, based directly on the male version, and the elegant garment soon became part of the wardrobe of any well-dressed woman.

Also indispensable was the designer hat. Fashionable hats at the time were either tiny little things that perched on top of the head, or large and wide-brimmed, trimmed with ribbons, flowers and feathers. Parasols were still used as decorative accessories and in the summer dripped with lace which added to the overall pretty impression.

The period marked the appearance of fashion magazines which were greatly sought after and had a profound effect on public taste. Talented illustrators, among them Paul Iribe, Georges Lepape and George Barbier drew exquisite fashion plates for the publications.

So much for the buoyant carefree aspects of the Belle Époque, whose glittering surface was underpinned by the availability of cheap labour. There was a downside, of course, as there always is during a boom time.

## CRIME

An increase in criminality at the end of the 19th century was attributed to rapid industrialisation, urbanisation and the explosion of the railway networks. This gave rise to a mindset on the part of the French public, the newspapers and some French politicians which held that criminal behaviour was innate and concentrated in certain classes of individuals.

So to protect society these criminals were to be banished to peripheral areas. The hope was that those devoted to crime would become agents in the service of France's larger colonial projects, as well as proving that such incarceration and punishment would be a further deterrent to crime.

In 1885 the French Parliament passed the Relegation Act whereby petty recidivists would be exiled as *relégués* to French Guiana and New Caledonia after serving prison terms in France. In these colonies they would occupy an intermediary position between the few free colonists and the condemned criminals known as *forçats*. It would prove to be a disastrous law, leading to brutalisation of the prisoners by sadistic guards (whose conditions were hardly any better than their charges'), and an uncaring administration with poor communication with the colonial authorities.

At home, the French took the lead in criminal investigation, forensic science and identification procedures, well ahead of the rest of the world including the much-vaunted Scotland Yard in the home of the traditional enemy, Britain. They also took the enlightened view that the background and psychology of the perpetrators of crime should be carefully examined and their sanity certified by qualified psychologists. The ultimate punishment for murder was the guillotine and extenuating circumstances were taken into consideration.

Then, as now, every criminal investigation was preyed upon by the Law's constant shadow, the Fourth Estate – *Le Quatrième Pouvoir* (literally, 'The Fourth Power').

## THE NEWSPAPERS

Newspapers in France and England and across the Atlantic were undergoing huge changes, driven both by the new technology and increasing battles for circulation. The telegraph and the telephone were transforming news into instant global communication. Linotype was introduced in 1890, using a keyboard to select letters and set one line of hot metal type at a time, thereby facilitating production.

There was also the emergence of what was termed 'yellow journalism'.

Yellow journalism is that which presents little or no legitimate or well-researched news. Techniques were the exaggeration of news events, scandalmongering and sensationalism. The term was used extensively to describe certain New York City papers about 1900 as they battled for circulation. The norm was scare headlines in big print, use of faked interviews, pseudo-science, a parade of false learning from so-called experts and dramatic sympathy with the underdog against the system. Circulation battles raged between Joseph Pulitzer's *New York World* and William Randolph Hearst's *New York Journal,* and Ervin Wardman's sedate *New York Herald* coined the term 'yellow journalism' (inspired apparently by a cartoon character The Yellow Kid which was run as a comic strip in both his rivals' papers). Yellow journalism became a recognisable and even bold genre in the late 19th and early 20th centuries and certainly could not be called predictable, boring or uninspired.

The *New York Times* established itself as the antithesis of irresponsible crass journalism. It often condemned the excesses of the genre, especially those of Hearst's *Journal*. Under the ownership of Adolph Ochs who acquired the newspaper in 1896, the *Times* nominally sought to position itself as an impartial, fact-based model of journalism that eschewed extravagance and flamboyance in presenting the news. The *Times* frequently challenged the wisdom and ethics of that active journalism which often created the news as opposed to reacting to events: for example, in 1897, a journalist springing a prisoner and then reporting on the fact of it. There were no pictures or outrageous headlines in the *Times* – serious newspapers considered illustrations inappropriate distractions from the newspaper's prose.

In general there was not much difference between imaginative writing and objective reporting. Matthew Arnold coined the term 'new journalism' in his 1887 essay 'Up To Easter' to describe what he considered a more sensational and less intellectually stimulating form of journalism which appeared in newspapers in Britain, France and the United States at the end of the 19th century.

*New York Sun* owner Charles Dana once described late 19th century journalism as a lawless field: "There is no system of maxims or professional rules that I know of laid down for the guidance of the journalist."

Leading newspapers believed that making news was a creative act. Pulitzer insisted that his reporters produce: "What is original, distinctive, dramatic, romantic, thrilling, unique, curious, humorous, odd, apt-to-be-talked-about, without impairing the confidence of the people in the truth of the character of the paper for reliability and scrupulous cleanness."

Dana of the *Sun* held a similar view: "The inimitable law of the newspaper is to be interesting. Suppose you tell all the truths of a science in a way that bores the reader; what is the good? The truths don't stay in the mind and nobody thinks any better of you because you have told the truth tediously. The telling must be vivid and animating."

In other words, the truth told in flat and objective terms would be boring, supposedly, however astounding the fact.

During a time when by-lines were scarce, anonymous reporters wrote and figured themselves into the news stories. *Sun* reporter Julian Ralph stated: "The reporter is a modern knight errant, whose work brings him in contact with a wide and varied collection of peoples, subjects and situations."

The main currents of the 19th century news ran through the telegraph wires, but first of all were collected by the intrepid reporters. When the wires companies, like Reuters Associated Press and the Press Association arrived in the latter half of the century, the reporters were reined in to an extent – there was at least some degree of censorship in operation. Now as a result the reporters were hunting in packs, because no individuals could hold up the lines. When on foreign duty information had to be shared. The day of the intrepid lone reporter was largely over. The reporters delivered copy to the telegraph office and their reports largely were syndicated through the agencies. It did not entirely wipe out the rush for the exclusive but technology helped on one hand and limited on the other.

By 1907, and before global news communication was a fact of life, the Monte Carlo Trunk Murder provided a classical example. But news reports far away from the ground in Marseilles and Monte Carlo proved that the newspapers and the reporters could rapidly follow up every lead in any country which had historical association through the travels of the perpetrators in the case.

This case burned the wires from France to England, Australia, New York and Ireland, serving at a relatively early stage of proceedings to prompt these remarks from a clearly tetchy *Irish Times* leader writer in an editorial:

One would be justified after perusal of last week's newspapers to conclude that the personages implicated in the Monte Carlo murder mystery are the most important people in the world at present. Every petty and morbid detail in connection with the crime is set forth with wearying minuteness. Surely there are other topics just as interesting and decidedly more edifying to which this space might be devoted. The literary productions known as 'penny horribles' are mild and harmless when compared with the way in which the most disgusting crimes are dished up for the public by the average newspaper.

The editor of the paper begged to disagree, however, for the newspaper carried extensive reports of the crime supplied largely by Reuters and the Press Association correspondents in Paris, Marseilles and Monte Carlo as did its sober counterpart the *New York Times*. Then, as now, reporting was characterised by a mixture of speculation, inventiveness and hard fact.

In that boom era of the Belle Époque in Europe, the Gilded Age in the United States and late Victorian Britain, murder of a certain kind was big news as was financial speculation on stocks and shares, both of which entailed a gamble which would decide success or ruin. As long as the Wheel of Fortune is spinning in the right direction, society is gripped by euphoria, an irrational exuberance which precludes any chance of the sequence ending. The lessons of the past are smothered by this optimism; history is of no consequence. All that matters is the rosy future. Gainsayers are thrust aside, prophets of doom cast out – those most apt to remember simple truths like that of Ovid on the matter of fortune: "The goddess who admits by her unsteady wheel her own fickleness; she always has its apex beneath her swaying foot."

In Monte Carlo in August 1907 the gaming rooms of the splendid casino were packed with the rich, the famous, the beautiful, the desperate, all hoping to break the bank before it broke them.

And in that other great casino, thousands of miles across the Atlantic, their counterparts were engaged in a similar exercise on the New York Stock Exchange. By the end of the first week and beginning of the second, unwelcome attention would be drawn to both houses of chance by the tragedy that always lurks in the midst of gamblers playing for stakes that have gone far beyond their control.

In both instances the fallout would reach a dramatic climax in November and December of that year.

On August 7th, the *New York Times* carried this report:

# W. S. Alley A Suicide

## Lost All In Stocks

The "Rocking Chair Fleet" on the piazza of the Larchmount Yacht Club, rocked away last night without its principal and chief member, its veritable Pooh Bah, William Alley.

Life at Larchmount, where Mr Alley lived the year round with his family, was placid and sweet. His house was within a toss of a stone from the sound, where in his palmy days, his champion sloop, the Schemer, showed her neat lines to him from his own piazza of a morning. But life in Wall Street, where Mr Alley strove to increase his fortune, proved a tempest he could not weather. His father before him, George B. Alley, had accumulated a large fortune and had died after a successful life, leaving much wealth to his family.

But "Bill" Alley as his fellow yachtsmen and members of "The Rocking Chair" coterie knew him hit the market at the wrong angle all the time.

Yesterday Wall Street heard that "Bill" Alley was dead.

"How?" was asked by broker after broker, for all of them knew he had been compelled to sacrifice his seat on the Exchange and that not only was every dollar of his money gone, but that he was also burdened with debt.

"Blew out his brains!" was the reply of those who had come to town from Larchmount. "In the club last night. He slipped away from the crowd and finished in a quiet corner."

Mr Alley left his home, a short distance from the club on Monday afternoon and spent the cool, early evening chatting with friends in the club and on the piazzas. He appeared in good humour, and a number of friends commented on his courage in standing up under the disasters he had met on the Street.

Then he excused himself, returned to a distant corner, where nobody could interfere with him, pulled a revolver from his pocket and shot himself through the right temple. He was still living when the club attendants and friends reached him. They hurried him to the New Rochelle Hospital but he died there five minutes after he had been put to bed.

Although he appeared to be jovial at all times, some of his friends say that when he was suspended from the Exchange because of a judgment obtained against him, he felt this keenly and protested that an injustice had been done him. The judgment was settled and he was reinstated. But another judgment was filed against him and he was crowded close to the wall. He sold his seat and filed a petition in bankruptcy. He gave the proceeds of the sale of his seat to his creditors, whose claims amounted to $191,000 and then retired to an obscure desk in the office of a brokerage in Exchange Place.

Yesterday when a Times reporter called at his home to inquire about the manner of his death, the place seemed a typification of the end of its owner. The lack of cash resources showed pathetically. The houses adjoining were spick and span, with velvety lawns and well-trimmed hedges and well-kept paths. The once bright abiding place of the popular yachtsman "Bill" Alley showed the unmistakeable signs of genteel poverty. His two young sons, bright little chaps, were playing ball on the untrimmed lawn, not realising their loss.

He is survived by his widow and two sons. He was 55 years old.

A report was current yesterday that Mr Alley killed himself so that his widow could collect the $10,000 insurance gratuity that the Stock Exchange provides for its members. Although Mr Alley had sold his seat on the Exchange, the transfer of his seat had not been made. The change in its possession will take place tomorrow.

Losses in the casino, especially in that Mecca of gamblers Monte Carlo, resulted in the same brand of desperation.

On August 9th, the *New York Times* reported a double suicide attempt:

# Woman Suicide an American

## Mrs Buckingham Brought a Fortune to Her Husband
## He Refuses Food

*Special Cablegram*

Rome, August 8th

The identity of the couple who attempted suicide at Castellamare, the woman dying and the man surviving, has now been established. The man, John Buckingham, who is now in hospital in Naples where he is constantly watched, is an Englishman, an engineer. His wife was a Miss Jenny Ensign, a native of Massachusetts, and lately of New York, whence she brought a considerable fortune. This fortune was entirely lost in gambling at Monte Carlo.

The couple drank a mixture of laudanum and arsenic, leaving a letter saying they wished to die together.

Since the death of his wife, Buckingham has made two attempts to jump out of the window. He refuses to take food.

Meanwhile in Marseilles another tragedy was unfolding which had its origins in the gilded halls of the Monte Carlo Casino.

# 2

## LA GUILLOTINE SÈCHE

The air is thick and heavy, the sky black as ink. A genuine day of death and burial.

How often there recurs to my mind that exclamation of Schopenhauer, at the spectacle of human iniquity:

*"If God created the world, I would not be God."*

Dry heat; the rainy season is near its end. I am covered with sores from the stings of mosquitoes and other insects. But all this is nothing! What are my physical sufferings as compared with the horrible tortures of the soul? Only infinitesimal. It is the aching head and heart which cry aloud with grief.

Such wild, fierce anger sometimes fills my heart against all human iniquity, that I could wish to tear my flesh, so as to forget, in physical pain, this horrible mental torture.

They will certainly end by killing me through repeated sufferings, or by forcing me to commit suicide to escape from insanity.

ALFRED DREYFUS: *Five Years of My Life* 1894-1899

## FRENCH GUIANA, 1908

The insufferable sun was high in the noonday sky, blazing down on the baked surface of the earth. Omnipotent, untouchable, dispensing the largesse of its unforgiving rays, merciless and unrelenting. All exposed melted; the rest, when they could, scuttled anywhere there was refuge of a shadow and when allowed clung to the base of the tall trees. The very trees that were to be felled by the blunt edges of their axes, cheating themselves of succour.

The skin, the brain boiled under the daily attention of that blinding orb in the sky. Other people in safe places would have raised their bodies to it in admiration and supplication. Not here. Here there was no protection other than the flimsy straw hat which offered no resistance to the constant whiplash of nature, all its contrasts in this part of the world extreme.

The dry season or the wet season made no difference; it was simply the replacement of one form of suffering by another. Standing stock-still might have offered a little relief but the effects were amplified by the hourly and daily exertion of felling, cutting and stacking wood to meet the insane daily quota.

In the intense heat, water sweated from every pore, and when the monsoon had its say, water poured into every pore, the whiplashes of a different but no less merciless nature. The punishing exertion was both physically and mentally debilitating. Every withered muscle creaked at every rise and fall of the axe, the flaccid legs groaned with weakness; the heart lurched and palpitated, the eyes stung in the glare and were blinded by the salt of perspiration. If there were a purpose to the work, a tangible objective, some even tiny incremental gain, some small comfort could have been derived. There was none.

The stomach emitted its gurgling from lack of nourishment, the black coffee of the morning long absorbed, the meagre midday ration quickly gone – nothing but emptiness, pain and degradation the daily sustenance. On top of it, the constant attack of the insects, the mosquitoes biting into every inch of exposed flesh, the sliding snakes a frightening threat. And then the trooping back to the ghastly huts and the prospect of the fear of the long darkness of the night.

Not even exhaustion provided relief. No such small mercy allowed in this man-made hell and intentional collaboration with nature. Nothing but darkness visible for the condemned.

He had been only there for a couple of weeks and the mental and physical torture was worse than anything he had feared; he felt already broken in mind and spirit. Everyone here was a prisoner of his own actions and conscience, everyone had expected punishment – but not one of such merciless construction. The purpose of its creation was to condemn the inmates to slow death by carefully planned increments. Little surprise the penal colony had been given the sobriquet of La Guillotine Sèche – 'The Dry Guillotine'.

However monstrous the crimes of the inmates, and his fitted this category but many others did not, this fate was beyond belief in the evil of its intent. Here was a retribution that even Robespierre's Reign of Terror could not match. The communication of the administration's past and present iniquities spread quickly among them in a very short time after their arrival. Which had the effect of obliterating every last vestige of hope that might be entertained.

Death bad, but death without hope incomprehensible.

The regime spared neither young nor old and even the most vigorous of constitution would be reduced to a physical wreck within six months. The climate alone without intervention could efficiently lead to mental and bodily deterioration. But the intervention of labour, harsh living conditions and awful food accelerated the process. There was no escape from the grand design to eliminate the convicted wretches of French justice.

He wasn't a young man, and older than his years as a result of the dissipated habits of his life. The drinking, the constant excitement of gambling, the pressures of failed business ventures and the inevitable consequences of his final gamble, the dreadful crime, had already taken their toll on his once athletic body. Not to mention the ravages all that produced in his mind.

The 'wet guillotine' would have provided the appropriate resolution. This by the process of law was denied him. Instead he was condemned to hell on earth, a place that Satan, it had been said, could not have invented. A hell that was amplified in the waking moments of night by the haunting remembrance of things past, phantoms ever present in the rafters of the hut like the blood-sucking bats. He was an educated man, intelligent, from the best of backgrounds, an aristocrat from a line dating back to and beyond the Crusades. Therefore he once had infinitely better expectations in life than any of his fellows . . . had he not been fatally attracted to the Wheel of Fortune.

But who knows the future? Least of all a gambling man who will throw the last dice in the hope that in that gesture the future will be assured, which of course is rarely the case. He, now in the throes of the consequence of his last throw, was the classical example. There was nothing at the time to tell him where it would end. It was beyond his imagination.

The nights were as terrible, in their own fashion worse than the days. Sleep was no more than snatched moments. There was a constant shifting of painwracked bodies, recovering from the exertions of the intolerable labour of the day. The groans and moans of men, itching and scratching the sores inflicted by the insects. The gurgling of those gripped by fever and illness and the fetid stench of human odours. All in the shadow cast by the oil lamp in the central isle. It was a time infused by the dire expectation of the rigors of the following day, the inescapable reflection on the past and terror of what lay ahead.

There was no relief from fear, tension and anxiety in this brutal existence. No inch of room to block it out from the constantly racing mind, the fever of the now ever-present, the fever of the past ever ready to pounce. His old body would determine how long he lasted but his mind was lucid and he knew that this would remain, until the last, a far greater affliction. That and the ghost of memory, reminding him of the curse of life. He had yet to fully grasp what brought him to this pass, a member of the colony of the damned. Where it had all begun now escaped him, but no doubt the longer he survived this abyss, the more it would become clear.

In past centuries many members of his illustrious family had experienced the vicissitudes of fate and survived, reputation ultimately untarnished. Reputation, the one thing that would always defeat the worms of the grave. And he, he alone, had with one awful act destroyed not only his reputation but that of generations. He had already searched in vain for some small clue to the chink in his personality that had led to his downfall. He had inherited a God-given talent for sport, he had received an education that had befitted his status in the Anglo-Irish aristocracy. So why?

During his time of incarceration in France before the passage to this hell, he had incessantly read the Bible and Milton to somehow assuage the enormity of his act. It had, he now realised, been an exercise of escape from and denial of the consequence of his murderous nature. His desperation at that time did not excuse him. He denied, he lied and then he confessed. He blindly attempted a pathetic rehabilitation in the comfort of his civilised cell. It had all been for nought. Like the many times he had bet on zero on the roulette wheel, it had rolled on, like everything else in his cursed journey under the sun.

The infernal bell rang at half past five in the morning. Another call to the savage routine of labour in the jungle. He pulled his aching limbs from the hard board and lined up to receive in the battered tin cup the half pint of coffee that was to sustain him until the paltry lunchtime ration. The stench of the night had not abated. If anything, in the cold light of the morning, it was worse. That was always the way. He watched his wretched companions tie the towels around their thin, wasted midriffs and collect the straw hats. He averted his sight, as much as he could, from the sights of deprivation – the foul evidence of disease, the yellow stains of dysentery colouring the skeletal legs, ribs breaking through the diminished torsos, the eyes sunken into the large-seeming heads, the crazed look of the hopeless. All watched over by the well-fed guards, with bellies tumbling over their trousers, ready to inflict more punishment whenever necessary.

Then they were handed the tools of the useless trade, the blunt-edged axes, and trooped into the harsh light of the day. The monkeys ran and grunted in the trees, the exotic birds cried, the mosquitoes swarmed, and ants scurried and bit.

Later, much later, the small exhausted army trooped back to the hut, collapsed on the boards and waited for the onset of the night. And waited for the next move of the administration. The next move would never be better; worse conditions were always waiting.

All part of the grand design. One move of perceived rebellion, one attempted escape, led to another level of punishment and then another. If there were many mansions in heaven, there were equally as many in hell and just so in this French-designed Hades. All of the inmates were aware of the consequences of breaking the rules. It did not stop many of them doing it. Simply because anything, they thought, might be better than the brutal regime that they endured.

As an older man, his mental and physical energy could not endure the huge effort that would be required to escape but he understood the ambition of youth to imagine some other alternative to the appalling reality of their lives and blighted future. If he had been a younger man, that would also have been his ambition. Even if he realised it was all but impossible. Such are the impulses of the young. But for him it was too late. He was resigned to his fate. He would die here.

The fruits of his education came relentlessly back to torment him. His old tutor was an enthusiast of Milton and the poet's words, once learnt, had never left him. As his situation now stood, they were all the more relevant.

*No light, but darkness visible.*
*Served only to discover sights of woe.*
*Regions of sorrow, doleful shades, where peace*
*And rest can never dwell, hope never comes*
*That comes to all; but torment without end*
*Still urges, and a fiery deluge, fed*
*With every burning sulphur unconsumed*
*Such place eternal justice had prepared*
*For those rebellious, here their prison ordained*
*In utter darkness, and their portion set*
*As far removed from God and light of Heaven*
*As far from the Centre thrice to the utmost Pole.*
*O how unlike the place from whence they fell!*

The words of this genius he accepted as being both descriptive of his state and an accurate account of the institution that had been created here to house the inmates, as if it had been taken literally from this blank verse poem of the 17th century. Could this have been in the minds of the architects of this place? Close enough matched.

*What can be worse*
*Than to dwell here, driven out from bliss, condemned*
*In this abhorred deep to utter woe!*
*Where pain of unextinguishable fire*
*Must exercise us without hope of end*
*The vassals of his anger, when the scourge*
*Inexorable, and the torturing hour,*
*Calls us to penance?More destroyed than thus,*
*We should be quite abolished, and expire . . .*
*To perish rather, swallowed up and lost*
*In the wide womb of uncreated night.*

Those words of *Paradise Lost* resonated and described accurately his experience and that of all his companions in the camp. And around every corner of the god-forsaken promontory were worse levels of torture awaiting. But the blind Milton was utilising his imagination to describe in words the House of Satan, never realising that man could match and better his wonderful creation. And within this construction there were even more states of punishment than its earthly architects, the Directorate of Napoléon III, could have anticipated. They sowed the seeds, but those seeds had produced weeds of ghastly growth that would turn them in their graves if their dark interment could possibly allow. "*Hell is here*," as Marlowe observed, "*nor are we out of it*." As an advocate of Cromwell, Milton should have known this. And here, in French Guiana, was the proof.

These things constantly revisited his mind, as indeed all the moments of his time on this earth did, like a constant reel, replaying the chapters of his life that brought him to this frightful conclusion. It is a process that all mankind must endure, but rarely in such heightened circumstances. There are, in the so-called civilised world, opportunities to diminish or block out its effects, the embrace of some sort of induced oblivion – drink, drugs or the ultimate choice of suicide.

He had already weathered some of those alternatives, without success. He had frequently in the past been tempted by the final one but the thought of what would happen to his wife and his innocent niece had stopped him. The result of shunning the option had been worse and he regretted now that he had not taken it. The consequence he realised was far worse for both, quite apart from the inevitable path of his present suffering. It was still an option, though diminished now by opportunity. No. He must accept his punishment and endure it to the last moment, for the alternative would be proof positive of utter cowardice.

He had been provided with great support and consolation by the Catholic chaplain in Marseilles prison who procured for him not only the Bible but other books that would help him prepare for his destiny in French Guiana, where he was to learn that such kindness by penal authorities was completely unknown. Among the books *Paradise Lost*, Alfred Dreyfus's account of his incarceration in this same penal colony and, even more importantly *The Consolation of Philosophy* by Boethius, the sixth-century Roman. The priest assured him that of all his reading, excepting the Bible, Boethius' work would provide him with the greatest help to understand and deal with his predicament. This was so, not just for its speculation on life and fortune, but because of his own obsession with that wheel of chance and the inviolable facts of his antecedents, his birthright from the start leading to a life of privilege and success. Nothing should have interfered with his path, but such paths can lead to perdition whatever the signs. History proves it, suggested the chaplain, and he must learn from that and hope to move to an acceptance of his fate. He offered this example of Boethius to demonstrate that to be born under a good star does not necessarily lead to a happy conclusion of life.

The Roman philosopher Boethius was a major source for the medieval view of the Wheel of Fortune. Writing about it in his *Consolation of Philosophy*, while in prison and his own doom looming, he said:

> I know how Fortune is ever more friendly and alluring to those she strives to deceive, until she overwhelms them with grief beyond bearing, by deserting them when least expected. Are you trying to stay the force of her turning wheel? Ah, dull-witted mortal, if Fortune begin to stay still, she is no longer Fortune.

He had good reason to analyse the Wheel of Fortune.

Anicius Manlius Severinus Boethius (ca. 480–524 AD) belonged to an ancient family which included emperors Petronius Maximus and Olybrius and many consuls. His father, Flavius Manlius Boethius, was a consul in 487 after Odoacer deposed the last Western Roman Emperor and became the first "barbarian" King of Italy. Boethius was growing to manhood when Theodoric, the famous Ostrogoth, crossed the Alps and, in the name of the

35

emperor of the Byzantine or Eastern Roman Empire, Anastasius, defeated Odoacer. Theodoric ruled Italy essentially as an independent monarch although he was the nominal representative of Anastasius.

Boethius' parents died early and he was brought up by Symmachus, a good and saintly man, and later became his son-in-law. Highly educated and talented, he excelled in a variety of disciplines – as an orator, musician and philosopher. He valued his integrity and his honesty shone like a beacon in the murky world of politics. He entered the service of Theodoric and was raised by him to the head position in the civil administration (*magister officiorum*). Not only successful, he also had a very happy family life with his wife Rusticana and sons Symmachus and Boethius. He could have been forgiven for assuming that Fortune would be his lifelong ally. This seemed to be confirmed in 522 AD when by special favour his two young sons were appointed joint consuls and rode to the senate accompanied by senators and with the approval of the public. Boethius delivered a speech in honour of King Theodoric. It appeared that his future was assured.

But within a year he was a solitary prisoner exiled to Pavia, 500 miles from Rome, stripped of his honours and wealth, facing death. He had been falsely accused of treason with evidence of forged letters composed by his enemies.

The Emperor Anastasius had died. His successor was Justin, who was also advanced in years, but who had a forceful young nephew Justinian. Theodoric himself, now in his seventies, had only Athalaric, his infant grandson, as an heir. Theodoric suspected that some within his own court were conspiring against him in favour of a return to direct imperial rule. Several leading senators were arrested on suspicion of conspiracy, including Boethius.

Boethius was distraught with grief, outraged at the injustice of his misfortune and sought relief from his depression by writing *The Consolation of Philosophy*. The result is one of the greatest examples in the history of the incarcerated of, for want of another term, the 'prison diary'. He spares little of his suffering in the account. Using a combination of verse and prose he constructed a scenario in which the Divine Figure of Philosophy appears to him in the guise of a woman of supreme dignity and beauty and during a series of conversations convinces him of the vanity of regret for the lost gifts of his fortune, raises his mind to the contemplation of true good and makes clear to him the mystery of the world's moral government.

She consoles him by discussing the transitory nature of fame and wealth (no man can ever be truly secure until he has been forsaken by fortune) and the ultimate superiority of things of the mind, which she calls the "one true good". She contends that happiness comes from within. One's virtue is all because it cannot be affected by the vicissitudes of fortune.

Boethius considers such questions as the idea of free will versus predestination and determinism. He discusses the nature of virtue, happiness, human nature and justice. Humans are essentially good, he concludes.

Significantly, he believes that criminals are not to be abused, but rather treated with sympathy and respect, using the analogy of the doctor and patient as the ideal relationship between prosecutor and criminal.

The book became one of the most popular works of secular literature in Europe, read by statesmen, philosophers and theologians. The Middle Ages, with its vivid sense of an overruling fate, found in Boethius an interpretation of life closely akin to the spirit of Christianity, at a time of great political and economic upheaval. Its themes echoed throughout the Western canon: the female figure of Wisdom that informs Dante's ascent through the layered universe in *The Divine Comedy*, Milton's *Paradise Lost*, the reconciliation of opposing forces that find their way into Chaucer's tales and the Wheel of Fortune so apt and revealing in all generations from the apogee achieved in the Middle Ages.

The opening verses of *The Consolation of Philosophy* encapsulate Boethius' feelings of despair at his predicament:

They were the pride of my earlier bright-lived days: in my latter gloomy days they are the comfort of my fate; for hastened by unhappiness has age come upon me without warning, and grief hath set within me the old age of her gloom. White hairs are scattered untimely on my head and the skin hangs loosely from my worn-out limbs.

Happy is that death that thrusts not itself upon men in their pleasant years, yet comes to them at the oft-repeated cry of their sorrow. Sad is it how death turns away from the unhappy with so deaf an ear and will not close, cruel, the eyes that weep. Ill is it to trust to Fortune's bounty, and while yet she smiled upon me, the hour of gloom had well-nigh overwhelmed my head. Now has the cloud put off its alluring face wherefore without scruple my life drags out its wearying delays.

Why, O my friends, did ye so often puff me up, telling me that I was fortunate? For he that has fallen low did never firmly stand.

As thus she turns her wheel of chance with haughty hand, and presses on like surge of Euripus's tides, Fortune now tramples fiercely on a fearsome king, and now deceives no less a conquered man by raising from the ground his humbled face. She hears no wretches cry, she heeds no tears, but wantonly she mocks the sorrow which her cruelty has made. This is her sport; thus she proves her power; if in the selfsame hour one man is raised to happiness, and cast down in despair. 'Tis thus she shows her might.

Fortune addresses him and says:

"I turn my wheel that spins its circle fairly; I delight to make the lowest turn to the top, the highest to the bottom. Come you to the top if you will, but on this condition, that you think it no unfairness to sink when the rule of my game demands it . . . In any way, let not your spirit eat itself away: you are set in the sphere that is common to all, let your desire therefore be to live with your own lot of life, a subject of the kingdom of the world . . .

"Wild greed swallows what it has sought and still gapes wide for more. What bit or bridle will hold within its course this headlong lust, when, whetted by abundance of rich gifts, the thirst for possession burns? Never call we that man rich who is ever trembling in haste and groaning for that he thinks he lacks . . .

"One man's wealth is abundant but his birth and breeding put him to shame. Another is famous for his noble birth but would rather be unknown because he is hampered by his narrow means. With how much bitterness is the sweetness of man's life mingled!"

Boethius was executed at the age of 44 on October 23rd, 524, either killed with an axe or sword or clubbed to death. His remains were entombed in the church of San Pietro in Ciel d'Oro in Pavia. In his *Paradiso* Dante refers to him as "*the soul who pointed out the world's dark ways*".

❧

This profound book was the spiritual treasure offered him by the chaplain in Marseilles prison who tried to impress upon him the idea that if he could preserve his mind and spirit then he could withstand the terrible physical rigors that awaited him. If mind and spirit should collapse, everything else would follow. How was the holy and venerable chaplain to know that the administration was equally aware of that fact and had it factored into the regime of the *bagne* (penal labour camp)? The very basis of the modus operandi of the camp authorities was slow death by a thousand whips. In France such a policy, such ghastly conditions and terrible punishments, would have created a scandal. Indeed, no man with a vestige of reason or logic could have grasped the rationale of such gross, fetid and merciless inhumanity.

But because of the fact that the colony was thousands of miles away and a light was thrown but briefly in its direction by the brutal 1894 slaughter of the anarchists and the infamous incarceration of Dreyfus, the plight of the large population of inmates was ignored, the methods of the administration never questioned and the concept and conduct of the death camps allowed to operate with impunity.

Not alone a machine for producing well-defined, well-regulated uniform punishment, it was a factory churning out misery without rhyme or reason – the purpose of it all to crush the prisoners, and the pieces could fall where they might. Hardly anyone survived, even in the mid-term, the ravages of the system.

Dreyfus had been constantly tempted to commit suicide and he was totally innocent of the crime that brought him to the colony. He had been sustained only somewhat by that fact in his four-year incarceration but also by the love of his wife and his children and few close friends who believed in him. It could be said that he did not suffer the worst excesses of the prison regime, not being thrown into the suffering, desperate and dangerous communal pit but locked up in a tiny cottage built for purpose. But he was exposed to the same crushing of the body and the spirit at the heart of the administration and, in common with the inmates that he was kept separated from, descended into regular states of deep depression and despair. And he felt another common sensation, one of being nailed to the rack, and another that his brain was melting and that he was going mad.

Unlike Dreyfus, *he* was guilty; his wife was in prison and his niece cast to the winds as a result of his weakness and his crime. There was nothing left but to survive until his body was thrown to the sharks.

However dreadful the prospect, he had to face it. He had read of the shame and punishment of Dreyfus when he himself was in a seemingly much better place. He was not, as he realised, so bitter now. He was consigned to utter shame, without possibility of redemption, but the fate of the Jewish military man, just in the past year restored by official pardon, curiously had inspired him to accept his own, last torturous descent into this hellish world.

He had read of the journey of Dreyfus at the time it had happened; it had but fleetingly caught his attention then, but now he was absorbed by it. It was an object lesson that he could take in the midst of his suffering. A lesson that the administration had ignored, but not he. The condemning of the innocent, the obliterating of the innocent, was an age-old phenomenon. His reading of the Bible and Boethius in prison in France had told him that among other things. For France now, Dreyfus was almost a Jesus figure, and in that there was consolation to be taken in some small fashion from despair.

"*The mind is its own place,*" Milton observed, "*and in itself can make a Heaven of Hell, a Hell of Heaven.*" This was indeed what the chaplain had asserted but had he considered the other side of the coin? The camp was the prison but its horrors could never eliminate that other place of incarceration – the mind – and worst of all the rattling shackles of memory and the hauntings that would never be erased. There were some recollections of the fleeting glory of his youth that pierced the dark clouds momentarily, but they were sadly outnumbered by the vast legions of dreary sorrow.

The vanity of the human and therefore the criminal mind dictates that we can learn by the mistakes of others, and that there is such a thing as escape from the consequences of any action. And so there is a constant cycle of human experience. Murder is no exception to the rule. What has been done is what will be done; there is nothing new under the sun. Fools can be separated from evil no more easily than a good man from God.

All these and many other thoughts flooded his brain, and

those of his fellow inmates. Together they were condemned to a constant examination of the errors of their ways, painful contemplation of their crimes and a never-ending search for an explanation of the blight on their short life on earth. What had led them, and not the rest of humanity, to end their existence in the colony of the damned? It was beyond any man's imagination that such a hell could have been invented on earth. And the why of it all.

Dreyfus captured in his journal the deadly depression induced by the constant conflict of the mind when exposed to an experience of such monumental cruelty:

> The sea beneath my window has always for me to be a strange fascination. I have a violent sensation which I felt on the boat, of being drawn irresistibly towards the sea whose numerous waters seem to call me with the voice of a comforter. Another tyranny. Where are the beautiful dreams of my youth and aspirations of my manhood? My brain reels with the turmoil of my thoughts. What is the mystery under-lining this tragedy? Even now I understand nothing of what has passed.

Not one disagreed that the guillotine would have been a mercy compared to what they had to endure before they were thrown to the sharks. The history and methods of punishment were known to all, through an oral telegraph as swift in communication as its mechanical counterpart. The past and present up-to-the-minute history breathed from the walls of the labour camps, transmitted from the mainland through the three islands, from the cages of the solitary-confined to the sanguinary halls of the dreaded Crimson Barracks (so called because of the killings committed among its prisoners, the most violent inmates, murders that were rarely punished because of the refusal of even friends of the victims to speak under torture –

murders that would be avenged in a continual loop of bloodshed).

One night in a state of fitful sleep the symbol of his terrible crime returned in a mixture of confused and haunting images. He was on a train, but not *the* train. There was a woman sitting opposite him, but not *the* woman. She was younger, beautiful, but mocking him, targeting his weakness which he had attempted to disguise for so long. But there was something else far more distracting. He could not dismiss it from his mind and every nerve in his body was jangling at the thought. He heard the next stop being called. He was on the wrong train and in rising panic realised he was going to Lyons. He was in possession of the trunk which contained . . . the trunk, the provenance of it all and the memory that seeped into the darkest hall of his diseased brain.

# 3

## L'AFFAIRE GOUFFÉ

A merchant in Baghdad sent his servant to the marketplace for provisions. The servant returned quickly, pale-faced and trembling, and told his master that whilst in the marketplace he was jostled by a woman who he recognised as Death and she made a threatening gesture to him. The servant begged his master for a horse and fled at great speed to Samarra, a town about 75 miles north of Baghdad, where he believed that the woman would not find him. The merchant went to the marketplace, found the woman and asked her why she had made the threatening gesture to his servant. She replied: "That was not a threatening gesture, it was only a jolt of surprise. I was astonished to see him in Baghdad, for I had an appointment with him tonight in Samarra."

*An old Arab tale from*
*the Babylonian Talmud*

In mid-November 1889, Dr Alexandre Lacassagne, head of the Department of Legal Medicine at Lyons University, received a request for his assistance in a bizarre and mysterious case. Four months earlier a body of an adult male had been found in a duck-cloth sack on a steep incline leading down to the River Rhône about ten miles south of Lyons. A post mortem had been carried out by a Dr Bernard, a previous student in the university. A cause of death had been established but there had been no positive identification made of the decomposed remains.

Dr Lacassagne had a considerable reputation in the matter of solving difficult murder cases and was regularly consulted when those cases seemed to be defying a resolution. He was not only an expert in legal medicine but a crime-scene expert and skilled pathologist. The body was believed to be that of a missing man from Paris by the name of Toussaint Augustin Gouffé. He was a court bailiff by profession, a widower with two children and worked from an office in Montmartre.

He was financially well off with a reputation as a bon viveur and with a vigorous interest in the opposite sex. Clearly his status as a widower allowed him indulge his taste for fine wine and women. Mature wine and unripe women, it was said. On July 27th of that year his brother-in-law, a man by the name of Landry, had reported him missing to the district police in Montmartre. It was a busy time for the force as it coincided with the Paris World Exposition and the report did not receive priority.

The report was brought to the attention of Marie-François Goron, chief of the investigative unit at the Sûreté. He was a man with a reputation for punctiliousness and doggedness in his methods of investigation and never gave up until a crime had been solved and the perpetrator brought to justice. He set his mind to finding the explanation for the disappearance of a man of some status who, as he had established from his initial enquiries, had no financial problems and had given no indication to anyone of plans to leave the capital in a hurry. He also learnt that a stranger had entered the bailiff's office on the evening of July 26th and had left in a hurry without stating his business.

Goron began, as was usual in such cases, to find out as much as he could about the missing man. He had last been seen by two friends on the Boulevard Montmartre at about ten minutes past seven on the evening prior to the report of his disappearance. Since then nothing had been heard from or about him, either in his office on the Rue Montmartre or in his house on the Rue Rougement. He was a man of regular habits in his working routine and even in the somewhat darker shades of his private life.

He was apparently in good health and spirits, so no reason why he should through melancholy go somewhere to take his own life. As a widower he lived with his three daughters, happily by all accounts. He did a good trade as a bailiff and process-server, a position in France that was more important and lucrative than in other countries and involved a lot of legal work.

At times, the detective learned, he carried around considerable sums of money in cash which he sometimes brought home. One night a week, Gouffé did not return home. His break from routine was in the pursuit of pleasure – wine, food and women to satisfy his vigorous sexual appetite. From an interview with the hall porter of the office building it emerged that in or around nine o'clock on the evening of Friday July 26th the porter heard someone he presumed was the bailiff going upstairs.

A short time later he heard the footsteps descending the stairs. He left the porter's lodge and, realising it was a stranger, was about to confront him when the man seemed to conceal his face and hurried out the door onto the street. As it was dark in the hallway he could not provide any useful description of the stranger. When the office was searched, there were no obvious signs of robbery or scattering of papers or documents. Quite the contrary. When the investigator moved aside some documents a sum of 14,000 francs was revealed.

If the strange intruder had been looking for money, he had made a poor job of the search. The safe had not been tampered with and there was nothing else to indicate an attempted robbery. There were ten long matches, half-burnt, on the floor. Perhaps Gouffé was a smoker – that would be easily confirmed. But on the other hand he did not appear to be the type that would just drop matches on the floor.

Strange, thought the detective. Indicative of haste, but for what? If the intruder was a robber in search of money, he was most definitely incompetent. Even the most cursory search would have provided an extremely good night's work. Perhaps he had been seized by some form of panic.

The reason for the visit thus was unclear and somewhat disappointed Goron, for if such a sum of money had been stolen then a solid motive and reason for the bailiff's disappearance could justifiably have been posited – and explain the visit by a man that the porter was absolutely sure was not the missing person. That would have connected two parts of the puzzle.

There was an additional element. Accepting that the matches had been left by the stranger, how else could access have been obtained to the office but by the bailiff's keys? In Goron's estimation the only way that would add up was if the keys had been taken from Gouffé by force. This, combined with his knowledge of the man's life and occupation, was enough to persuade the Sûreté chief that wherever he went it was not of his own accord.

The team carried out further questioning of Gouffé's family, friends and business associates, among them a man who could have provided an early and vital lead but, for weak reasons that would eventually be ventilated, chose to remain silent. A review of the statements produced a lot of good information but nothing to indicate how or why the bailiff had melted into thin air.

The investigation stalled. There was nothing to do but wait. There is a time all good detectives recognise when all the pushing will lead nowhere. It was time for a pull and it came without any use of energy in the Sûreté.

On August 15th, in a thicket at the foot of a slope running down to the River Rhône, from the road that passes through the district of Millery, ten miles south of Lyons, a roadmender was overpowered by a foul odour and discovered human remains. The body had been wrapped in cloth and placed head-first inside a duck-cloth sack. It was in a fairly advanced state of decomposition, accelerated by the means of wrapping and the warm climate of the season.

The Lyons police were informed and, in the company of a forensic team and doctor, arrived at the scene. It was confirmed the corpse was male and was completely nude inside the sack. There were no clothes, nothing to aid in establishing the identity. Detectives judged by the position of the sack that it had been rolled down the incline with the purpose of reaching the river, where it would have been taken away by the current.

Again Goron pondered on the fact that, in such an isolated location, the person or persons responsible for the dumping of the body had not taken the time to ensure that it had, as intended, been deposited in the river. The matches on the floor of the office came to mind. A further indication of similar haste, by the same person?

Goron was energised by the find and was sure that the body was that of Gouffé and the investigation could go into full swing. Another event raised his hopes even further. Two days after the discovery of the corpse, a broken empty trunk was spotted by some snail-gatherers in the woods and when the police examined it a transport label was still attached. It showed that the trunk had been dispatched from Paris to Lyons on July 27th 188– . The final figure of the date was obliterated. After a further search, a key was unearthed which fitted the lock of the trunk.

Goron urged the Lyons judicial authorities to establish a link between the body and the trunk. It was beyond the realm of coincidence. He telegraphed a description of Gouffé, including facial features, hair colour and approximate height and age.

The post-mortem findings by Dr Bernard revealed that there

were two breaks in the larynx indicating that strangulation was the cause of death. He also concluded that the man was about 35 years of age, of average height with black hair.

Gouffé was 49 years of age with chestnut-brown hair.

Nonetheless Goron sent the brother-in-law Landry to view the corpse which had been temporarily deposited in a makeshift morgue on a nearby barge. The state of decomposition rendered the facial features unrecognisable and, probably shocked by the viewing of the corpse and influenced by the different hair-colouring, he could not make a positive identification. He said that the body was not that of Gouffé.

This was a blow for the investigation, and the body after being photographed was buried in the pauper's plot of a local graveyard. That seemed to be that. But Goron was not tempted by this setback to consign the case to the missing-persons file to gather dust. He was positive that his instinct in the case would prove to be correct.

He took the label found on the trunk to the Gare de Lyon and, interviewing the clerk who handled it, established that it had been brought there on a train from Paris as confirmed by the company records.

But that was not the main purpose of the visit. He wanted to know the weight of the trunk. The recorded weight of the trunk amounted to that which would match the container plus the weight of an adult man. Goron did not have any difficulty deducing that it had almost certainly been the receptacle of the body found in the vicinity. The detective was excited by the discovery. It fired his determination to get to the bottom of the mystery. Another part was inserted into the board of the puzzle.

Moreover, he suspected that the trunk had carried the body of Gouffé. Nonetheless, he could not prove, as things stood, that the body in the pauper's grave was that of the missing man. Quite to the contrary, given the pathologist's findings and the failure of a family member to identify the body as his brother-in-law.

He pondered the matter in his office in the Sûreté. There was no rational explanation for Gouffé's disappearance. He had not informed any of his family or friends that he had plans to travel, and to just go away without notice was completely out of character. The more he thought about it, the argument for Gouffé being the body found was overwhelming.

Was there something that the pathologist had missed? Landry could hardly have been blamed for not recognising his brother-in-law's face, bloated and blackened by the process of de-composition.

The hair was black not brown. Could that be a result of the rotting? He contacted Dr Bernard and travelled to Lyons. The doctor produced samples of the hair he had kept in a test tube. Gouffé's hair was brown and worn short, while the hairs from the body appeared to be black and longer in length.

He asked the doctor for distilled water and immersed the hairs. After a few minutes, cleansed of black residue, the hairs were brown and shorter. The doctor admitted to the shortcomings of his examination. The detective realised that the doctor was a young man with limited experience. He needed a pathologist with a proven track record and did not have to look far to find one.

On this basis Goron applied to the authorities to have the body exhumed and examined by another pathologist. Despite the protestation of the local authorities he secured permission for the exhumation and sought the involvement of Dr Lacassagne. On both counts he succeeded. While Lacassagne shared his instinct in the case, he did not hesitate to state that the only way of proof was by science.

Identification was aided by the act of a clever lab assistant who had a hunch that the body would be needed again, and had scratched his initials on the outside of the coffin and put a hat on the corpse's head in anticipation of such an eventuality.

Lacassagne was faced with a huge task. Not only had the body deteriorated further in the grave but he found that the first post mortem was a botched job. The skull had been opened with a hammer and the chest while being opened with a chisel, a usual method of the time, had been damaged. But since the death had luckily not been caused by blunt-force trauma, he got on with the job.

The breaks in the bones of the throat were still evident, supporting the idea of death by strangulation. Manual strangling.

The next thing he looked for was the signs that would establish the age of the deceased more accurately. He examined the pelvic bones and in particular the teeth. There was only one missing so he had a lot to go on. Over the ageing process there is a loss of gum and deterioration in the bone around the sockets of the teeth. He concluded that this was the body of a man well over forty and near to fifty. That was a match: Gouffé was 49.

Next was height. The standard practice was to stretch the body and add one and a half inches. The doctor had the benefit of a study by a student Étienne Rolet who had examined the bodies of 100 men and women, calculating the relationship between measurements of bones and the height of the deceased. From this study, Lacassagne calculated that the height of the body was 5 foot 8 inches. In Paris Goron made confirmation by reference to Gouffé's military record and interviewing his tailor. A match.

There was the problem of the hair colour which the pathologist did not fear as he was aware from his previous test that it had been altered by the putrefaction process. By careful washing, the black post-mortem residue was stripped away to reveal chestnut brown. He made a microscopic comparison between strands of hair on a brush that Goron had retrieved from Gouffé's apartment and strands taken from the cadaver. The diameter was exactly the same. A match. To be absolutely certain, he asked a medical colleague to make chemical tests to establish if the hair had been dyed. The tests proved that it had not.

He then made a close examination of the bones to see if there were any deformities or old injuries unique to the body. The heel and ankle-bone of one leg revealed an old fracture which had not fully healed. He concluded that this might have produced a slight limp. There was also an abnormality in one of the knees. He discovered a ridge on the bone that attached to the right big toe which the doctor suspected was associated with gout, a disease caused by a build-up of uric acid in the bloodstream and resulting in inflammation of the joints. When located in the big toe it is an extremely painful condition. He received a second opinion from another medical colleague whose examination of the bones confirmed Lacassagne's findings. He contacted Goron and asked him to interview Gouffé's family and doctor and anyone else who could corroborate his conclusions.

Goron found out that Gouffé had a fall as a young child and sustained a fracture which resulted in his dragging his right leg slightly in a minor limp. His cobbler had compensated for the affliction by making a wider right sole and also had used particularly soft leather so as not to put pressure on the right big toe which caused him chronic pain. His physician confirmed that Gouffé suffered from gout, resulting in great discomfort in the right toe. He also suffered from swelling of the knee. Despite medical recommendation to deal with the gout, it had persisted; seemingly the pain did not act as a restraint to the patient's fondness for good food and wine, often but not always the cause of the condition.

After eleven days of post-mortem examination, Lacassagne was able to announce to his audience of attendants and police: "Messieurs, the body found at Millery is indeed the corpse of Monsieur Gouffé."

Goron was overjoyed; all his hard work and instinct had been confirmed by the work of a brilliant doctor and criminologist.

The way was clear now to hunt down the perpetrators.


## PARIS, NOVEMBER 1889

It was now the end of November. Four months had passed, and the police were no closer to identifying a prime suspect for the murder of Gouffé. A friend of the victim had come into the frame but after questioning was eliminated from the inquiry.

But a solid lead was established when a man who knew Gouffé was being interviewed. "There is another man who disappeared around the same time as Gouffé," he said. "The man's name is Eyraud, Michel Eyraud." He had not thought of this before, he said, he had not made the connection. Since it was a good lead the detectives did not make a fuss about the lateness about the information.

Goron made enquiries about this Eyraud and learnt he was a married man aged 46 with a chequered career, who had left a trail of debt and was implicated in a number of financial swindles. He had a mistress Gabrielle Bompard who was half his age and who had engaged in prostitution. Sometime after Gouffé was reported missing they disappeared and had not been heard of since.

Goron had a replica of the trunk constructed and put on show in a Paris morgue where it was viewed by no less than 25,000 visitors. A reward of 500 francs for information had been offered by the family of the victim to anyone who could identify the trunk. Later, photographs were carried in the French and foreign press. Apart from a large amount of crank mail and anonymous letters, these measures did not immediately produce anything of interest.

Then in December, the police chief received a letter with a London postmark from a boarding-house owner, informing him that Eyraud and a woman he only knew as Gabrielle had stayed in his house and on July 14th the young woman had left for France via Newhaven and Dieppe, taking with her a large trunk with little or no contents. The boarding-house owner's wife remembered having expressed surprise to Gabrielle at the large size of the trunk, into which she had put one dress. "That's alright," replied Gabrielle with a beaming smile and a laugh. "We shall have plenty to fill it with in Paris." Having departed on the 14th, she returned on the 17th. On the 20th, she and Eyraud travelled back to Paris.

Goron sent members of his team to London who confirmed the veracity of the story. They also found the shop on the Euston Road where the trunk was purchased. The assistant confirmed that a man answering Eyraud's description had bought the trunk on July 12th.

Having established the identity and descriptions of the killers the police chief began to make further investigations into their movements after the commission of the crime. His right-hand man Jaume, wearing out a lot of shoe-leather, found out that on the 27th the couple had purchased train tickets from Paris to Marseilles but had got off at the Perrache Station in Lyons. Travelling there, the detective confirmed that a couple matching their description had stayed in the Hotel Bordeaux with the trunk.

The following morning the couple had taken the trunk away from the hotel in a horse-drawn cab. The owner of a livery stable told Jaume he had hired the cab by the day to a couple, one a middle-aged man of respectable appearance and dress and a small and slender brunette in her early twenties. Staff at the railway station said that later that day they had deposited luggage in the cloakroom. In the evening they returned to the station and took the express train to Marseilles. There the trail ran cold.

Piecing together what he had to date, Goron concluded that this unlikely couple were indeed the killers and had committed the crime on the night of the 26th, since Gouffé was last seen around 7p.m. on that date. Concealing the body in the trunk, they had travelled to Lyons, spent a second night with the corpse and then had driven in the cab to the countryside and disposed of both trunk and corpse near Millery. Then they'd travelled to Marseilles, for what reason he did not know, and then presumably came back to Paris and sometime later took flight.

The police contacted French government agencies and consulates abroad with details and description of the fugitives which were also disseminated in newspapers internationally, carrying stories saying that Michel Eyraud and Gabrielle

Bompard were wanted for questioning in relation to the trunk murder.

The year 1889 faded into oblivion, the sensation of the Gouffé murder undiminished by the bells of the New Year. No one needed to guess what Goron's resolution would be. The tentacles of information were out there in the world and he had no doubt that somehow, somewhere, someone with something relevant to say about the case would contact him. Time was no longer running out for the investigation; that situation was left for the perpetrators. Albeit, he realised, it was a big world out there.

## PARIS, JANUARY 1890

As January moved on, nothing. The chief did not despair. He was exhausted and later in the month he contracted a nasty flu but after a few days in bed dragged himself into the office before he had fully recovered.

On the morning of January 16th when he entered his office there was a large letter on his desk. Picking it up, he noted the postmark was New York, dated January 8th. Not even his clever mind could have anticipated the contents, never mind the author.

He read the first paragraph with a sense of the incredible. Another astonishing twist in the strangest case of his career. He jumped briefly to the last page. There it was, the signature: the writer was none other than Michel Eyraud. He turned the letter back to the first page.

Why had Goron, the writer complained, made him the object of a worldwide manhunt? He admitted he had fled from Paris the previous summer but he had done so due to his financial failure. Much of his misfortune was down to the Jews and Miss Bompard.

He had, he wrote, not harmed his good friend Gouffé but he suspected that Gabrielle and one of her many lovers were guilty of the evil deed. He protested against the suspicions directed against him. It was all as a result of improbable coincidences. His misfortune was his association with that "serpent Gabrielle Bompard". He had certainly bought a large trunk for her but she told him that she had sold it.

They had gone to America together, he to avoid financial difficulties. There Gabrielle had deserted him for another man. He concluded the twenty-page letter by attacking his accomplice: "The great trouble with her is that she is such a liar and also has a dozen lovers after her." He promised that as soon as he heard that Gabrielle had returned to Paris he would, of his own free will, place himself in the hands of Goron.

When he had finished it did not take long for the officer to recognise the epistle as longwinded and entirely self-serving and a pathetic attempt to pin the blame on Gabrielle, more than likely prompted by her deserting the sinking ship. It was an expression of rage for this betrayal more than anything and he was so stung that he revealed his admittedly very large hiding-place. Goron was somewhat bemused. He could have spent a lot of time in conjecture about where the wanted couple had ended their flight. Here, without any effort on his part, was the answer.

Eyraud was a man who could not apply a harness to his emotions, whether rage, panic or fear. So much so that the rejection he suffered at the hands of his mistress must be punished, even at enormous risk to himself. His hatred was evidenced by two more letters on the 18th and 20th renewing his accusations against Bompard. Goron was struck down again by his illness and was forced to take to the bed. Shortly there was to be another, again, entirely unpredictable development.

The very next day, a short attractive young woman with a neat figure, dyed hair, greyish-blue eyes and a lively intelligent expression arrived in the front office of the Prefecture of Police in Paris, seeking an interview with the Prefect (Préfet). When asked her name, she replied in a haughty tone: "Gabrielle Bompard." She was accompanied by a middle-aged man who identified himself as Monsieur Garanger.

They were brought to the office of the Prefect Loze to whom she detailed her version of events, stating that she had been an unwilling accomplice of her lover Eyraud in the murder of Gouffé. She gave the location of the crime as No 3 Rue Tronson du Coudray. She was not there on the night in question and relied on the account of her lover for what happened. They had later gone to America where they had met the man now with her and, finding themselves in the usual pecuniary difficulties, Eyraud proposed killing him and robbing his money.

She divulged the plot to Garanger and asked him to take her away from the pernicious influence of her lover. They had travelled to Vancouver where he persuaded her to make a clean breast of the affair, return to Paris and face the music.

She was prepared to give evidence against Eyraud and on that basis both she and her companion clearly assumed that they could just leave the building to be contacted at the Préfet's pleasure. Garanger said he would vouch for the greater part of her account. Loze had other ideas. He sent for a detective inspector who produced an arrest warrant for Bompard.

Bompard was brought to prison where she did not seem to be unduly perturbed by her situation, probably under the misconception that she would walk away from her part in the ghastly act. While the investigation had suddenly made a big jump in progress and one of the accomplices was under lock and key, the other had to be found and brought back to face justice. Goron was under no illusion that would be an easy task but it would prove far more protracted than he could have predicted.

Two detectives, Jaume being one, travelled to New York to begin the operation of tracking down Eyraud. He would prove to be a very able and inventive fugitive despite leaving a trail littered with clues due to the necessity of thieving and swindling for funds to keep on the move. The trail led from New York to San Francisco and then to Mexico. In one location he "borrowed" an exotic oriental robe from a wealthy Turk and disappeared with it. This act would way down the line prove to be his undoing.

His inventiveness was displayed by his conning of a naïve actor who was staying in the same boarding house. Eyraud, befriending him, railed and ranted about his wife deserting him and running off with another man. He wanted to wreak revenge but did not have the funds to do it. He wheedled 80 dollars from the actor who later told the French detectives that the conman delivered a performance that he as a professional would scarcely match.

A myriad of such incidents littered the journey the detectives took in the effort to hunt him down. He still managed to stay ahead of the posse. He ended up in Mexico where he could not resist writing a letter to a French newspaper insisting that Gouffé had been murdered by Bompard and an unknown. He was obviously still deeply affected by her flight and was determined to cast her as the real villain of the crime. But he could not temper his rage, a fact that would later be revealed as an ingrained aspect of his character. It did not seem to occur to him that nobody could possibly interpret his efforts as anything other than an attempt to save his own hide.

## HAVANA, FEBRUARY 1890

By whatever subterfuge, he managed to make his way from Mexico to Havana. In the Cuban capital a Frenchwoman by the name of Madame Puchen ran a business as a clothes merchant and dressmaker. In February 1890 a man of haggard appearance and dressed in clothes that had seen much better days came into her shop. He introduced himself as Gorki. He was clutching an exquisite oriental robe and asked her if she was interested in buying it.

Not knowing its provenance and he making no attempt to explain it, she was reluctant to engage in the matter, all the more so because of his bedraggled state. For all she knew it might have been stolen. She declined the offer. She quickly forgot about the incident until in May of the same year she was reading an

American newspaper and came across an item that brought it back to her and confirmed her original suspicion. The article mentioned the fact that an expensive Turkish robe had been stolen by a Michel Eyraud who was the chief suspect in a murder and was wanted for questioning by the French authorities.

Later in the day she spotted the same man who had offered her the robe walking past the door of the shop. She called him and asked if he still had the robe and he replied that he had sold it. They had a general conversation. He mentioned that he had been in Mexico and Madame Puchen enquired if he had come across the murderer Eyraud who was believed to be hiding there. He replied in the negative. When she asked him if he had been in Paris at the time of the murder he became somewhat nervous. Half-jokingly she said that he looked rather like him. He laughed in a hollow way and said: "I will see you again." Any other man in his position would have never darkened the street, not to mind the door of Madame Puchen's establishment, given the content of the conversation. But Michel Eyraud, typical of a particular category of killer, had a peculiar habit of seeking attention at a time when he should most avoid it.

On the other hand, her observation "You look rather like him" more than likely rang in his ear with the impact of a tolling church bell. And he could not make up his mind whether the dressmaker was half joking or half in earnest. Either way, Eyraud was without doubt thinking that she was a danger to him. He could brazen it out or disappear; he chose the former.

Madame Puchen in retrospect felt greatly uneasy that she had been so bold and was not looking forward to seeing him again.

He duly reappeared carrying a copy of a newspaper which he said he had found in a café. He pointed out a photograph of Eyraud which was fuzzy and indistinct.

"What a blackguard!" he remarked.

"Indeed!" replied Madame Puchen, affecting a more forthright attitude in his company. "What an awful end he gave to that poor bailiff! He truly deserves the guillotine when he is caught."

The vagabond's eyes narrowed. "I suppose that is true."

He then abruptly left the premises with a hurried farewell and no promise of coming back. In the rush, he left the newspaper behind and the more she examined the photograph the more she felt that it resembled the man who had just left.

It then struck her that the unusual act of coming back with the newspaper was a bungled attempt to allay any suspicions she might have harboured, by sheer brazenness. His performance did not impress her one bit; in fact, the very opposite. Her remark about the guillotine was foolish in retrospect. If this man was indeed Eyraud then she could be in danger. No one, not even the newspapers, knew he was in Havana. All presumed that he was still in Mexico.

She decided to act at once and made her way to the French consulate where she gave a statement to the consul, outlining her suspicions and detailing the substance of the encounters she had with the man she believed to be Eyraud.

"I believe," said Madame Puchen, "that these encounters are beyond the realm of coincidence. Whatever suspicions that I had, when the man had the temerity to return with the newspaper and made remarks about Eyraud in the third person, this confirmed what was simply an uneasy feeling at the start."

"Certainly," replied the consul, "there is more than enough from what you have observed to check this man out. And I agree with you that there comes a time when fate takes over from coincidence. If this man is indeed Michel Eyraud then it would appear that his past has caught up with him."

The consul thanked her and promised to take the matter in hand immediately. They shook hands and Madame Puchen left the consulate.

A pair of eyes sunken in a haggard countenance followed her progress down the street. What she did not know was that Eyraud had been observing the building to cover such an eventuality. It was as well for Madame Puchen that she had followed up her instinct so quickly or she might have suffered a similar fate to Gouffé's. The killer's back was against the wall and he was more dangerous than ever. But, luckily for the French dressmaker, the advantage for killing her had passed.

But Providence was going to have its way. By another twist of fate that had been at the heart of the case from the beginning there was a man living in Havana who had worked for Eyraud when he ran the distillery at Sèvres, the collapse of which had sent him on the road to financial ruin. The consul, aware of the fact, summoned this man and told him that it was suspected that Eyraud was living in the capital and if he encountered him to immediately inform the consulate.

The consul then contacted the Spanish authorities and arrangements for a search for the fugitive were put in place. No sooner had the man left but he encountered Eyraud who was still keeping the consulate under surveillance. He took the former employee to a café and there admitted who he was and begged the man not to betray him. It was after midnight when they left the café. Already the killer was regretting making himself known to the man and murderous thoughts seized his mind as they walked down a dark street. Simultaneously fear gripped his companion and he hailed down a cab and made off.

Earlier in the day Eyraud had moved out of his hotel to another establishment near the station, but he was afraid to go back there. He decided to spend the night in a brothel but was turned away from the door because of his ragged clothes. The down-at-heel killer wandered the streets, gripped by tension and apprehension. It was as if his victim was exacting revenge from beyond the grave. Eyraud had been at the end of the tether many times but now the rope had frayed right through.

He again encountered the man from Sèvres like a ghost in the street. "It's all over for me now," Eyraud croaked and melted into the darkness.

He was haunted by the apparitions of his blighted and depraved past. He was drowning in a despair that he had never experienced before. The noose was now around his neck and he was choking and gasping. He staggered along the empty street and felt the ground moving up to meet him. He was suddenly aware of another presence. He turned, a police officer approached.

"Who are you? What is your address?"

"Gorki, Hotel Roma."

The officer recognised the name he used as an alias and a hotel they had visited earlier. He handcuffed the fugitive and brought him to the station where he was questioned and thrown in a cell. The police took his luggage from the other hotel. He attempted suicide in the early hours but did not succeed. For Michel Eyraud the game was up.

On June 16th he was handed over to the French police. They reached France on the 20th and Eyraud was at last incarcerated in a Paris prison.


## PARIS, JULY 1890

By July 1st when Eyraud made his first appearance in a Paris court in front of an examining magistrate, Bompard had already been subjected to intense questioning and medical examination to determine principally her mental state. A favourite defence ploy in the face of overwhelming odds was to plead insanity to avoid the razor-sharp edge of the guillotine. As part of that process of examination, to which Eyraud was also subjected, the background history of the prisoners was considered an important component.

Bompard was 22 years of age at the time of her arrest. Investigation of her family history was, as it turned out, very revealing. She was the fourth child of a respectable merchant of Lille, a hardworking man of good moral principle. His wife, who had suffered from delicate health, died when Gabrielle was 13, thereby removing an important element in her parenting.

She was a rebellious and difficult teenager who was expelled from four boarding schools and managed to stay at the fifth for three years. There she developed her worst instincts – for lewd behaviour, lying on a grand scale and a foul tongue most unusual for a girl of her age. At 18 years of age she returned to her father's house but soon ran off with a lover who she later said had hypnotised and seduced her.

Her father asked the family doctor to induce her into a hypnotic state in an effort to reform her errant ways. It was a popular method at the time for dealing with mental aberrations, particularly hysteria. It made no difference, the doctor diagnosed her as a neuropath and, worse still for her afflicted father, said that there were no home influences that would help her overcome her instincts. The doctor was held by experts who examined her later to be too ready to empathise with his subject.

The 20-year-old was immoral, unduly self-centred, vain, lewd, intelligent but with no grasp of the difference between right and wrong. After the murder, she spent the night alone with the body in the trunk as her accomplice went back to stay with his wife.

Goron asked what she had been thinking during that most unusual of circumstances. Most would shiver at the memory.

Not Gabrielle who with a broad smile replied: "You would never guess what a funny idea came into my head. You see, it wasn't very pleasant for me being in this tête-à-tête with a corpse. I couldn't sleep. So I thought what fun it would be to go into the street and pick up some respectable gentleman from the provinces and bring him to the room and, just as he was beginning to enjoy himself, say: 'Would you like to see a bailiff?' Then open the trunk suddenly and, before he could recover from the horror, run into the street and fetch the police. What a fool the respectable gentleman would have looked when the officers came!"

Goron was taken aback by the sheer callousness of the young woman who gave not a thought to the murdered man but in her fantasy used his body to perform a bizarre act of malice on a "respectable" person who she would lure back to the death room for sex and then shock and deliver to a form of punishment. Clearly, in her depraved imagination, conventional respectability was not a status that she cherished. Little wonder that the investigation team nicknamed her "the little demon".

Eyraud's adolescence followed a parallel path. At 13 his conduct was so troublesome that his father had to have him put into a reformatory school. At 19 he enlisted in a chasseur (light infantry) regiment from which he was transferred to the Foreign Legion. He served in the war between France and Mexico, then deserted his regiment and joined the enemy guerrillas under General Juarez. He betrayed the position of the French forces and when captured was tried by court martial and sentenced to death.

He was spared by the amnesty of 1869 and returned to France where he then embarked on a career of ruinous business activity first, followed by crime, mainly theft and swindling, and was committed to a life of drink and debauchery. He was subject to outbursts of violence especially towards women and had great difficulty in keeping control of his temper.

For some reason he thought himself above labouring for a living. "Understand this," he told detectives who brought him back to Paris, "I have never done any work and I will never do any work."

Such a statement, given his grave circumstance at the time, was an indication that he was just as much a fantasist as the young woman he was destined to meet on July 26th, 1888, a year to the day before the murder. At that time he was, as usual, scraping the bottom of the financial barrel – a bankrupt and discredited in every way. And he still lived with his wife. Apart from her small dowry, Eyraud was bereft of resources. If he had pursued a frugal existence or worked at menial tasks as others had to, he would have got by. But like his new consort he had delusions of grandeur, quite at odds with his situation. Most women would have quickly departed the company of a born loser but Gabrielle had a similar appetite for vice and chaos in life.

Even her earnings from prostitution could not support their habits and faced with poverty they hatched a plan to bring a customer of hers back to a place where, dead or alive, he would part with money. Dead would be the better option as then there would be no witness and no retribution, or so they thought.

Through separate interviews with the accomplices, whose versions differed less about the general narrative than who was the prime mover and therefore took major responsibility, the police got as accurate an account of the events as possible from the perpetrators and then nailed it with corroboration.

In July 1889 they went to London. The first stop was the West End where a red-and-white girdle of plaited silk was purchased by Gabrielle; this was to be the means of snaring their chosen victim both literally and metaphorically. Next the trunk to act as temporary coffin. They also acquired thirteen feet of rope and a pulley. Back in Paris they got hold of twenty feet of duck packing cloth which Gabrielle sewed into a large sack. A ground-floor apartment was rented at No 3 Rue Tronson du Coudray.

The bed of the apartment was in an alcove separated by curtains from the rest of the room. To the beam forming the cross section at the entrance to the alcove, Eyraud fixed a pulley. He ran a rope through the pulley so that, concealing himself behind the curtains, he could provide an improvised gallows and hang the man by pulling strongly on the rope.

It was an extraordinarily complicated mechanism that had no guarantee of success but no doubt the pair thought it nothing short of ingenious.

Eyraud already knew of Gouffé's existence but during a conversation with a friend on the 25th of July discovered that the bailiff was in the habit of carrying large sums of money and spent Friday nights away from home in pursuit of pleasure. The following day Gabrielle stopped the bailiff on the way to his lunch and they arranged to meet at eight that evening. Little did he think that it was a rendezvous with death in the shape of a young woman.

The afternoon was spent setting up the infernal mechanism.

The plan was to sit Gouffé on a chair with his back to the curtained alcove. Gabrielle would sit on his knee and playfully knot her plaited girdle around his neck. Then she would surreptitiously attach the end of the girdle to a swivel at the end of the rope and pulley operated by the hidden Eyraud.

At eight Gabrielle met Gouffé on the street and fifteen minutes later they entered the apartment.

"You have a nice little nest here," remarked the bailiff.

"Yes, a fancy of mine. Eyraud knows nothing about it."

"Oh, you are tired of him?"

"Yes," replied Gabrielle, "that's all over."

She then slipped into a robe, with the red-and-white silk cord girdle around her waist, and sat him down on the chair.

Perching on his knee, she took off the girdle and playfully looped it around his neck, laughingly remarking: "What a nice little necktie it makes!"

"Very elegant," said Gouffé, "but I didn't come here to see that!"

She then attached the end of the girdle to the swivel behind his back. Behind the curtain Eyraud then pulled on the rope, hauling Gouffé aloft and according to his statement "within two minutes he ceased to live".

In her statement Gabrielle disagreed and said that while it rendered the bailiff insensible, he was not dead. She said that Eyraud finished the unfortunate man off with his hands, strangling him, which was confirmed by the post mortem finding of manual strangulation.

Eyraud removed the victim's watch but, searching his pockets, only came up with the meagre amount of 150 francs. All their best-laid plans seemed to have been in vain.

Worse was to follow. He found a set of keys and then rushed off to the bailiff's office. Letting himself in, despite being in a panic he was too careful not to disturb the papers and documents on the desk. In his haste he missed the 14,000 francs that might have rendered all the effort worthwhile.

He was now gripped by a dreadful sinking feeling. All that

planning and travel and expense for nought. Cold perspiration sprouted on his forehead. His hands shook as he tried to light a cigar to induce calm and he threw one half-lit match after another on the floor. He tried to collect his thoughts which were wildly swinging like a pendulum through his brain. The safe was locked, he had no combination.

The folly, the arrogance of his best expectations, were now laid bare as well as the total inadequacy of his preparation and intelligence. If he had threatened and questioned the bailiff before prematurely despatching him he could have established where the money was hidden or got access to the safe. Gouffé could have been trussed up with the rope, a scarf tied around his mouth and guarded while Gabrielle kept watch. He then could have got a large amount of money. Now he had nothing but a corpse. His head was bursting, he was beginning to lose his reason. She would go mad when he arrived back empty-handed.

In a sweat at the danger of being caught, he left the slightly concealed booty behind and quickly made his way down the stairs leading to the office.

It was on the way out that the porter approached but he rushed out into the street. The plan had been a ghastly failure and he returned to the apartment in a rage of frustration and despair. Gabrielle started screaming at him when she heard. He slapped her across the face and threw her on the bed. He gulped down brandy and champagne, now no longer for the purpose of celebration but to ease his shattered nerves.

They stripped the body, put it in the improvised shroud and placed it in the trunk. They then apparently had sexual intercourse on the bed which would have been consistent with their depraved character, after which Eyraud went home to his wife leaving his mistress alone with the trunk. According to his account he slept soundly, "worn out by the excitement of the day". The consequence of his act would come back to haunt him much later. In the interim he would have to concentrate on the next part of the ill-conceived plot to get rid of the body.

After travelling to Lyons the next day and spending the night with the trunk in the Hotel Bordeaux, they disposed of the body and trunk and took the evening train to Marseilles where they dumped Gouffé's clothes and boots in the sea. While there he borrowed 500 francs from his brother. Back in Paris, Gabrielle raised another 2,000 francs from her stock in trade. They later travelled to England and from there sailed to America.

After Eyraud's imprisonment in Paris he was brought to the murder room and, in the presence of Goron, a number of officials and an examining magistrate, he was confronted with his accomplice. Each denied with unrestrained hatred each other's account of events. One blamed the other, she claiming that he was entirely responsible for the plan and had strangled the bailiff with his own hands when the hanging did not work.

The judicial witnesses to this confrontation were astounded by what they had seen. Not one whit of remorse was displayed by the actors in this ghastly scenario, not one ounce of pity for the victim, just selfish efforts to distance themselves from the blame for the awful killing that both had planned and carried out – both clearly entirely removed in their own minds from the looming consequence.

It was also obvious to the investigators that Eyraud did not care at this juncture about going to the guillotine but he was determined that his former mistress would share his fate. Her defence argued that she had acted under hypnotic suggestion by her accomplice. Three doctors approved by the examining magistrate to assess this argument and her mental state came to the conclusion that, while she was susceptible to hypnotic suggestion, there were no grounds to find that she was acting under such influence when the murder took place. She was alert, intelligent but completely lacking when it came to the matter of morals. As indeed was her accomplice and perhaps guiding hand. The matter would be decided in a court of law on the evidence presented.

The trial took place over four days beginning on December

16th 1890 before the Paris Assizes Court. It had been delayed by an outrageous example of newspaper contempt on the part of a journalist who had interviewed some members of the jury panel whose composition had been previously published. The article which appeared in the *Matin* newspaper was full of doctored and invented quotes, an exercise in fertile imagination for which the writer was sent to prison for a month to reflect on his woeful grasp of journalistic ethics. There was another scandal.

There was naturally a huge demand for tickets of admission to this sensational case; they could not be obtained for love or money. The Presiding Judge M. Robert circumvented this problem by distributing tickets to favoured friends in high places, attracting the ire of the Minister for the Interior who made sure that this would never happen again.

The trial was naturally mainly concerned with establishing and proving the facts of the case but it was marked by Eyraud's arrogance, lack of emotion or remorse and the defendants' insistence that each was responsible for the plan, details and execution of the crime. At one stage Bompard was seized by a fit of hysteria and was carried kicking and screaming from the court to a cell to calm down. Whether this was genuine or performed was not remarked upon.

Much time was taken up on the matter of hypnotic suggestion, a defence witness Professor Liégeois of the University of Nancy giving a four-hour dissertation on the subject which unduly strained the patience of all present. The chief prosecutor demolished his theories, quoting his side's eminent medical expert, Dr Brouardel: "As to the influence of Eyraud over Bompard, the one outstanding fact that has been eternally true for 6,000 years is that the stronger will can possess the weaker. That is no particular part of the history of hypnotism; it belongs to the history of the world."

Her advocate, in his address to the jury, ignored the hypnotic theory, resting his plea on the moral weakness and irresponsibility of his client. The upshot was that the jury found that in her case there were extenuating circumstances, namely her accomplice's influence over her allied to her moral weakness and she was sentenced to 20 years' penal servitude.

Eyraud received the death sentence. At first he seemed to accept this, writing to his daughter from prison that he was tired of life and his death was the best thing that could happen for her and her mother. But, as his advocate tried to get the sentence commuted, he became hopeful.

*"There are grounds for appeal. I am certain that my sentence will be commuted,"* he wrote in a letter.

But the Cour de Cassation (the French Supreme Court – *'cassation'* literally meaning 'breaking', referring to its power to break a previous judgement) rejected his appeal.

A petition was sent to President Carnot but he also chose to turn it down. On the morning of February 3rd 1891, Eyraud noticed that the warders who normally finished their shift at 6 a.m. remained at their posts and an hour later the Governor of the Roquette prison entered his cell and announced that the time had come for the execution of his sentence. He remained silent for a while but then burst into a rage directed toward the Minister for the Interior, Monsieur Constans.

"It is he who is having me guillotined – he's got what he wanted. I suppose now he will decorate Gabrielle!"

Not even facing death did the killer think of anything but the perceived injustice of his mistress escaping the same fate. Perhaps he thought that he was a loser to the last and this was correct. As he lived so should he die, but he accepted the upshot without grace. What about the man he had despatched to his uneasy grave without the slightest reflection? To Gouffé he gave no consideration.

Eyraud went to the guillotine in a mixture of self-pity and rage, and thousands lined the streets hoping to get a glimpse of the notorious killer.

Street vendors sold miniature replicas of the infamous trunk. Inside each was a small toy metal corpse bearing the inscription: *"L'Affaire Gouffé."* A bizarre postscript to an equally bizarre crime.

But someone somewhere, such was the knowledge of the crime spread through newspapers all over the world, may well have taken notice of the salient features of this extraordinary case.

All the more so because this could have been the perfect murder but for some avoidable blunders and slip-ups made by the killers. The purchase of the trunk at a London location was clever – a little too clever by half since Eyraud was confident enough to sign his own name on the receipt – nonetheless distant enough to make the origin hard to establish. And the plan to dispose of the body was good enough if not visited by an element of panic, perhaps brought on by the fact that no money was to be had at the end of it all. If they had made sure that the body had made it into the river, that might well have assured success.

There seemed little excuse to leave the label on the trunk while crudely trying to smash it up. But if the body had been given up to the depths and currents of the Rhône that would not have mattered.

But again such slip-ups would have been of even less consequence had not the case involved two distinct but brilliant minds, both tirelessly devoted to the task at hand, whose skill and dedication would justifiably be beyond the comprehension of even the most ingenious of killers. It was the efforts of Goron and Lacassagne that prevented the case from becoming a perfect murder and all the more so as the odds were all stacked against them.

There is hardly doubt that their fictional counterparts, Holmes and Watson, could not have cracked this one because as Lacassagne, an admirer of the pair, remarked: "Why don't they ever carry out a post mortem?"

The outcome was hailed as a miracle, as if it had been fashioned by some divine intervention. The doctor's best and most famous student Edmond Locard put this into its proper perspective. "It was no miracle because modern science is contrary to miracles. Yet as a work of deduction it was truly a masterpiece –

71

probably the most astonishing I suspect that has ever been made in criminology."

But it might well have been different and that is how the criminal mind operates. It would not be the last time a trunk was employed to house and transport the victim of a horrendous murder.

Financial speculators and murderers have notoriously short memories when it comes to considering consequences.

# 4

## LE TIGRE

Most men submit to the whirlpool of life, helpless in the face of the slings and arrows of outrageous fortune. It takes a man of great fortitude, strength, endurance and action to face and overcome the tide of fate. Georges Clemenceau was such a man – French statesman, physician, journalist, who was nicknamed Le Tigre – The Tiger.

Clemenceau was active, alert, capable and highly intelligent, his face an index to his character, giving an impression of tremendous energy. A teetotaller all his life, he was active and fit. He had a rapidity of perception, a quickness of wit and was a master of irony. He didn't hesitate to attack in order to defend. Nevertheless his voice was rarely raised above conversational level and as a rule he was quiet and unemotional in his manner. He possessed a power of logical and connected argument and was a brilliant orator. He was 65 beginning his first period as Prime Minister (1906-1909) and 79 when defeated in the 1920 elections after his second period in that office (1917-1920), but had great physical energy for a man of his age, an insatiable appetite for work and the endurance to bear it.

Good or bad luck, success or failure, made no difference to him. Invariably he told the truth about any situation which in a political sense was probably the opposite of conventional practice by politicians. Unlike those, he was not afraid of the consequences of making mistakes. Principle was more important to him. As Aristotle remarked: "Great masses of men are more easily led by personality than they are roused by principle." Clemenceau had both in abundance. He was not named The Tiger for nothing.

He always upheld the right of free speech and the press, a dangerous position during times of great political and economic flux. The words of the American banker David Harum might have been his motto: "Do unto others as they would do to you *and do it first*." He had a firm opposition to compromise. Men in every age become ministers, aware they will refuse in power to do that which they promised in opposition. Not this man. Anyone who takes, like Clemenceau, high principle and serious endeavour into political life is not playing the game.

## EARLY LIFE

Clemenceau's father Benjamin was a passionate Republican who had been sentenced to exile in Algeria by Napoléon III but set free in Marseilles before the deportation order was carried out.

Clemenceau was born in 1841. He studied medicine in Paris and in May 1865 qualified as a doctor like his father before him. During his student years he had founded several magazines and written articles attacking the Imperial regime. He spent 77 days in prison in 1862 for putting up posters announcing a demonstration. In 1865 Imperial agents began cracking down on dissidents many of whom ended up in the penal colony Devil's Island. In July 1865, Clemenceau left for the U.S. where he ran a medical office and was New York correspondent for a Paris newspaper. Then he took a post teaching French and horseriding at a girls' school, later marrying one of his students,

Mary Elizabeth Plummer, with whom he had three children before they divorced. He returned to Paris around 1870 when the Third Republic was established, after the collapse of the Second French Empire due to French defeat in the Franco-Prussian War.

Clemenceau then threw himself wholeheartedly into a political career and in 1876 he was elected to the Chamber of Deputies, joining the far left and quickly becoming leader of the Radical section. In 1880 he founded a newspaper, *La Justice*, which became the voice of Parisian Radicalism. He held his Chamber of Deputies seat until defeat in the 1893 elections, after which he turned his full energies to journalism.

## THE DREYFUS AFFAIR

In December 1894, Captain Alfred Dreyfus, a member of the general army staff was found guilty of treason by court martial on the basis of a unanimous verdict. He was given a terrible punishment – condemned to Devil's Island, the notorious prison camp in French Guiana, and the prolonged torture of solitary confinement in a tropical climate.

The *bordereau* (detailed memorandum) used to convict Dreyfus had been retrieved in a wastepaper basket at the German Embassy by a cleaning lady who was in the employ of French military counter-intelligence. This document had been torn up into minute pieces but was pieced together. It contained information on French field artillery.

As Dreyfus was a man of means, there had been considerable doubt as to whether he would really have sold secrets to Germany for financial gain when he did not need money. And what else could be the motivation?

The trial had lasted for four days, held in camera, and the accused was defended by one of the country's most able advocates. However, an element that escaped comment at the time, probably because it was simply not known, was that the evidence for the prosecution was never disclosed to the defence. This was a travesty of justice.

Dreyfus was of Jewish Alsatian origin. Alsace, located on France's eastern border with Germany, had long been a contested territory which was annexed by Germany in 1871 after the Franco-Prussian War. It remained a German province until 1918 when France reclaimed it. In 1871 between 100,000 to 130,000 Alsatians (of a total population of about a million and a half) chose to remain French citizens and left the province, many of them resettling in French Algeria.

Dreyfus' family moved to Paris at that time. They had long been established in the area of Alsace that traditionally was German-speaking, and his father Raphael spoke Yiddish and conducted his business affairs in German. The first language of most of Alfred's elder brothers and sisters was German or one of the Alsatian-German dialects. Alfred and his brother were the only children to receive a fully French education.

Therefore, in French eyes, his background was suspect and the fact he also was a Jew played into the hands of racists and anti-Semites.

Not long after the condemnation of Dreyfus, the military counter-intelligence section at the French War Ministry had a change of leadership. Colonel Georges Picquart, who had been in charge of reporting on the Dreyfus case to the War Minister, received the appointment. He was a young, brilliant and extremely conscientious officer, like Dreyfus of Alsatian origin.

During a further inquiry into the evidence in 1896, he came to the conclusion that the incriminating papers were not in the handwriting of the condemned Dreyfus but rather of another officer, Major Charles Marie Ferdinand Walsin Esterhazy. He suspected that Esterhazy was a Prussian spy and he had forged the *bordereau* which convinced the court of the guilt of the accused.

Picquart was told by the authorities to keep silent about his discovery. He persisted and was removed from his post and abruptly sent to inspect the intelligence service in the east of France. From there he was sent to Marseilles and later Tunis, to keep the lid on the cover-up. (Revisionist historians put forward the hypothesis that Esterhazy may have been a double agent.)

The new facts about the Dreyfus case were leaked and Clemenceau resolved to start a campaign for the revision of the case. At that stage he was not convinced that Dreyfus was innocent of the charge but was nevertheless sure that he had been wrongly convicted.

Once he doubted that there was fair play, he immediately displayed those qualities of personal and political courage, persistence, disregard of popularity and concentration of the powers at his command that had distinguished his political career. He was, as always, indifferent to the strength and numbers of his opponents. Which in this instance were in the vast majority.

Together with the author Émile Zola, the socialist Jean Léon Jaurès (editor of *La Petite République*) and other radicals, Clemenceau claimed that, even if guilty, Dreyfus could not be legally condemned on what was false evidence and forged documents, none of which had been provided to the defence to challenge in court. He and his friends faced the most powerful forces in the State and the newspapers in their quest for justice. At that stage they had no inkling of just how far those forces were willing to go to maintain the status quo in the Dreyfus Affair.

The *affaire* dragged on with suicides, apparent suicides in custody – and duels (several fought, successfully, by Picquart).

On January 13th 1898, Clemenceau published Zola's *J'Accuse*, an open letter to President Félix Faure, on the front page on *L'Aurore*, outlining the facts of the case and the cover-up that followed. Zola was charged with treason and libel. The case was lost and Zola fled to England to avoid imprisonment.

After the trial of Émile Zola, Picquart was himself accused of forging the note that had convinced him of Esterhazy's guilt, and arrested.

A retrial of Dreyfus was eventually ordered in 1899 and he

was brought back to France. On September 9th before a military court he was again found guilty with "extenuating circumstances" and sentenced to 10 years' detention.

The verdict caused public outrage, however, and he was hastily pardoned by the President and released. He accepted the pardon on condition he could still continue to try to prove his innocence.

In 1900 a bill was introduced declaring that all actions for matters connected with the Dreyfus affair, except murder and treason, were null and void. It was the "policy of the sponge" and met with opposition from the supporters of Dreyfus who saw in it a stifling of justice. It was adopted on 24th December 1900. Picquart, indignant at the amnesty, resigned from the army by way of protest.

In 1906 the first report of the committee appointed to examine the whole affair was released. It exonerated Dreyfus of all blame and declared him to be a victim of conspiracy based on perjury and forgery. It secured the overturn of the second trial and restored him to his position in the army after years of martyrdom.

This of course also absolved Picquart, who was then promoted to Brigadier-General. He was Minister of War in Clemenceau's first Cabinet (1906-1909).


## IN OFFICE

In 1902 Clemenceau was elected to the Senate and, on March 12th 1906, was appointed Minister of the Interior in the Ferdinand Sarrien government with its parliamentary majority of the *Bloc des gauches* (Left-Wing Coalition).

As Minister, Clemenceau bent his formidable mind to the problems of establishing and maintaining law and order. He supported the scientific methods of policing developed by Alphonse Bertillon. Among other advances, Bertillon had created anthropometry, an identification system based on physical measurements and other individual physical features. Before that, criminals could only be identified by eyewitness accounts. The method was eventually supplanted by fingerprinting, but his other contributions like the mug shot and crime-scene photography remain in place to this day.

Clemenceau and his Director of General Security, Célestin Hennion, founded the *brigades mobiles* ("mobile squads") which were nicknamed *brigades du Tigre* ("The Tiger's Brigades") after Clemenceau himself. He reformed the police force and implemented repressive policies towards strikes by workers in the mining, wine and electricity sectors.

Just two days before Clemenceau was appointed Minister there had been a mining disaster in the Courrières-Lens district which claimed the lives of over 1,000 workers stifled by gas or burnt alive in a series of underground explosions. The mine had made a profit of over 1000% the previous year and safety measures had not been adhered to. The surviving miners went on strike.

Clemenceau went to Lens and addressed a mass meeting of the miners. He said that the government supported the right to strike but also the right to keep the mines open. The strike went ahead and the military were ordered in to support the non-strikers and were attacked by the strikers. Clemenceau would not support the breaking of the law – especially as he perceived it was supported by agents of anarchists and reactionary forces exploiting the situation.

Speaking at Lyons on May 3rd he said:

> My position is between the political demagogues of the Church, the clericals and the reactionaries on one side, who tried to hound on the troops (that I had been forced to call in) to fire on the strikers, who greatly provoked them. This the ecclesiastics and restorationists did with the hope of fomenting a revolt against the Republic – a revolt supported by certain military chiefs inspired by the clericals and their shameless

lack of discipline. The plot was frustrated, butchery was avoided.

On the other side, I am accused by the revolutionary socialists of indulging in brutal military oppression because I suppress anarchist rioting. This though no striker was wounded or killed. I acted for tranquillity while the monarchists fostered disturbances. The anarchists helped the monarchists, who had agents throughout perturbed districts, by denouncing the Republic and excusing mob violence.

Yet how stood the case? Was it I who organised a campaign of panic? Was it I who was responsible for the original explosion and strike? Was it I who brought about the state of things which resulted in general disturbance and might have tended towards another coup d'état? Nothing of the sort. I was suddenly called upon to deal with unexpected troubles. I acted for the maintenance of the Republic and kept the peace under the law.

Another test of his resolve was the strike of the electric engineers and workers of Paris.

## SCENE: CABINET OF THE MINISTER OF THE INTERIOR

The Minister, M. Clemenceau, is at work at his desk, dictating to his secretary and everything is going nicely. Suddenly the lights go out and darkness falls. Candles are obtained and oil looked for. The consequences of this lightning strike is brought home to the Minister as he sits with his wax tapers and old-world lamps glimmering around him. Dangers of every kind are lurking on the streets in the black night. The electric workers are on strike and he is to surrender and admit the rights of the few to blackmail the needs of the many. That is exactly how he perceives it.

Immediate action is necessary. Light is a necessity for security and for life. He calls on the State engineers under military control to light up Paris. It is done.

But here is the socialist Jean Jaurés and leader of the French Section of the Workers' International (SFIO), his companion-in-arms in the Dreyfus Affair, asking of him: "What are you doing, M. Clemenceau? You are outraging all your principles. You are interfering with the liberty to strike, which you say is sacred. If you were true to yourself you would convert the electrical supply of Paris now in the hands of the monopolists into a public service and give strikers every satisfaction."

Clemenceau replies: "This was a bitter fight between two irreconcilable antagonists against inoffensive people. The people of Paris for whom I am concerned had nothing to do with the matter. I knew nothing about the decision to strike until my own work was made impossible. There was a matter of public safety, the threat of the Metro by immersion by water, due to the suspension of electrical pumps and lifts. Lives could have been lost in the flooding unless the sappers and the firemen came to the rescue. I decided in favour of the people against the strike of the electrical engineers for more wages."

Clemenceau's image as a strong and practical Radical leader, who was nevertheless sensitive to the rights and conditions of the working class, considerably diminished the popularity of the socialists.

## THE POLICE

One of Clemenceau's main objectives for many years was to reform and improve the police force which was a complex legacy of a number of regimes from the revolution through royalist, imperial and republican regimes. The practice of hiring non-commissioned officers from the army, who qualified after five years' service, brought a rough, drunken and lazy element into a force which was already riddled with corruption.

Dr Edmond Locard, pioneer in forensic science, gave a damning assessment of this practice:

> Nothing is more harmful for the police than its obligation to hire non-commissioned officers. I accept that the army is a school of honour and courage. But it is not a school for police, and these officers bring three inutilisable virtues, of insolence, habits of revelry and laziness into their new careers. I do not conclude that the fact of having been a non-commissioned officer should prevent them from becoming policemen. I only believe that it is not sufficient reason by itself to oblige the police service to annually absorb a certain amount of men who become an encumbrance.

The Third Republic was the first political regime in France in which the organisation, errors, abuses and achievements of the police became the object of Parliamentary debate and an electoral issue. Police were forced to adapt their working methods, especially with the introduction of telegraph, telephone and eventually the car. It was an era that saw the rise in popularity of the detective story and the notion of the sleuth.

There were several police forces, all of which were complicated by a Kafkaesque administrative structure and the rivalries that existed between the different types of police organisation.

First, the uniformed police who were concerned with maintenance of order in its broadest sense. It was to these that the governments of the Third Republic paid most attention, especially in Paris. Their responsibility was to keep order on the streets.

Secondly, the judiciary or criminal police (*police judiciaire*) who concentrated on the repression of crime and the tracking down and arrest of criminals.

Finally, the political police concerned with the surveillance of public opinion and political movements. Their role was to make forecasts as an aid to government decision-making.

There was also a fourth part if the gendarmerie, a military corps, dependent on the Ministry of the Army, is taken into the equation. It took on a policing role in towns of less than 5,000 inhabitants.

While in theory the other three forces depended on the Ministry of the Interior, their statutes, level of autonomy, jurisdiction, organisation, size, means and real power were each very different.

The Sûreté Générale in Paris dealt with the whole of France, except Paris and the Department of the Seine. As the government's police arm its role was extensively political until 1907 and its budget came directly from the Ministry of the Interior. In addition, it had some rights over the municipal police as it took part in appointing the commissaires de police though it did not pay them. On the other hand, all the lower-ranking municipal police personnel were totally outside its jurisdiction, which was why the Sûreté was called 'a state without troops'.

Paris and the Department of the Seine came under the Préfecture de Police in Paris. Despite a law passed in 1884 which allocated the direction of their police to the municipal electorate and despite the claims of the Parisian municipal council, the Paris police, together with those of Lyons and later Marseilles, came under the Préfet de Police (Police Commissioner), a civil servant directly responsible to the Minister of the Interior. The Préfecture employed more police than all other forces put together and the budget greatly exceeded that of the Sûreté Générale.

No government, of which there were many under the Third Republic, would consider reducing such a resource. It was in Paris that revolutions and changes of regime took place. They all paid the greatest of attention to the Paris police and its chief was of greater importance than that of the Sûreté.

As for the municipal police, its status was complex and the administration of the Third Republic never succeeded in putting forward a clear view as to who was responsible for its powers – torn as it was between the tradition that these police powers should emanate from the local authority and Napoleonic ideas of centralisation. The fact was that the force was dependent on the Ministry of the Interior in some matters and on the local authority in others. The Ministry, and thus the Sûreté and the Préfets, were responsible for the appointment of the Commissaire de Police, an obligatory post in towns of over 5,000 inhabitants. The Ministry was also responsible for fixing the size of the force and that of the municipal budget in towns of over 40,000 inhabitants. The local authority was responsible for all the rest.

Towns of over 5,000 had their own police who theoretically came under the authority of a commissaire appointed by the Ministry but who were paid by the local authority. Apart from the commissaire, all other police appointments were made by the mayor who decided on their salary levels.

The system had several questionable consequences. Firstly conflict between the mayor and commissaires when the latter were seen to be too submissive to central government and thus too detached from local authority. The commissaires had great difficulty in getting local authority to obey them and in general they slid into the pocket of the mayor and his cronies if just to have an easy life. It required a great deal of tact and diplomacy if a commissaire was to keep both his masters happy.

The state of the municipal police was pretty awful. In most towns with a population of under 40,000, the mayor and municipal council decided how large a police force was necessary and to save money kept them as small as possible. The standards of men and resources were very poor. The criminal force was equally inefficient, because it was dependent on four different police authorities. This resulted in vast areas left at the mercy of gangs and criminals who prospered and sowed terror throughout whole regions.

## PRIME MINISTER

In October 1906, after six months as Minister of the Interior Clemenceau was called back from Carlsbad where he had gone to treat uncharacteristic gout in order to form his own Cabinet in place of that of Ferdinand Sarrien. There he assumed the post of Prime Minister while still keeping his former office. He would face even greater challenges and prove equal to them, as he had done during his career to date.

Time had affected him little. He had still the same energetic and determined frame and aspect of the fighter that he'd had decades before. His head was now bald but his eyes looked out from under heavy white brows with the old fire, and his long white moustaches heightened the 'tiger' impression. Nothing, it seemed, had mellowed a man who by age should have been in slippers in front of a fire, reminiscing over his past glories and defeats. He was as alert as someone twenty years his junior, power still apparent in his every movement.

Despite the seriousness of his pursuits, he had an impish sense of humour. A tale he was fond of reciting was a passage from Lucian's *Dialogues of the Dead*. Minos, the appeal judge of the Underworld, where people pass after death, is confronted by Sostratus a notorious pirate, who is brought before him for punishment.

Clemenceau delivered every line, word for word:

*Sostratus:* A word with you, Minos. See if there is not some justice in my plea.

*Minos:* What, more pleadings? Have you not been convicted of villainy and murder without end?

*Sostratus:* I have. Yet consider whether my sentence is just.

*Minos:* Is it just that you should have your deserts? If so, the sentence is just.

*Sostratus:* Well, answer my questions. I will not detain you long.

*Minos:* Say on, but be brief; I have other cases waiting for me.

*Sostratus:* The deeds of my life – were they my own choice, or were they decreed by fate?

*Minos:* Decreed, of course.

*Sostratus:* Then all of us, whether we passed for honest men or rogues, were the instruments of fate in all we did?

*Minos:* Certainly, Clotho prescribes the conduct of every man at his birth. *[Clotho is one of the Three Fates in ancient Greek mythology, responsible for spinning the thread of human life and making decisions on men's fate.]*

*Sostratus:* Now suppose a man commits murder under compulsion of a power which he cannot resist, an executioner, for instance, at the bidding of a judge or a bodyguard or that of a tyrant. Who is the murderer according to you?

*Minos:* The judge, of course, or the tyrant. As well ask whether the sword is guilty, which is but the tool of his anger which is the prime mover in the affair.

*Sostratus:* I am indebted to you for further illustration of my argument. Again, a slave sent by his master brings me gold or silver. To whom am I to be grateful? Who goes down on my tablets as benefactor?

*Minos:* The sender. The bringer is but his minister.

*Sostratus:* Observe then your injustice! You punish us who are but the slaves of Clotho's bidding, and reward these who do but minister to another's beneficence. For it

86

Minos:    will never be said that it was in our power to gainsay the irresistible ordinances of fate!

Minos:    Ah, Sostratus, look closely enough and you will find plenty of inconsistencies beside these. However, I see you are no common pirate, but a philosopher in your way; so much you have gained by your questions. Let him go, Hermes, he shall not be punished after that.

Clemenceau would let out a large roar of laughter after recounting the story from the pen of the ancient satirist, with a caveat that if taken seriously, there would not be a prison in the country. One thing he loved, practised and admired in others was a well-constructed argument. He won most of his but not always.

He and his friend Célestin Hennion (the country's best intelligence policeman and soon to become Director of General Security), would take that passage and discuss its implications within the context of their own opinions and beliefs. How much did destiny and fate play a role in the ebb and flow of the tides of men's affairs, as opposed to free will?

Hennion liked to quote Machiavelli in *The Prince*: "He says that Fortune only rules one half of man's fate, the other half resides in their own will. He reminds the reader that Fortune favours the strong or even violent hand, the more aggressive and bold young man rather than the timid elder."

"Well, then, Hennion, that puts you in the favoured position as I could be described as elder – but certainly not timid. We consider destiny as a sequence of events that is inevitable and unchangeable. Many Greek legends and tales tell us the futility of trying to outmanoeuvre an inexorable fate that has been correctly predicted. Can that possibly be the case?"

"I suppose that precludes any effective intervention from

man? If we accepted that notion, well, then, we would resign our positions right now. So can we seriously believe that fate is destiny? A power or agency that predetermines and orders the course of events?"

"Truly neither of us could ever have predicted that we would be in our respective public offices at this time," said Clemenceau, "particularly if you look back and put it into the context of both of our roles and stances in the Dreyfus case. Given the tides of that affair, at least in the early days, more than likely disgrace and exile should have been our lot."

"But can we see the hand of fate in that?" asked Hennion.

"Perhaps. Or was it because our collective will did not cave in under the most powerful forces against us? We survived and thrived. But I still ask myself what force of destiny or fate decreed the sequence of events that all but destroyed Alfred Dreyfus?"

"Yes, even the great and perceptive Machiavellian theory cannot explain or encompass such foul injustice. It does not fit the compass."

For all their philosophising, both men were of necessity pragmatists. They accepted that the preservation of law and order was paramount.


## THE IMPACT OF THE 'BLOND GIANT' ON POLICING

Clemenceau liked to joke about himself being *"Le premier flic de France"* ('the chief cop of France') though he knew, and proved it when he made him Director of General Security, that was rightfully Hennion's crown.

He and Hennion had many urgent issues to deal with, among which was the further reform and centralisation of the police force, the vast increase in crime in Paris and also in the provinces. The port city of Marseilles was becoming a problem both on the streets and in the matter of organising and controlling the police force. There was also a growing swell of civil protest by the wine growers in the Southern region which was being supported by the municipal authorities. It was of course being exploited by political factions including radical socialists and anarchists.

The blond, tall and handsome Hennion, nicknamed *Le géant blond* (the blond giant), was just the man to tackle any one or all of the problems. Born in 1862, son of a farm labourer, he joined the army at the age of 18 and campaigned in the 110th infantry from 1880-5 in Tunisia. He joined the police in 1886 and at 24 was an inspector in the specialised railway squads. He had a rapid rise through the ranks and was moved into intelligence work where he investigated organisations intent on overthrowing the Third Republic. He was engaged in surveillance on spies and investigated General Boulanger, once seemingly poised for a coup d'état.

He was appointed Police Commissioner in Verdun in 1890 to study the functioning of the police in the provinces, then Special Commissioner of the Police in Paris in 1893. During the 1890s he investigated the counter-evidence provided by Georges Piquart during the Dreyfus case, becoming a strong supporter of Dreyfus. Despite political pressure, he was one of the few police to seek the truth. At the retrial of Dreyfus in Rennes, he was responsible for his safety and keeping order in the city.

He was responsible for the security of Félix Faure, President of the Republic (1895-1899), especially during his travels in Russia. In September 1901 he thwarted an attack against the Tsarina during the second visit to France of Czar Nicholas II, and in 1905 he foiled an assassination attempt on Alfonso XIII, King of Spain, when an anarchist's bomb was thrown at him as he led a procession in Paris with President Loubet of France.

On January 28th 1907 he was appointed Director of General Security by Clemenceau. He was part of a modernist movement within the French Republic with Aristide Briand and Louis Lepine. He advocated great reforms and improvements in the police forces, modernising them both administratively and operationally with the introduction of mobile brigades, vice squads and forensic services, and the utilising of all modern methods of communication, telegraph, telephone and the establishment of fingerprinting and photographic archives.

With Clemenceau he also implemented more rigorous and exacting recruitment and promotion standards and more central control of the municipal police force. Hennion was, above all, concerned with the 'judicial' or criminal police where there was a lot to do to institute a professional service adapted to the conditions of the modern world. But also he had long been preoccupied with the recruitment and training of all police, inspired by his own experience and Clemenceau's assessment in 1906:

The wielding of authority is always a delicate matter; the more so, in a democratic regime where the borderline of respect necessary for the liberty of others is easily overstepped. The function of the police is almost entirely concerned with imposing constraints on the liberty of some for the protection of others.

One seems to find it natural, while demanding a fairly long training period for most state employees, even if their employment requires more routine than initiative, to throw young policemen straight into work dealing with all manner of material and moral interests, after nothing more than a feeble exam which hardly allows one to judge the most rudimentary extent of their knowledge.

They are given no effective guide or directives to help them in a task where they frequently dispose of the interests, liberty and honour of their fellow citizens who they are called upon to counsel and punish. This is why we need a school of police. A tentative start has been made; it must be extended. It is truly strange that at the start of the 20th century, after 35 years of the Republic, we should still need to ask for an institution to teach theory and practice to men destined for a profession that has no equal in its complexity.

Hennion established proper training, notably the School of Professional Practice in the Préfecture de Police. He wanted to teach the police "how to think for themselves and appreciate the importance of their function and the services which they could offer the community." He wanted a police school that would live up to its name.

In training, use was made of film of typical Paris street scenes and events that enabled instructors both to elicit the students' response and teach them the correct ways for the police to intervene – whether dealing with a brawl, street fight or accident. And of course there was the use of film for surveillance.

Other reform concerned the promotion system. He had two main aims here – to ensure promotion took place on clearly defined terms and to link promotion to higher professional qualifications.

It was but a few decades before that Yves Guyot, journalist, politician and economist, wrote about a police commissioner, not untypical of the time, and one whose type Hennion wanted to prevent ever getting into the position again. According to Guyot:

> There is a man in certain communities who nobody calls by his name, but by his title. The administration chose him from amongst the absinthe drinkers, chasers after women and drunkards whose habits prevent them from taking part honourably in social life in order to earn their living. Pushed out of the army, good for nothing, good enough for everything. This villainous, cowardly, aggressive, gossiping, venomous, ignoble and superfluous being, detested and abhorred by everybody. The representative of authority, the moral order, the family and property is: the police commissioner.

It was during Louis Lepine's long career at the head of the Préfecture that the outlines of professional police knowledge began to emerge. This was largely based on the new criminology in which France held the leading position. But if Lepine prepared the way, the most important step was taken by his immediate successor Hennion who is now considered the father of modern policing.

In 1907 Hennion had a file of newspaper reports which were clamouring for action, the consensus agreeing with a strong article published by the sensationalist and hugely popular *Petit Journal* which wrote that violent crimes in France had increased to unbelievable proportions, and produced the latest statistics to back it up.

The statistics quoted showed that over the past years, even when the population was not increasing significantly, criminals were never so numerous. The number of proceedings were: 114,181 in 1835; 200,000 in 1850; 300,000 in 1875; 400,000 in 1880; 500,000 in 1892; 520,868 in 1901 and 546,257 in 1906. Murders had increased by 40% – all due to the audacity of gangs, rogues and scoundrels of every kind.

The Apaches were kings of the streets. These were street gangs numbering 30,000 and consisting of young men between the ages of 15 and 20, who terrorised the capital. And according to the *Petit Journal* this threat was being exacerbated with weak laws, the extraordinary indulgence of the courts and insufficient numbers in the police force.

There were many causes offered for this proliferation of crime: alcohol, too much freedom in access to bars, shady hotels and "the unfortunate spirit of humanitarian sentimentality – for the criminals but not for the good people". According to the *Petit Journal,* gang members were arrested and then let go or given minimal sentences when they deserved good sentences with hard labour instead of parole and reduction of sentences. When in prison they were well housed and fed, given books and not enough work. Under such conditions how could rogues fear justice? It was common for judges, so lenient on criminals, to reserve severity for the police.

"Policing on the streets has become impossible," offered one police source.

They needed staff, ten times more than they had. The *Petit Journal* asked: "What more is needed for the triumph of the wicked but to see police agents accused in court by mercurial judges?"

It was as bad in the provinces where vagrants terrorised rural roads and farmers. What could 32,000 rural police do against an army of 200,000 nomads, a population of tramps wandering around rural France, some of whom terrorised locals and farmers? Rural police were primarily servants of the mayors and their duties already absorbed them. The steady increase of crime, the number of Apaches growing in cities, and tramps in the countryside only served to show the need for more police. But even if there was an increase in the police force, to effect improvement "childish humanitarianism must be given up".

"You want to moralise the condemned and not make them suffer? If [so] work the criminals . . . work alone is moralising." So concluded the article which conveniently ignored the fact that France, despite its undoubted high reputation in the fields of academic, literary, scientific, judicial and criminal investigation techniques had off the coast of South America in French Guiana the worst system of penal retribution in the world. While it did house inmates with abominable crimes on record including some of the above-named Apaches, there were many more who had committed relatively minor offences.

## THE PROBLEM OF MARSEILLES

In the late 1860's local administrators in Marseilles were calling for the nationalisation of the municipal police with partial support from the State on the model of Lyons. But the government refused to do it, by arguing that the largely working-class city of Marseilles did not have the same risk of political turmoil as Lyons. But that would change as the port city grew in size and there was an increase in the trafficking of prostitutes from Africa and South America. There were territorial fights between pimps controlling different sections of the red light district. Lawlessness increased on the streets.

But there were also political considerations. A socialist mayor Simeon Flaissieres was elected in Marseilles in the 1890's. Central government was not too happy about that development.

It was time for the Sûreté to exercise control in Marseilles. And this necessity was spurred on by another event of economic and political nature. In 1907, responding to a major crisis of regional economic development, winegrowers, vinedressers and artisans in the Aude, Hérault, Gaudes and Pyrénées-Orientales took to the streets in an effort to compel the government to impose controls on the production and marketing of wine.

As a form of regional protest, it was significant in that it drew together all classes of wine producers and workers in a combined and united front. The region-wide wine-market depression in the spring and summer of 1905, causing municipal resignations and tax protests, persisted through the following two years into 1907. Between March and June 1907, a series of huge meetings and demonstrations shook the whole wine-producing south of the country.

500,000 gathered in Montpelier on June 9th. In demonstrations the image of hunger and misery recurred on the banners and symbols displayed. These symbols provided a dramatic reminder of the grinding poverty that winegrowers and workers faced. Appeals were made to the government to take action against producers of 'fraudulent wines'.

The local populations were electrified by the revolt that galvanised the entire Midi. Proprietors lent workers wagons and horses to travel to demonstrations and train fares were also reduced to accommodate protestors. There were confrontations with troops and police. There was a massive tax strike, resignations of municipalities and a military rebellion following the army occupation of lower Languedoc. Departments agreed to suspend not only collection of taxes but all municipal operations.

When Clemenceau responded by arresting several of the prominent leaders of the movement and sending troops to occupy the south, tensions escalated. Police and troops were attacked and demonstrators killed by gunfire in Narbonne. These tragic events provoked a storm of reaction. The killings and the subsequent riots in Montpellier provided a turning point in the 1907 revolt.

Demonstrations died down and the government passed legislation requiring all winegrowers to declare the size of their vineyards and harvests each year. Addition of water was forbidden and a surcharge was put on sugar. By July calm had been restored.

In response, Clemenceau on the advice of Hennion set about creating in 1907 mobile brigades, one of the first being established in Marseilles.

Clemenceau had agreed that Marseilles had to be sorted out and already Hennion had succeeded in getting one of his own men in as head of the police department, who had in turn gathered together a top-quality team of men who were dedicated to criminal investigation. Hennion then got rid of the useless cronies of the municipal authority and initiated a campaign carried out by the head of police to stamp out and legally punish corruption in the force. The mayor and the Préfet did not dare protest or interfere, such was the public and media outcry against crime in the port. And the President had criticised the inadequacies of policing in the port in Parliament.

❧

The attention of the most powerful politician and the greatest policeman in France was on Marseilles – winds of change were blowing from the direction of Paris.

# 5

## CASINO ROYALE

### MONTE CARLO, AUGUST, 1907

It was a sweltering August in Monte Carlo, the exotic Monégasque playground, a setting of wealth, glamour, intrigue and – inevitably where money is involved – scandal, jealousy, greed and crime. In this gem of luxury and Mecca of gambling, located between the sparkling Mediterranean Sea and the majestic Alps in one of the smallest countries in the world, there was the aroma of wealth on every street. And money always attracts unwelcome guests.

It was populated with larger-than-life characters, some of whose obsessions and decadent tastes were touched by evil and some of whose actions would have led to tragic consequences with or without the influence of the famous casino. The casino was the focal social point, like its companion the Opera House, for the titled, the rich, the hangers-on, the professionals and the desperate.

Just over four decades before, the ruling Grimaldi dynasty and Monaco faced bankruptcy. The first effort to establish a casino was teetering on the point of failure. The main problem was the lack of customers caused by the difficulty of reaching Monaco from the rest of Europe.

Then, in 1863, the twin brothers François and Louis Blanc, successful casino owners in Germany, took over the gambling operation. Like many a gambler, the Blancs epitomised the famous expression later coined about the Principality of Monaco: "A sunny place for shady people."

Born in 1816 to a poor tax collector, they showed from an early age an intense interest in gambling and financial operations. By careful gambling and speculation in stocks, they accumulated some modest capital and opened a bank, by any other name a firm specialising in stock speculation. They understood that to win in the stock market they needed to acquire exclusive information. They were able to infiltrate a communications system owned by the French government and bribe a few well-placed employees. In the next two years, they enjoyed steady profits from buying and selling government stocks. Eventually their scheme was uncovered. They were charged with corruption but, by hiring a top lawyer and pleading that they were doing nothing different from what the Rothschilds did, they were acquitted.

The bank was closed and they decided to concentrate on gambling. They acquired a concession and opened a casino in Homburg in 1863, which was an immediate success. Dostoevsky wrote his story "The Gambler" on the basis of his gambling on roulette in Homburg, where he lost all his royalties on future works.

François Blanc, keeping his eye on potential competition, went to Monaco and made an offer to Prince Charles III to buy a concession on the casino for 50 years for the sum of 1.7 million francs. On March 31st 1863, the prince approved the deal.

The Blancs lavishly decorated the casino. New hotels and villas were built, work began on a railway to connect Monaco with other coastal cities, and a new service of bigger and better steamers was instituted between Nice, Genoa and Monaco.

They also insisted that the place where the casino was located – Les Spélugues – had to be renamed. The name basically meant

"The Caves" but had the connotation of "a den of thieves". The new owners of the concession must have thought it was a little too close to the bone. After some thought Prince Charles agreed to commemorate his name and call it Monte Carlo – Mount Charles.

The railway opened in 1868 and the flow of visitors increased dramatically. Over the next decades the profits grew to such an extent that the Prince was able to abolish all taxation on the principality's citizens. The number of hotels expanded from 2 to 48; the numbers of jeweller's and florist's from 3 to 15 and 1 to 15 respectively. In 1900 there were 85 wine merchants and the Opera House and Oceanographic museum were established.

The Blancs paid the Prince of Monaco a yearly subsidy of millions of francs for permission to carry on their business in his territory. The administration paid a revenue to its shareholders of over 25 million francs per annum. The authorities were pledged, for the state of their own continuance, to pay any player on the spot, no matter how great the winnings. The coffers of the principality overflowed beyond belief, so much so that the head of the Grimaldis was able to abolish taxation on the citizens of the state. Even greater evidence of wealth was provided by the death of Louis Blanc in 1879, who left control of the Casino and a fortune of 72 million francs to his son Camille.

At the end of the 19th century almost a million tourists were visiting annually. Monte Carlo had become the favourite play-ground and gambling destination for players, aristocracy, royal families, self-made millionaires, great artists and inevitably con-artists and chancers of every nationality – and of course women of loose morals and intent.

## SHADY PEOPLE & HIGH SOCIETY

During 1873, Joseph Jagger, an engineer from England, gained world publicity by 'breaking the bank' at Monte Carlo.

Born in the village of Shelf near Halifax in Yorkshire, he had gained his practical experience of mechanics working in the cotton-manufacturing industry. He extended his experience to the roulette wheel, speculating that its outcomes were not purely random sequences but that mechanical imbalances might result in a bias towards particular outcomes.

In 1873 he hired six clerks to clandestinely record the outcomes of the six roulette wheels at The Beaux-Arts Casino at Monte Carlo. He discovered that one of the wheels showed a clear bias in that nine of the numbers – 7, 8, 9, 17, 18, 19, 22, 28 and 29 occurred more frequently than others.

He placed his first bets on 7th July 1875 and quickly won a considerable amount of money – £14,000 (roughly £896,000 nowadays) – and over the next three days amassed £60,000 in earnings, with other gamblers in tow to emulate his bets. In response, the Casino rearranged the wheels, which temporarily threw Jagger into confusion.

After a losing streak, he finally recalled that a scratch he had noted on the biased wheel was not there any more. Looking for the telltale mark, he was able to locate his preferred wheel and resumed winning. Coming back at him again, the Casino began to move around the frets (the metal dividers between numbers), daily. Over the next two days, Jagger lost and gave up, but took his remaining earnings, then about £65,000 (roughly £4,160,000 nowadays) and left Monte Carlo, never to return.

Jagger resigned from his job at the mill and invested his money in property.

Of course, the Blancs wanted the publicity generated by stories of big winnings . . . as long as no run of luck cost the Casino too much . . . or ran too long. If a gambler won more money than available on a particular table, he was said to have *"faire sauter la banque"* ('broken the bank' or, literally, 'blown up the bank') and a black shroud was placed over the table until a new game was set up. No gambler, however, came even close to winning the whole reserves of the casino and the Blancs could rest confident that no one ever would.

Charles Deville Wells was a gambler and confidence trickster.

From his childhood, he dreamed of being rich. He referred to himself as an inventor, which in itself was an invention, and sought bank credit to help him develop his ideas. He also got funds from private investors who were as always looking for quick and easy returns. They would only find out much later that the con artist was investing their funds in a very old invention called the roulette wheel.

In July 1891, Wells went to Monte Carlo with £4,000 he had collected from investors and in an eleven-hour session broke the bank twelve times, winning a million francs. At one stage, he won twenty-three times out of thirty successive spins of the wheel. Wells returned a second time to Monte Carlo in November. During this session he made another million francs in three days, including successful bets on the number 5 in five consecutive turns.

Despite hiring private detectives to check out his actions, the Casino never found any evidence of a particular system employed by the winner. Wells later said it was just a lucky streak in which he employed the high-risk strategy Martingale which was simply doubling the stake after a loss in a bid to catch up on winnings on previous spins of the wheel. He put his gambling feats down to bravery and guts. "Anyone is free to watch me play, but the general defect of the ordinary casino player is that he lacks courage," he said. Crowds constantly surrounded any table he was playing at, many copying any bets that he made.

In April of 1892, Fred Gilbert wrote the song, well known to this day, which was a hit when sung by musical-hall star Charles Coburn, entitled "The Man Who Broke The Bank At Monte Carlo". It was apparently inspired by Wells – it certainly helped Wells to become a celebrity.

> *I've just got here, through Paris, from the sunny southern shore;*
> *I to Monte Carlo went, just to raise my winter's rent.*
> *Dame Fortune smiled upon me as she'd never done before,*

*And I've now such lots of money, I'm a gent.*
*Yes, I've now such lots of money, I'm a gent.*

*Chorus*

*As I walk along the Bois Boolong*
*With an independent air*
*You can hear the girls declare*
*"He must be a millionaire."*
*You can hear them sigh and wish to die,*
*You can see them wink the other eye*
*At the man who broke the bank at Monte Carlo.*

*I patronised the tables at the Monte Carlo hell*
*Till they hadn't got a sou for a Christian or a Jew;*
*So I quickly went to Paris for the charms of*
*mad'moiselle,*
*Who's the loadstone of my heart – what can I do,*
*When with twenty tongues she swears that she'll be true?*

When Wells entered a night spot, the orchestra would strike up the tune of the popular hit. It seemed he had it made; even if he paid off his investors and creditors with a good profit, he would have plenty left over. But it was not the road the rotund little conman wished to travel. And like many of his kind he was just as adept at spending the money, living a lavish lifestyle.

He maintained the myth that he was a brilliant inventor and had come up with the idea of a fuel-saving device for steamships. He persuaded many wealthy investors to again sink money into this spurious venture. In the winter of 1892 he made another trip to Monte Carlo in a large yacht, the *Palais Royal*, with his young mistress Joan Burns, on the pretence that the yacht was being used to test his device.

He had another lucky streak, breaking the bank six more times, but then proceeded to lose all his winnings and the additional money he had conned from investors in the interim with the excuse that the fuel device had to be repaired.

The game literally was up and Wells was later arrested at Le Havre and extradited to England to face charges of fraud. He was found guilty at the Old Bailey and sentenced to an eight-year prison term.

He was another of those rogues who ignored the lessons of the past. He later was again imprisoned for three years for fraud and, after serving his sentence, left England for France of all places where he got up to his old tricks, under the name of Lucien River, and a financial scam involving no less than 60,000 depositors promised interest of 1% per day – which landed him another prison sentence of five years.

Apparently this time he flew the coop again and was arrested in Falmouth, in a finely fitted steam yacht and with some of his ill-gotten gains on board, before being returned to France to face a tune of an entirely different melody than the one that made him famous.

He died in poverty in Paris in 1926.

Florenz Ziegfeld, the American master showman, went to Monte Carlo in 1906, won a million dollars in the casino and saw the *Folies Bergère* in Paris. Inspired by this, the first Ziegfeld Follies appeared on Broadway in 1907-08. He was famous for lavender shirts, long telegrams, long-distance telephone calls and frequent unreasonableness. He owned six custard-coloured Rolls Royces and travelled in a private railroad car.

Lily Langtry, the famous British actress and mistress of royalty (Oscar Wilde was quite smitten with her), liked to visit Monte Carlo in her spare time and visited the Casino regularly, losing frequently before in 1907 becoming the first woman to break the bank. She was 54. Her final home was a villa in Monaco which she named 'Le Lys'. She had married Hugo De Bathe, 19 years her junior, in 1898. He lived in Nice and was only called on occasionally to take the bare look from her on social occasions. When his father Sir Henry de Bathe died she took on the title Lady de Bathe, despite the fact that her marriage was nothing but a sham. Her constant companion, friend and confidante was Mathilde Peat, the widow of her butler.

The French Riviera was the destination, winter and summer, for Europe's élite. Queen Victoria, the Czar of Russia, King of Bavaria, and merchant magnates such as Thomas Lipton were among the familiar faces in the area. Between rounds of clay-pigeon shooting and roulette at the Casino in Monte Carlo, the wealthy travellers moved about on their private yachts, anchoring in the bay of Villefranche-sur-Mer.

In 1907, the Belgian King Leopold II owned most of Cap Ferat and was prevented from expanding his domain by Parisian baroness, Mme Beatrice Ephrussi de Rothschild of the famous banking family, who purchased seven hectares on the narrowest strip of the isthmus. She had fallen in love with the area after visiting her husband's cousin, Theodore Reinach, who was building a Grecian-style villa in Beaulieu-sur-Mer. She decided to build a summer palace inspired by the Italian Renaissance. Pink was her favourite colour and she would dress from head to toe in it with matching parasol and handbag. Her villa in Monte Carlo was called "Rose De France". There she invited her friends to lavish parties reminiscent of the best days of the ancien régime.

These were the "rock stars" of Monte Carlo's heyday, living a life of leisure, luxury and wealth, but behind the glittering façade the truth was they were all at the same time both parasites and prey of the all-devouring Casino.

## THE LURE OF THE CASINO

An empire built on a simple premise: lust for money. The centre of it all: the Casino, that magnificent edifice, a glittering, white palace set in gorgeous gardens with their palm-trees, giant geraniums and mimosa.

Away across the white balustrade of the broad magnificent terrace could be heard the whistle of the express "Flower Train" which travelled daily from Cannes to Boulogne faster than the *passenger-de-luxe*, bearing carnations, mimosa and violets from the Côte'Azur to Covent Garden flower market. Beyond stretched the sapphire Mediterranean – in the distance the blue hills of the Italian coast.

The privileged denizens of this fantasy palace were inevitably clad in evening dress, the *monde* and *demi-monde* temporarily on equal footing. Eagerly they climbed those fateful steps and entered an enormous hall of great height with a polished parquet floor, the walls covered by huge pictures let into the gilded panelling, separated from each other by pilasters of gold. Ceilings, where electric lights glowed, were painted and the general effect was of almost overpowering magnificence. At one end of this hall a series of swing-doors constantly opened and closed again. At the doors stood alert sentinels in long frock coats, watching in grave silence as the crowd moved to the inner sanctum – for beyond this huge room there was another and even a larger one, crossing it at right angles, and beyond that, still another.

Inside these salons, at intervals, under the domed roof, long tables were set, each one as long as two billiard tables. The glorious Mediterranean sun was kept out by thick expensive curtains, while over each table, as well as electric light, oil lamps, shaded green with billiard-table effect, cast a dull, ghastly illumination on the strained and flushed faces of the players. People may have wondered at this antiquated addition to the electric light. It was purely pragmatic in purpose and added as a result of a raid one night on the tables when the perpetrators cut the supply and in the darkness grabbed all they could get.

On each table, a long expanse of green baize cloth, marked with numbered squares and triangles, while at one end were two huge diamonds of red and black in either corner. Dividing each table at the centre was the wheel and the croupier with an ivory ball.

The ritual at the roulette tables was as predictable as a

religious ceremony, though the congregation as a whole would scarcely be welcome in a church of any denomination. They were all to a man and woman more like participants at a masked ball, with feelings, fear, tension, apprehension to be buried behind the disguise of indifference, win or lose. The upper-class players should not give way to euphoria or annoyance; money in their world should be so subservient to gentility as to be above thought and certainly expression. They were supposed to be ignorant of the realities, but even this breed was not immune to the consequences of speculation. There were enough of their kind resting in a certain weedy 'Suicides' Graveyard' not far distant to prove that point. And the palpable atmosphere of acute tension gave the lie to the indifference on the faces – the atmosphere and the combined odour of nervous perspiration and for the most part very expensive perfume.

The little ivory ball spun and fell on a numbered spot. The whirling of the wheel at the bottom, the opposite course of the ball, and the triangular silver stars which broke it, all made it a matter of chance into which apartment upon the wheel the ball was going to fall. So rapid was the paying out and gathering in of the money at the tables, the wheel was spun every minute and a half. The little cards, printed in red and black, which were provided by the casino authorities for recording the play, were pricked each time the wheel was spun. The flow of pernicious chance was hardly interrupted. The gamblers, the great and the greedy herd, imagined all sorts of repetitive patterns. Notes were taken feverishly in a sweat-induced haze to establish a repeating sequence and then bet on the opposite for the following run. Money was placed on the numbers from every part of the table. Sometimes the people pushed it themselves onto the chosen numbers, sometimes when they were too far away they gave it to one of the croupiers, who sat round among the crowd and pushed coins to the destined spot with their long Indiarubber-tipped rakes.

Behind each croupier, a higher seat was occupied by the

official in charge and constantly from his lips came the famous line:

*"Faites vos jeux, messieurs! Faites vos jeux!"*

The croupier swung the capstan and spun the ball which emitted a low humming tone as it whirled.

The croupiers were not as indifferent as they seemed. That was a role that they played to perfection. In fact, they were anything but indifferent to whether the bank won or lost. They were given instructions to attract players, to keep a close eye over the bank's interests and for their services were awarded prizes and premiums.

*"Rien ne va plus!"* was the signal that no more stakes could be put on the table.

When the wheel stopped, the number was called out: *"Rouge – dix-huit!"* Then the long rakes of the croupiers shot out from every part of the table, threading their way in and out of the masses of gold, silver and bank notes with extraordinary rapidity and well-practised manipulation.

A small fortune was swept into the bank until the table was almost bare. All done with the precision of a machine, without a single mistake, and hardly completed when the stakes of those who had won were added to in a shower of golden coins. It took a croupier in Monte Carlo a year to learn his business, but when he had mastered it, no magician could provide a more startling exhibition. No single coin rolled off its appointed square, but fell flat and motionless within an inch of the stake at which it was aimed.

Within no time at all, the stakes were again being spread over the board, for the next coup.

Despite the assumed indifference of the gamblers, one who could stand back from the concentrated play could observe the greed of the collective gaze at the table with its scattered *louis d'or* and streams of gold and the constant chink, chink of the money. So near, yet so far away, torturing those losers who were reduced to playing for the smallest stakes, praying for the lucky break . . . standing watching the play for some sort of pattern, some hint, some sign, even some superstition that would postpone their own personal destination of zero. The colour, the number to bring them back from the dead. Surely, in this game of chance, there was one small certainty?

*"Messieurs! Faites vos jeux!"*

The room was always crowded and the atmosphere quivering with the tension so common and peculiar to the act of gambling. It seems that down through generations the act of throwing money on chance has that effect. As it should, for why should people expect that acquiring money without toil should be free from some form of nervous retribution?

Aristocracy rubbed shoulders with women of ill repute and men laughed heartily with beautifully attired cocottes from Paris or stars of the film or stage. From such wealth and glamour, robbers, conmen and thieves are never very far away, all bathing in the glow of the light of the greatest casino in Europe and probably the world, for a brief time escaping the vicissitudes of the world outside and indulging in a collective fantasy.

Among the crowd the casino police moved silently, incognito, watching out for the pickpockets and swindlers who infiltrate the salons, and always present to settle the inevitable disputes that break out when gamblers are at play.

*"Messieurs, faites vos jeux!"*

Here, women and men seized by the demon of speculation, an addiction as powerful as that to drugs and drink constantly cast their nets into the sea of chance, despite all the odds against retrieving a fortune.

The red and black wheel spun, the little ivory ball clicked over the numbered spaces, slowly lost its impetus and, after spinning about unevenly, made a final jump and fell with a loud click.

*"Zero!"* cried the croupier.

⌒⌒⌒

The casino for all its glamour, fashion and innate excitement could, by the very nature of its ability to break a man by transforming his wealth to nought in instant, provide a motive for desperate even deranged behaviour. And desperation can drive a man or woman to extremes that in their previous life would have been beyond contemplation. In the matter of gambling, no different than any other human activity that becomes an obsession, there is a generational amnesia: however long they stretch back in history, or however harsh the consequences, lessons are not learnt.

Fortune, right back to the days of antiquity, was represented by a symbol that never lost its relevance in the passing of millennia. The Roman image is that of Fortuna, with the wheel which she blindly turns, emblematic of the endless changes in life between prosperity and disaster. It was the personification of luck in the Roman religion. She might bring good luck or bad, and could be represented as veiled or blind.

In Shakespeare's *Henry V* are the prose lines:

> "Fortune is depicted as blind, with a scarf over her eyes, to signify that she is blind. And she is depicted with a wheel to signify – this is the point – that she is turning and inconstant, and all about change and variation. And her foot, see, is planted on a spherical stone that rolls and rolls and rolls."

Not much different from the roulette wheel in Monte Carlo.

Legend or myth claimed that François Blanc said he had sold his soul to the Devil for the secret of roulette, the total of the wheel numbers adding up to 666. Whatever about that, there was plenty to occupy the devil's disciples in this strange and exotic place where extravagance and well-disguised penury mingled, where beauty and depravity were not far removed and where sanity and insanity were quickly interchangeable.

Beside the glamour, the fashion, the trappings of wealth,

lurked men and women of notorious reputation, and others waiting to be damaged by ill-met association. Foreigners were preferred – one among them a certain Emma Levin, the Swedish widow of a Danish stockbroker. There congregated Russian Archdukes and their mistresses, South American women awash with jewels, and other great figures of doubtful fame. The scent of expensive perfume was everywhere and rumours abounded – rumours of orgies and satiation of illicit appetites of all kinds – men with men, women with women and the interchange of both. The so-called noble mixed with the most depraved, depravity being a dubious badge of honour in this seemingly most glamorous of worlds. There were fancy-dress parties and the enactment of dubious and ancient rites. There were few of the collected mob whose reputations had not been sullied in one way or another in their past lives. The whiff of odious vice and scandal was ever-present.

And there was also an undercurrent of desperation, because gambling in the casino was not the simple preoccupation of those who had the capital to fritter away. There were those whose existence and future absolutely depended upon the roll of a wheel, the throw of a dice, the fall of a card. Such was life in the great Casino of Monte Carlo. In addition, a stroke of ill fortune, an unseemly incident, could consign any of them to official, societal and actual oblivion.

A succession of sharp taps, as the little ball was tossed hither and thither, furiously jumping from one side to another, flung back for an instant upon the sloping side of the basin, returning to its mad career over the slots. And then a sudden final click as it fell to rest. The hyperventilating audience were, as always, reduced to silence. Not far away lay the ghosts of the hostages to the misfortune inherent in devotion to this ritual.

For some the disaster that accompanies great loss under this gilded roof was too much to bear. In one room there was a seat called The Suicides' Chair, for over the preceding years no less than ten men and women who were occupiers had taken their lives and were buried in secret in the Suicides' Cemetery. One man who had lost a quarter of a million in a month threw himself under the Paris Rapide train at the long bridge over the Var.

The cemetery is situated in a small overgrown piece of land, not a long distance away, because there is no such thing as real distance in Monaco. There is the hidden graveyard; nobody then knew where it was. And in that forlorn plot lay the bodies of nameless gamblers who had sacrificed all their happiness, honour, life to the ebony basin. More than evidence, if it were needed, about the fear and desolation that existed among the glamour under the gilded roof of the Casino. The chronically addicted who lost great sums were allowed to apply to the administration for a *viatique* (from Latin *viaticum* meaning 'provisions for the journey') – sufficient sums to pay expenses to any destination after losing everything. It was never refused but many preferred to take the short trip to the little cemetery.

At Monte Carlo, the talk was always of a run of sequences, the times zero-trois had turned up, how little one ever won on en plein or thirty-six. The yellow cards of admission were monthly granted to those who were approved by the committee of inspection who judged by appearance whether one had money to lose. That, of course, was not always possible – the very art of the gambler is to disguise the mind's construction in the face.

Nonetheless even the best of them with the greatest of resources could have all that they possess reduced to zero by the gaming tables and the roulette wheel. It is an old adage that a fool is easily parted from his money. It was all the more applicable when the purse was threadbare from the start.

A lot of the women were more prone to gamble and prepared to go to the last throw. The smart women from Paris, Vienna or Rome never lost the head. They gambled discreetly. The fashionable cocottes seldom lost much, and always kept their eyes on the men. If they lost they generally secured a loan from someone, no doubt in return for a reciprocal favour, not of the monetary kind. It was an old adage that when people went to Monte Carlo, they left their morals at home. There was little caution in the wind that blew over the polished parquet of the elegant *sales-de-jeu* in the casino.

## APPOINTMENT WITH DEATH

Emma Erika Levin was one who revelled in the atmosphere of Monte Carlo, the lure of the roulette wheel, and the fun of attracting men from 18 to 80 – anyone who could remove the money from her account or the jewels from her neck. She was surrounded by them but unaware of her danger in her blind love for the world of excitement, her caution cast aside by the death of her husband and the release of her inheritance. Eighteen years previously she had married a Jewish stockbroker Leopold Levin of the firm Levin & Sons with offices in Copenhagen and Berlin. Her husband had died two years previously and left her well off. Her new-found freedom and life indicated that she had led a closed and conservative existence under the eye of the older man. Her previous life therefore had made her a very unsuitable candidate for the society of Monte Carlo – or a very suitable one from the point of view of the many predators who lurked there.

A couple whose acquaintance she would make had arrived in the Principality the previous October to stay for the season: Sir Vere and Lady Goold. They had taken up residence at Villa Menesini with a young pretty woman who was introduced to neighbours as their niece. According to a chemist and Englishman, Mr Reilly, who knew him as a regular customer, Sir Vere was a quiet unassuming man, well spoken, and Reilly let it be known that the couple were well off and had taken a suite in the villa for the whole season.

Lady Goold was French but spoke English fluently. The couple mixed with the best society and were frequently seen at the tables in the Casino. The villa they lived in was close to the Carlton, the celebrated night restaurant along the new road which runs parallel but below the Boulevard des Moulins. The villa was a large building let out in ten suites and the Goolds lived on the fourth floor. The niece, Mademoiselle Giroudin, was about 25 years of age and was friendly with the daughters of English doctors who practised in Monte Carlo. The couple visited the chemist shop and always paid their bills regularly. There was nothing much more known about them at the time.

They were, it would emerge, devotees of the house where Lady Fortune's spinning wheel ruled her subjects, all slaves to the game of chance, watching her wheel turn with a rapt mixture of hope and fear.

There, Sir Vere and Lady Goold subjected themselves to the vagaries of the Wheel of Fortune until the arrival at zero prompted a gamble of somewhat different consequence in August of 1907.

# 6

## LE TRAIN

**MARSEILLES, AUGUST 1907**

In the early morning of August 6th, shrouded in steam, the 5.38 a.m. train from Monte Carlo pulled up at the designated platform of Gare de Marseilles Saint-Charles. It was the height of the tourist season and the platform was thronged with disembarking passengers and marked by the feverish activity of the overworked porters.

One, Beraud, was given the task of bringing a large trunk to the baggage section where it was due, according to instructions, to be forwarded to London. Sweat sprouting on his forehead from stress and effort in the heat, he brought it to the appropriate section where he placed it on the last existing space on the bottom part of the large wooden rack. He noticed an unpleasant smell emanating from it and wondered what it contained. He then speedily returned to the platform to retrieve more luggage and suffer extra punishment for his now constantly aching bones.

Meanwhile station commissaire Louis Pons, famous for his punctilious follow-up and examination of his underlings' work, was doing his rounds of the room, making sure that every bag and item of luggage was in the right section and placed correctly for quick and efficient removal. His devotion to duty was much lauded and he was personally proud of the performance of the service under his tutelage.

His team of porters did not resent or hate Pons because he was considered tough but generally fair. Everyone knew the lie of his land and knew never under any circumstance to get on his wrong side. So respected was he by his employers that his judgement was final. Beyond him there was no court of appeal.

His life outside his work was equally regimented. He tolerated no excess and in his life there was no room for the unexpected. When it turned up he dealt with it quickly and firmly, thereby keeping it at bay.

He noticed the recently delivered trunk and re-adjusted its position slightly to his own satisfaction. As he approached the next rack, he stopped in his tracks. Some instinct which he could not explain at the time, or afterwards, made him turn his attention to the trunk once more. The perennially prepared superintendent was not ready for the grim scenario which was about to unfold.

As he stood over the trunk, within centimetres of his gleaming black shoes he saw a small dark-red spot and then another fell on it and then another, forming a small pool. The origin seemed to be somewhere on the underside of the trunk. It looked like blood. Pons instantly recognised that to investigate it was not his business and momentarily was paralysed by a wave of anxiety which went from his toes to his stomach and then to his head and back to his stomach again. For him a most disturbing, unusual and unwelcome sensation.

How, he thought, would whatever might prove to be the explanation for this aberration reflect on his well-oiled operation and his department, hitherto run to within half a centimetre of perfection? He was no fool. Like at a port, all life passes through a train station, and quite a lot of unsavoury things can and did happen. Many of sufficient interest to the newspapers. The congregation of travellers were under the constant attention of a gaggle of robbers, pickpockets, conmen and prostitutes. Who in turn were the subject of observation of Pons, his security personnel and the undercover police. But all those eyes and all the precautions could not stem the whole tide of criminal intent. There had been numerous arrests made in the station, many unreported, and most of the rest attracting what could be described as cursory attention and a few paragraphs on the inside pages of the local newspapers. But a couple of incidents made the front pages – a stabbing after a row between two pimps, the arrest on a just-arrived train of a notorious fraudster. Pons winced at the memory and the perception that the wonderfully constructed station, so efficiently managed, accommodated within its august portals a den of iniquity.

In this instance, he recognised that if his dawning, anxious suspicion proved to be true, the local, national and the foreign press would come crawling like a plague of rats over his territory and, worst of all, his name would be dragged into reports. The object of newspapers, in his opinion shared by many, was to create sensation rather than further the cause of truth. It was of no comfort to Pons that he might be lucky enough to be portrayed in a favourable light. He detested the idea of such attention; his privacy meant everything to him. But as always, he knew, whatever his misgivings, he had to do his duty and properly. There was no question of cleaning up and disposing of the now-coagulating pool which had formed under the rack.

But of course, the thought had, even for an unacceptable instant, crossed his mind.

The cacophony of noise, the hissing of the steam, the shrill whistles of the guards, the shunting thunder of the trains had departed Pons' range of consciousness. He might as well have been solitarily confined in a cell, so occupied was he with his thoughts and the direction of his actions.

For a moment he felt dizzy with a confusion completely

foreign to his experience. His palms became wet with a cold sweat and he felt his heartbeat soar uncomfortably. He took several deep breaths and pulled himself together, considering such panic intolerable.

The anxiety having receded, he took one more deep breath and removed a notebook and pencil from his inside jacket pocket. He bent down and from the tag on the trunk took a note of the details. The names of the owners, destination and their current address which caused Pons some inexplicable comfort.

He returned to his office, shut the door, sat at his desk and from the drawer removed his pipe, filled and lit it. Momentarily he relaxed in his chair, then began to mull over what he perceived as his two immediate choices. He must, he realised, bite the bullet.

He could contact the owners. What would they say? That the trunk contained fresh meat or slaughtered poultry. He laughed inwardly at an explanation so outlandish that he would have to instantly ignore it. Of course he would be offered a bribe which he would also not countenance. There was no one that could not do with more money. People could have enough of sex, drink and food but never of money. And Pons of all people, given his character and behaviour, believed that any unlimited need leads to destruction. He was happy with his salary and his legitimate percentage of his porters' tips, on account of which he smoothed their daily passage. He kept them happy and the favour reaped a double return, cash and loyalty. A fair bargain. No whiff of corruption. Bribery was different in his book. Being bought meant being owned and Pons valued his independence. His employers acknowledged it as did his workers.

Too much to lose for too little. Because as sure as tobacco was in his pipe, the owners would try to buy him off.

He had only one choice. No other.

He picked up the phone and rang a valued friend but strictly on official business.

In his office at the Préfecture de Police in the Town Hall, central Marseilles, Inspector Charles Dupin was drinking a comforting cup of coffee. He was in an idle mood which was uncharacteristic of the best detective in the port city and indeed in the whole Côte d'Azur. He was well used to the unexpected nature of his job and simply became galvanised when anything came his way.

He loved what he did and considered it not work but a particular study of the human criminal act, most particularly of killing and its consequences. He was an advocate of the relatively new science of criminalistics currently most completely expressed by Hans Gross, the examining magistrate and Professor of Penal Law at the University of Graz. And of course that of Alexandre Lacassagne of the University of Lyons who had established a great reputation in France for criminal investigation and who had taken a young man Edmond Locard, a qualified doctor and lawyer, as his assistant – a young man who in time would become known as the Sherlock Holmes of France and would formulate the basic principle of forensic science: "Every contact leaves a trace." This became known as Locard's Exchange Principle. (The young Georges Simenon, detective writer, is known to have attended Locard lectures in 1919 or 1920. He would have been no doubt struck by Locard's statement that policemen "should have the method of mathematicians and the imagination of poets".)

For the past three years Dupin had kept in constant contact with Lacassagne and Locard and he recognised that their work would have a huge impact on criminal investigation. Already he was putting into practice Locard's principles, particularly in the preservation and examination of the crime scene.

Both he and Locard had embraced the methods of Adolphe Bertillon of the Paris Préfecture who had pioneered crime-scene preservation through the use of photography. For this purpose, in the tradition of Bertillon, Dupin had promoted a clerk, Lazare, who had studied art and sketching, as his official photographer. And of course he espoused Bertillon's anthropometry, the identification system based on physical measurements.

Dupin's character was in perfect tune with Bertillon's belief in cool and objective reasoning in his approach to his task and the separation of premise from the process of deduction. He never allowed the weight of his workload or pressure from his superiors to interfere with this method of investigation. And, as the mayor and the police commissaire learned very soon after the Inspector's appointment, he would brook no interference in the matter of his working agenda.

He was less concerned with the swiftness of his results than the sureness of them. He had also learned to be immune to the clamour and sensational behaviour of the newspapers but knew how to use them when he saw fit. He had learnt to be very careful, because a reporter could and would gut him as quick as a fisherman who had just landed his catch.

Dupin knew, and he drummed it into the psyche of his men, how important it was not to be swayed by gossip on the one hand and the easy and temporary eulogising the reporters and commentators employed. They looked for a hero and a villain but the roles could be easily interchanged. Solve the crime and you play the hero, fail to and you are handed the part of the villain.

He developed a relationship of trust with Pierre Gazeau, editor of *Marseille Dimanche*, who treated the reporting of crime with seriousness and responsibility, unlike his local counterparts and the national stringers who could be reporting a municipal meeting in the morning, a crime in the afternoon, a sports game or entertainment event in the evening. The same brigade had an alarming habit of falling back on 'creative journalism', especially in the face of looming deadlines. Crime came under the category of shock-horror and murder provided the excuse to throw any remaining journalistic ethics down the drain, most graphically by always attempting to predetermine the outcome long before the facts had been established or court process concluded.

Dupin had learnt from experience that when a crime of note is committed, opinions become extreme and that then bias rears its ugly head. The police were sought out and flattered at the early stages of an investigation but could afterwards be set up as a target and sacrificed on the altar of sensation. Dupin knew that he was an object of hatred because he kept the newshounds at a long arm's length and never let them within a quarter of a mile of a crime scene. The days when they could trample over the scene, contaminate evidence and photograph victims were over. Naturally this created huge resentment among the Fourth Estate and Dupin was perceived as an enemy of the hegemony of the press and so-called freedom. Freedom, as far as the Inspector was concerned, came with responsibility.

Dupin's best defence was his impeccable record but he knew that one mistake and his reputation would count for nought.

On the other hand he was a realist and crime had become a major target not just for the newspapers but also for the politicians, particularly in Paris, whose duty it was to stem the tide of lawlessness that had increased dramatically during the past decade. Marseilles being the second city and a large port had more than its share of criminal activity.

As a city commission report over two decades before noted, it seemed to be a particularly auspicious site for crime since it had a population at the same time changing and diverse, so different in habits, views and sentiments, and there was, as was said, a constant ferment of "perversity". As the city and port grew in the interim, crime also accelerated.

Also because of inefficiency, poor resources, corruption, in a matter of five years from the turn of the century the apprehension of armed robbers had halved and one year before, out of 3,700 thefts, almost three-quarters were without suspects. The city was under the control of the Bouche-du-Rhône Department which had a 50% higher theft rate and a 300% higher murder rate than the Department of the Seine.

Marseilles was the scene of spectacular crimes, including murders by organised gangs and regular territorial wars between the controllers of the lucrative trade of prostitution and traffickers from North Africa and the colonies.

And there was the enemy within the force. Dupin had investigated and prosecuted a ring of bent policemen who had been making up to 1,000 francs a month for protection. This added to the corrupt image of the city.

The municipality wanted to double the size of the force and wanted this subsidised by central government without any loss of control of the force for them. Naturally Paris would have nothing to do with such a poor bargain, despite the newspapers and local business looking there for a solution. Dupin and his team could well do without the small-time and oftentimes corrupt control of local influences and knew that their resources, numbers and effectiveness would be vastly increased by central control. They all knew, even though the Préfet was appointed by Paris, he played second fiddle to the mayor who was the effective head of police. The Préfet of the Bouche-du-Rhône depended on the mayor for the staffing of the force, who recommended favourites of his who were invariably accepted. There was one policeman for every 370 citizens and even though this might be considered a good ratio, their duties were not all related to fighting crime. There were visits to boarding houses, lodging houses, inspection of brothels and acting as messengers and guards. In the city, all these obligations having been satisfied, there were only 150 men per shift available for patrol service – one for every 4,500 citizens. Little wonder the criminals were running riot and little wonder that the focus of the top authorities in the capital were on Marseilles.

Thus there were other pressures, emanating from Paris. The previous year the Minister for the Interior, Clemenceau, now Prime Minister, wanted to put the municipal police in the hands of the central state and had earlier this year appointed his right-hand man Célestin Hennion as Director of the Sûreté Générale. The devolution of power to municipal governments in the Third Republic created a bulwark of resistance to the central state and Clemenceau wanted to break it. He was haranguing Parliament about the need to stem the growth of crime, pass reforms and implement investigation techniques that Dupin had long espoused. In this matter Dupin was at one with the President and Hennion.

Clemenceau had targeted Marseilles because, as Dupin and his bosses the mayor and the commissaire agreed, it was a large city and they controlled a territory three or four times that of the Paris headquarters. Apart from Paris and Lyons, no other French city rivalled Marseilles in size or significance.

So the politicians, knowing full well that the city was over-burdened and under-resourced, painted a picture of Marseilles as a city where crime had run amok: "On the Canebière they steal and rob people in broad daylight."

Dupin knew that he and his team's record in serious crime was a matter of admiration in Paris and the only insult that could be thrown was in the area of petty crime. Fair enough. Part of the game.

All the same it was clear that the Sûreté wanted control of Marseilles and that would ultimately make the police's job of fighting crime in the city easier. It was a time for change and this must be embraced. For someone in his position it was also exciting because, in the matter of criminology and forensic policing, France was heading the international forces.

Even though in his view politicians should be left to politics, the police to crime, and never the twain should meet, the Inspector knew the reality was that in France politics was never far from the surface of anything.

He feared that even if Hennion succeeded it would not be long until the bureaucratic umbilical cord would be cut. In this instance de jure would not be de facto. There were plenty of other factors that would intervene to prevent the best intentions of the Paris establishment from being carried out in the immediate sense.

Nevertheless, all parties knew that when Le Tigre and Célestin Hennion were on the case there would be only one result. Yes, all things considered, change would arrive and it was only a matter of time.

In any event, Dupin was a subscriber to Voltaire's dictum that it is highly dangerous to be right on a matter where the established authorities are wrong. He could play the game and exercise caution and restraint when the situation demanded.

On this August morning he had a lot on his plate but he was determined to enjoy his break and his coffee. His phone rang and he just let it ring. It prompted a memory. At his age memories were increasingly occupying his consciousness, a fact of life which he could not and did not resist. It was the ringing of the phone which prompted the visitation to the past.

He was nine years of age when his father brought him to the Universal Electrical Exposition in Paris. In the Pavilion there were booths in which people could listen to, by telephone, recitals from the Paris Opera House. There were two rooms, each divided into two compartments, fitted out with a dozen headphones through which visitors could hear the music.

As a child he found the effect magical. In the austere, dimly lit rooms, equipped with a row of headphones placed along the walls, there was complete silence. Then as he and his father lifted the two headphones to their ears, they were transported directly to the Opera stage. Closing his eyes, the reality was complete. It was as if he was in the audience listening to the great Krauss, hearing the orchestra and the applause of the audience.

Ever since, music was his greatest delight together with opera and the stage. It was the end of the earth compared to what he did for a living but he was not alone. Lacassagne and Locard were also, outside the parameters of their profession, greatly attached to the arts which provided soothing alternatives to the dark arts of crime and murder.

Dupin reflected on yesterday's monthly conference in Lyons with his team of police and investigators. They might have preferred to call it a lecture but one which they conceded was never boring. The purpose was to keep them motivated on one hand and abreast of the lead the French had established over the world, including the famous Scotland Yard, in methods of criminal investigation – most particularly in the area of murder.

The address was by Professor Lacassagne who had been accompanied by his assistant, the Inspector's friend Dr Edmond Locard.

The professor was on every level a fascinating character, a specialist in toxicology, bloodstain-pattern analysis and ballistics. He also had a keen interest in sociology and psychology and the correlation of those disciplines to criminal behaviour.

In appearance he was anything but the academic type, with a large handlebar moustache, the girth of an opera singer and a mischievous twinkle in his eye. He had the gait of a circus strongman.

His school at Lyons was widely influential. The basis of his theory was that the social environment was the breeding ground of criminality. The criminal was the microbe and was of no consequence until the conditions were present to enable it to breed. He was of the firm view that society has the criminals that it deserves. He became prominent as a result of his involvement in a number of high-profile cases such as the assassination of President Sadi Carnot, stabbed by the Italian anarchist Caserio, but most publicly by his roles in the conviction of the French serial killer Joseph Vacher and the Gouffé Trunk Murder.

Locard was born in Lyons in 1877. He qualified in medicine in 1902 and then became an assistant to his mentor Lacassagne. He passed the bar examination in 1907 and qualified as an advocate. The criminal courts of the city were housed in the old Palais de Justice, an enormous and impassive building with a sweeping exterior staircase that led down to the Saône river.

A much less salubrious door in the rear of the building led to cramped jail cells and next to them, cluttered rooms bursting with large police files including dossiers on criminals and their activities. Just off the file room, a narrow staircase led up four stories to the pair of attic rooms that would house the first police forensic laboratory assigned to Locard. The basic equipment was a microscope, a spectroscope, a collection of basic chemicals and a Bunsen burner.

Locard was a slim man with an aquiline face, pencil moustache and thick dark-brown hair who was a devotee of music and theatre and wrote reviews on them for Lyons newspapers. He was also a fan of Sherlock Holmes and urged his colleagues and examining magistrates to read Conan Doyle's works and those of Edgar Allan Poe. Locard, like Holmes, vigorously researched and wrote papers on fingerprints, trace evidence, tobacco, seeds, insects and the host of potential evidence found at crime scenes. His work was responsible for the incarceration of countless criminals.

While the Palais de Justice would house his laboratory, he'd had access to one in the university for many years before. He had what Dr Watson referred to as a "peculiar facility for deduction". He was influenced by his mentor Lacassagne, Dr Hans Gross the Austrian professor and criminologist, and Alphonse Bertillon of the Préfecture in Paris who introduced the first system for documenting personal identification, firstly on cards with physical and facial characteristics and later added to with photographs. By 1891, Gross pointed to the advantages of fingerprinting over Bertillon's system. But the Frenchman greatly assisted the development of forensic science by the introduction of photography not just for identification but also at crime scenes with measuring scales recording the size and relationships of evidence. He was routinely sent with investigators to document crime scenes. He photographed bodies of victims and their relationship to significant items of evidence including footprints, stains, tool marks and points of entry.

Bertillon also instructed and lectured students and investigators including Locard. Both he and Gross advocated the application of scientific methods to criminal investigation. This all led to Locard's conclusion that when any person comes into contact with an object or another person, a cross transfer of physical evidence occurs – Locard's Exchange Principle. Thus by collecting and analysing such evidence criminals could be tied to both a location of the crime and the victim.

All of the circumstances of the crime must be taken clearly into account and submitted to a strict logical analysis from the commencement to the last stage of the examination. Locard said that the criminologist re-creates the criminal from the traces the latter leaves behind, just as the archaeologist reconstructs prehistoric beings from his finds.

At the previous day's conference Professor Lacassagne had outlined the logic of his cautious approach to crime-scene investigation. Everything should be viewed with healthy doubt until proved. Nothing but the facts should determine the path the investigator was to take, thus the importance of crime-scene analysis including the vital post-mortem signs in the corpse.

All theories were to be put to the test, not only by close analysis of the scenes but also by reconstruction of the crimes. Important factors were the collection of physical evidence, objectivity, the employment of logic and the viewing with suspicion of witness and offender statements. The examination and reconstructions should be carried out by logical, sequential frame-by-frame analysis.

Dupin now recalled with pleasure the highlights of the address.

"One can start from the point, for argument's sake that nothing is ever what it seems. But then it is up to us to prove that is the case. The important thing is to avoid any pre-conceived theory and keep in your mind healthy doubts about everything that is presented to the naked eye. However tempting, never jump to a conclusion. That always arrives at the appointed time and never before.

A simple example. Some 12 years ago I was called to the scene of a death in Lyons. An elderly man was found in bed in the locked bedroom with a head wound and his hand firmly gripping a pistol. There was no evidence of forced entry and two physicians called to the scene stated that the manner of death was clearly suicide. Which seemed a reasonable deduction in the circumstances.

I might well have agreed even before enquiring whether the door had been locked from the inside and checking the possibility of an alternative convenient exit. I did not have to go that far. The first thing that struck my attention was that the bed linen was neat and almost covering the man's arms. Also his eyes were closed. His skin lacked the usual gun-powder burns of a close-range shot.

I made some enquiries with colleagues and nurses who had experience of dealing with the after-effects of violent deaths. The consensus was that the eyes would remain open in a fixed stare which matched my own observations in such events. I turned my attention to the gun in the man's hand. Such a tight grip would be hard to achieve by placing the weapon after death. I asked medical colleagues to inform me immediately of a death.

When one arose I placed a pistol in the hand of a man. It could be manipulated to grip, but not tightly. However when rigor mortis set in, the gun placed in a loose grip now tightened. This eliminated the possible earlier contradiction. The police questioned the victim's son who confessed to the crime when confronted with evidence that contradicted the finding of the physicians. He had closed his father's eyes and rearranged the bed linen after the murder out of 'respect' – which was his undoing."

To the delight of the rapt audience he then brought the case of Joseph Vacher to attention as a classical example of the persistence of a magistrate that paid off and the crime-scene investigation that linked the perpetrator to the savage murders of one adult woman, seven teenage girls and seven boys in different parts of the country.

"A serial killer of cunning savagery and deliberate sexual depravity, a bloodthirsty psychopath," the professor said.

He pointed out behaviour in Vacher's childhood that gave clues to his nature such as the mutilation of animals. The fourteenth of fifteen children, he once shot dead his dog because he would not eat the food Vacher had laid out. Later when a soldier he fell in love with a pretty maidservant Lousie Barrant who laughed when he suggested marriage. This rejection drove him into an uncontrollable rage. As a result he shot her four times and tried to kill himself. They both survived, he with a partially paralysed face. It was clear that Vacher had as little respect for his own life as that of others.

After a year in an asylum he was released by the doctors, according to them "cured". He took to the roads as a vagrant, one of 400,000 roaming the countryside in search of food and work. This vast army of tramps provided the man with a killing instinct with unintended cover.

His first victim was a 21-year-old female mill worker who he strangled and stabbed and then mutilated after death.

Over the next three years he murdered at will, moving on rapidly from location to location. Many of his victims were young shepherds working in isolated places which facilitated the perverted killer.

Émile Fourquet, a magistrate in the town of Beley, was the first to identify and link the murders and he gathered witness statements from all over the country. When the killer was caught assaulting a woman by her husband and son and jailed, he confessed to the murders in the hope that by pleading insanity he would escape the guillotine.

Lacassagne visited and assessed each crime scene and established a modus operandi that implicated a single perpetrator.

"At each of the murder scenes it appeared that a predatory animal had gone on a rampage. But there was an unmistakeable pattern to each one. The killer always stalked the victims, approached them from behind, slit their throats with the professionalism of a hunter, sodomised and then disembowelled them. The killer had left his signature on the bodies of the victims. One man responsible for all."

While incarcerated he claimed in a letter to the judge that while young he had been bitten by a rabid dog which poisoned his blood and drove him to lifelong insanity and murder. This also, he said, explained why he drank blood from the neck wounds of some of his victims. His defence was going to plead that he was insane, which if successful would mean he would avoid execution.

Certainly, the professor admitted, it could be perceived that the sheer depravity and horror of his impulsive slaughter could not be other than the acts of a madman. But then where does one draw the line between insanity and evil? Or the Shakespearean dilemma at the heart of Hamlet: was the Prince mad or simply feigning madness to justify his brand of bloodletting?

What occurred to him was that the killer was self-obsessed and showed not an ounce of remorse for his victims or the terrible effects that he wreaked on the families of the young people he had despatched. He was devoid of feeling, compassion and conscience. The insane by contrast were capable of human emotion.

He therefore examined and closely studied the background of Vacher over a five-month period before his trial in the town of Bourg-en-Bresse, a time during which he put together a psychological profile of the serial killer and established that he was not insane but was responsible for all his depraved and evil actions.

During his evidence the professor held the packed courtroom in thrall and made a significant contribution to the prosecution case. Even the prisoner was prompted to complement his expertise by remarking that he was good.

Vacher was executed on December 31st 1898, and even nine years later the horror of the killings still haunted the public imagination. The professor had become a legend who introduced a national system of post-mortem procedure and helped devise techniques in crime-scene analysis proposed by Bertillon and later improved upon by Locard.

To say he fired up his audience with enthusiasm is in the realm of understatement. More importantly, he heartily approved of the uptake of his techniques and their implementation under Dupin in the Marseilles force.

∼∽∾

While Dupin took his coffee break, there was a body of a young woman in the morgue awaiting the pathologist Dr Dufour's cutting attention. Dupin and the pathologist were two sides of the forensic coin and both shared the same philosophy regarding their task. On his office wall the pathologist had a large poster with the Latin quotation:

MORTUIS PRAESIDIUM ET VOCEM DARE NECESSE EST. *"The deceased must be protected and given a voice."*

Once when Dupin had the temerity to sympathise with Dufour on the gruesome nature of his work, he pointed out that while the Inspector had his hero Bertillon and now Lacassagne and Locard – he also had his.

"My dear Dupin, mine is the great Carl Von Rokitansky, the founder of modern post-mortem technique. In his career he supervised 70,000 post mortems and personally performed 30,000, which averaged two a day, seven days a week for 45 years. And I should complain?"

*Touché.*

A straightforward suicide by drowning, the result of love's rejection it seemed, but Dupin had been around long enough to know nothing might turn out to be as it seemed. Like the fact that the victim's scarf was found tied around her neck. With a knot at the back that no woman would have made. There was a lot tides could do, the Inspector thought, but tie a scarf?

While the scarf had no role to play in the death, it was a message. An insult, not only to the victim. It made the Inspector feel that someone had just spat in his eye. But without the force to blind him, not for an instant.

This was the third in three weeks. Suicides, Dupin knew, often occurred in spates, as if the knowledge of one made it easier for others on the edge to take the plunge. The other young women had died, one by hanging and the other by poisoning. All three were prostitutes, open to all sorts of characters and dangers. It was a hugely profitable trade in the port and the Inspector was aware that there was a territorial war bubbling between controllers of the two main red-light districts. These glorified pimps would stop at nothing to maintain their profits, including murder.

There were terse notes. But a strange echo:

*"I can't go on anymore."*

*"I can't live anymore."*

*"He doesn't love me anymore."*

The tenor of those notes, it struck Dupin, was too singular. There was one persistent note in all three. And of course one word: anymore. The same author, he began to be convinced. The notes, he suspected, were dictated. But he needed more physical evidence to back up his suspicion.

It was just a suspicion but there was another aspect of singularity which he noted. If the images of the victims' features were placed in a line they bore a remarkable similarity. Coincidence, perhaps, but even if so he felt it invited explanation, the purpose of which at this point in time he simply did not know.

He had Lazare's photographs at the scenes of discovery and prior to, during and after post mortem. In looking at them, whatever their evidential value, he found he was viewing them as if at one remove, as if they were mannequins. In pictorial repose, they lost the real sense of the human quality of the victims. By the same token, they were more disturbing. A representation as opposed to the bare fact. This experience sickened him in a way that the real body did not. He could identify better with what was flesh, however brutalised.

There were occasions when he had to draw breath, as any human would, faced with man's inhumanity. To place himself exclusively in the temple of *raisonnement* was not possible. It was excusable on the odd occasion to sigh when poring over the photograph of a dead young woman, whose last minutes and seconds on this earth he could only imagine.

Time is of its very nature relative and not always measurable. One second of terror could be equal to a lifetime, before the veil of darkness was drawn over for eternity. It was that second that he often contemplated. For it was that short space of time that drove him in the most measured fashion to get justice for the departed and incarcerate the perpetrator who then must wait out his moment before the guillotine deposited the head in the basket and hurtled the killer to the afterlife.

He had asked Dufour to re-examine the body of Marie-Anne who had apparently hanged herself.

Dufour consulted with Locard. It was his opinion that it is very difficult to stage a hanging and well nigh impossible to persuade a victim to hang themselves under threat. Most would opt for death by the manner threatened. Locard said that hanging always produces an almost identical mark pattern on the neck and slight rope burn. He provided sketches of the four most common knot positions found in hanging suicide. One was a knot at the back of the head, two a knot on the right side of the head, three on the left side behind the ear and four on the left side in front of the ear. In further illustrations he sketched the pattern of ligature impressions that should be found on the neck of the victim. Any difference in the patterns which he had illustrated could indicate staging. Locard also recommended that the pathologist look for any other signs of prior strangulation – a mark or impression that was not consistent with the impact of the rope. He also recommended checking for recent sexual activity.

Dufour followed his instructions and found no ligature mark that conformed to the sketches in any of the positions indicated and on the front part of the hanging victim's neck an impression that could have been a thumb indentation. And by careful measurement found that the pattern of compression on the neck did not conform to the pattern illustration provided by Locard. In the first two victims there were signs of sexual activity before death and he took swabs for analysis.

Dupin's team had also collected fibres from the living quarters of the victims and from their clothes which he had sent to Locard for analysis and comparison. He awaited those results.

It was beginning to be obvious to Dupin that he had three murder victims, young women from the provinces working on the night streets of Marseilles, away from their families and living solitary existences outside their workplaces. He would await Dufour's post-mortem report to formulate his investigation now that the scientific signs had altered his view.

Thanks to Locard's advice he had not released the first two bodies for burial and postponed the inquests. This gave him pause for thought as did the fact that some months ago the first crematorium opened in the city, only the third in France. The opposition of the Church had hindered the progress of the use of crematoria. Dupin had no truck with the clergy but on this occasion he agreed wholeheartedly with Bishop Freppel of Angers whose opposition some years ago on a number of issues to the introduction of a cremation bill included the potential to allow murderers escape undetected.

Now that forensics, he suspected, had frustrated the perpetrator's effort at covering up one of the crimes, he would turn his thoughts to the mind that would plan and carry out such dastardly acts. An investigative tool that he favoured was trying to look at the world from the killer's point of view.

Understand the mind of the killer, to better understand his crime. It had the effect of being better able to reconstruct the crime and of particular benefit during interrogation. Such use of psychology was another tool of his trade that the Inspector was beginning to value more.

Of course Dupin's qualification in psychology was limited to his life and professional experience so when the occasion demanded he consulted Professor Lacassagne. The professor had given expert evidence at a number of trials on the mental state of perpetrators and had more than a passing interest in the criminal mind.

Of late, pleas of insanity were becoming increasingly common, the awful prospect of incarceration in a lunatic asylum being deemed preferable by killers to the prospect of the hell that might await them after the guillotine.

He planned to contact the professor after he had received and read the post-mortem report. While he was musing during the silent moments of his break he was as usual doodling on a page of the large notebook on his desk – a word that had entered his mind with no prompt: *narcissist*.

He knew the myth of Narcissus, the beautiful young man who falls in love with his own image in a pond, having treated admirers with cruel disdain and in the end perishes as a result of this obsessive self-love and attachment to the beauty of his reflection. He remembered the narcissistic Mathilde in one of his favourite books, Stendhal's *Le Rouge et Le Noir*, who looks at herself rather than the protagonist Julian Sorel and creates a fantasy of him as a hero of her dreams and not as he really is.

But without knowing what, he felt there was more to the condition than being in love with a reflection and made a note at the end of an arrow: *Ask Lacassagne about this*.

Then, as he finished the dregs of his coffee, a phone call.

"Ah, my good friend Pons!"

He listened, his handsome creased face lighting up as the news from his friend sank in.

"Hmm. Wait there – we will be there shortly."

Pons led Dupin with his assistant Froissart and photographer Lazare to the wooden rack and pointed towards the trunk. The Inspector noted the coagulated blood on the floor. Pons looked at him nervously and handed him the note he had made about the tag.

"Excellent, Pons, very good, you have touched nothing – very important when it comes to evidence. Aha, British aristocracy no less. Odd but people, given the circumstances, can be very odd."

Pons had become anxious all of a sudden as if reality had just come home to roost.

"What do you think, Charles?"

"Not a lot, Pons, until we see what is in the trunk."

"You mean break it open?"

"Not for the moment, of course, my dear fellow."

The Inspector noted a twitch appear in his assistant Froissart's eye and watched Pons' face blanch. All no longer in doubt and cognisant of what the outcome might be.

Dupin, as always, when faced with the inevitable, relaxed. He asked Pons to close and lock the door to the area. He told him that he was unconcerned about the chaos that would ensue in luggage handling and placement. They were faced with a far more serious situation.

"My dear Pons, this is now a crime scene. We must all do our duty."

He told Pons to advise his team of porters of a problem but under no circumstances to reveal its nature. In time they could resume their duties after he had finished his business.

He took Pons, now pale-faced and agitated, aside.

"My friend, I know how you must feel. Don't worry, when we have finished, you can resume your work. If you are bothered later with enquiries, particularly from the wolves of the press, refer them to me under instruction. There is no need for you to be an accidental victim of someone else's dastardly act. I will ensure that you are not affected and that your employers are aware of your total co-operation in our enquiries and your professionalism in all aspects of this unfortunate situation."

Pons seemed comforted by his words.

"Now what I suggest is this," said Dupin, "but you do not have to do it. Go to the owners' hotel – Hôtel du Louvre. Tell this couple that you have to enquire into the details of their luggage and say that they must come here to assist you. We will then confront them with whatever we find."

Pons then left to go to the hotel.

Dupin directed Lazare to begin photographing the trunk from a variety of angles and acquire images of the blood that had pooled beneath the rack.

The Inspector then asked one of his team to force open the trunk to establish what was inside. When the top was pushed back the young man's face drained of colour and he fell backwards into the arms of one of his companions.

The Inspector moved forward and was confronted with an unspeakable sight. Inside the trunk there was a bloodstained torso, partially covered by blood-soaked material. The legs had been hacked off. The neck was severed. There was no head. The female genitalia indicated that it was the body of a woman.

Lazare, without prompting, moved forward and took more shots of the dismembered corpse.

Dupin took a deep breath. "Nothing is to be touched or handled."

Pons would be back shortly with the owners of the trunk and then, Dupin surmised, the investigation would begin in earnest. His mind instantly jumped to the Gouffé case. Another trunk but an entirely different scenario and with no less a sensation as far as the press were concerned. Nothing, he determined, in this case could be left to chance. When news of this broke, he knew with certainty that Célestin Hennion would be on the phone.

The Marseilles police chief looked again at the transport label retrieved from the side of the trunk. The destination was Paddington Station, London. The owners Sir Vere St Leger Goold and Lady Violet Goold.

# PART TWO

# 7

## LE BAGNE

### Deus Mihi Providebit

**FRENCH GUIANA 1908-9**

He had been moved from the prison in Monte Carlo back to Marseilles and then readied for the train journey to La Rochelle. That last-named port had a special resonance for him. An ancestor of his, Elisabeth Goold, daughter of Alderman Stephen Goold and his wife Helen of Cork, Ireland, had been married there to James Nagle in 1705. When Mrs Nagle died two decades later she left money and a house in Paris. Now how far had the ancestral line sunk in the mire? The next Goold to go there would arrive a manacled prisoner destined for French Guiana, an overseas region of France located on the northern Atlantic coast of South America.

*DEUS MIHI PROVIDEBIT* . . . *God Will Provide For Me*. With a bitter sense of irony he remembered his family motto. The crest: a lion rampant.

French Guiana was originally inhabited by a number of

indigenous American people. It was settled by the French during the 17th century. The first French effort to colonise Guiana was in 1763 when 12,000 Frenchmen were induced to accept free offers of land there. They arrived expecting to scoop sacks of gold and diamonds from the ground. Unprepared for the tropical climate, they died in their thousands. Lacking proper dwellings they were caught in drenching storms, after the rains they reeled through the steaming jungles, caught in floods, assaulted by clouds of mosquitoes carrying malaria.

Only 2,000 of the original group survived the first year. They were saved by taking refuge on three islands, ten miles from the mainland. These islands became known as the Isles of Salvation (Îles du Salut): Île Royale, Île St Joseph and Île du Diable, the smallest and separated from Royale by a vicious tide. It is said that this island got its name Devil's Island from the cloud of black birds that nested on the island. In time the whole penal colony came to be known as 'Devil's Island'.

By 1775 there were 1,300 whites and 8,000 slaves in the colony. All three of the neighbouring Guianas – French, Dutch and British – were dependent on slaves for their existence. This resulted in thousands of blacks fleeing into the bush. For more than a century they formed renegade bands and made forays against the plantations and white settlements, killing, looting and liberating other slaves.

The slaves were emancipated in 1794, only to be re-enslaved when the fortunes of the colony diminished. A second emancipation occurred in 1848. However, by this time, the reputation of Guiana was so evil that white colonists could not be persuaded to emigrate. Napoléon III decided to solve the problem by transporting political prisoners to the colony, which from that time became a penal colony.

So awful were the conditions there that the French government decided that only Africans, Arabs and Annamese (from French Indochina) would be transported. From 1884 white prisoners were also brought there. It was not for nothing even now, over half a century after Napoléon III had created his hell on earth, that it had become known as the Colony of the Damned.

He was at the same station in Marseilles that he had come to the previous year to submit to his well-deserved fate.

He was taken with some others in a van from the prison and brought to a freight entrance, where railway carriages specially built for the transportation of convicts to the penal colonies were waiting. The carriages were divided into small cells, three feet by four. Each cell had a small bench and a sliding panel through which food was passed. Each contained a prisoner, feet securely fastened by chains, wrists handcuffed and irons placed on the ankles. There were three armed guards in each of the carriages. Such carriages arrived at La Rochelle from all parts of the nation, hitched to passenger and freight trains, stopping by the prisons to pick up men banished to the hell of the penal colony.

Sometime around noon the train arrived at La Rochelle to a crowd of onlookers at the station. His stomach churned with fear. It was the first time that the reality of where he was destined sank in. Before that it was tomorrow and tomorrow, with always the thought that something might intervene. Nothing did. It was the last stop before leaving France.

The convicts were marched through La Rochelle. There was a crowd watching, some weeping relatives and wives and sweethearts, all bathed in tears. It was a heartbreaking spectacle. He had nobody and felt all the better for it. Those people knew that they would never see their men again. They were put on a ferry for Saint-Martin-de-Ré on the Île de Ré, an hour's crossing. The prison here was in former days a grim embattlement from which the musketeers of Louis XIV once repulsed the forces of the Duke of Buckingham.

They entered through a great drawbridge into a large court. The convicts there were stripped naked and given a rectal examination. This was to look for suppositories or *"plan"* in

French criminal jargon. This was a hollow cylinder inserted into the anus by convicts to contain money or other articles of value to them. They were given prison clothes and wooden-soled shoes. There was an inventory taken of possessions such as letters and photographs which could be sent on to family or if not, destroyed. More often the latter.

They were then given the attention of a barber, clipped, shaved and put into icy showers. Then to the *quartier cellulaire* where guards let them into a large cell. They were lined up at the edge of a tier of bare boards which served as bunks. The sergeant keeper of cells appeared and asked for all the names and length of sentences. Chains were then put on the prisoners. In the morning each was given a number and sent to workshops. Silence was insisted upon and there was a regime of brutal discipline. For the slightest thing, the turn of a head, a beating ensued.

Prior to the departure of the convict steamer, each was given a canvas sailor's sack containing two sets of clothing and a blanket. They were then taken to the courtyard where they saw the prison guards from Guiana and Senegalese soldiers. They were counted and handed over to their new captors. They now belonged to the prison administration of Guiana. All 450 men were marched back over the drawbridge and into the town. They began to take their last steps from the soil of France.

They were watched by the same crowd of spectators including grief-stricken members of family, mothers, wives, girlfriends and children. There were newspapermen and photographers to record the transportation. As if the humiliation was not sufficient.

None more than he had previously been subjected to this form of attention. His foul crime had already been the focus of worldwide attention. He kept his eyes firmly fixed on the ground. No photographer picked him out; he was now just a number among the detritus of French society, not given the dubious privilege of being incarcerated in their own homeland.

They reached the pier where a number of barges took the army of convicts to the waiting steamship. On board they were forced into a series of cages. Each cage held up to 90 men, counted as they entered. Hammocks were distributed and the cages were locked.

The cages were 60ft long, 12ft wide and the same in height. There was a hardly an inch of room to breathe, the heavy air awash with human sweat and the acrid stench of vomit. Younger men had some hope in their hearts, mostly because the possibility of escape was in their minds. He and the older men were deprived of all hope as they knew that they had no chance of any other life than the one that faced them.

The reality would prove that neither age nor youth would provide any protection from the awful tortures that would compose their future incarceration.

The intense heat inside the cages overwhelmed the prisoners. For half an hour a day they were marched on deck for air while sailors sloshed out the cages with salt water to get rid of the detritus of their stay. They were forbidden to talk and were forced to stand facing the sea. One more lash of the whips – the thousands that they faced when they arrived at their destination.

It quickly became apparent to him that the cause of the brutality they were already exposed to, quite apart from any larger design, was that the guards were, to a certain extent, not a whole lot better off than their charges. They were subject to the same conditions, diet, climate and apparently poorly paid for their efforts. They would resort to anything to ease their lot. And their resentment was transmitted at every turn to the convicts.

In the cages the discipline was relaxed and they were allowed to talk, smoke and play cards. Leaders and bullies, mainly strong-arm men called *fort-à-bras*, many of whom were tattooed head to foot, with experience of African prisons, took control and struck terror into the weaker convicts. Even in this stinking quagmire there was a hierarchy established.

This vicious mentality pervaded the cages. They organised

gambling games, with playing cards drawn on bits of paper, checkers and dominoes fashioned from bits of bread or lumps of sugar. It was a far cry for him from the tables at Monte Carlo. Gambling was, it was confirmed, part of life for all classes, and these were the lowest of all. The results, he found out, would not be much different. On the high seas, the game of chance was still being played born of the same desperate need.

Dreadful food was brought in slop buckets and the old and feeble were given little. The laws of the jungle prevailed. If this was a foretaste of what was to come, it had the effect of hope being created for men by discussing plans for escape when they arrived in the colony.

They entered the Mediterranean and, three days after departure from La Rochelle, the ship docked in Algiers where 200 hundred more prisoners, Arabs and Black Africans, were taken on board. The ship then headed straight to Guiana, passing between Gibraltar and Tangiers and out into the Atlantic once more.

As it reached the tropics, the heat and humidity of the air became even more intolerable. The prisoners were hosed down by the guards. The drinking water became contaminated and was mixed with rum to make it acceptable. Most of the men wore nothing but towels around their waists. The twice-daily hosing with cold seawater proved the high point of the stifling experience of human incarceration in the heat and humidity of the holds.

When the ship slowed down, which it frequently did on the journey, a shiver of fear shot through the seaborne community. It signalled a death and the deposit of the corpse into the sea. There were some poor souls who would not make it to the colony, and they would prove to be the lucky ones.

After what seemed an interminable time the shore appeared and the ship reached the mouth of the Maroni River after a journey which had lasted a day over three weeks. The ship shuddered to a halt and waited for the high tide. An air of expectation and excitement gripped the men instead of the dread that should have been their reaction. It was but a temporary escape from reality.

When the tide was right the ship moved off and into the mouth of the Maroni, a name that would become etched in the consciousness of every prisoner. It steamed slowly along the bank, flanked by the immense wall of a green jungle, a more effective obstacle than anything the penitentiary authorities could have built. The natural ramparts were as crushing as the appalling habitation of this forgotten but very much alive penal colony.

The convicts were ordered to dress for the landing. The whistle blew and the ship stopped again. They had arrived at St Laurent de Maroni which, bathed in tropical sunlight, looked almost pleasant – from the outside. A crowd had gathered to watch the arrival of another human cargo, among which were white-attired colony officials, colourfully dressed black women and more ragged denizens. Whatever their status, they were free to stop and stare at the miserable band of humanity that was disembarking and being marched in a line along the pier.

There was a strange atmosphere of expectation. The sort, incredibly, that he and countless others might have had when arriving at a holiday destination. It resembled somewhat a feeling of pleasure, an irony that all too soon would become obvious to all. The sunlight, the sensation of normality, the gathered crowd was almost seductive.

The walk, he thought like all the others, confirmed this feeling. St Laurent de Maroni was a pretty little place, neat and clean. There was, like in any French town, a Hôtel de Ville and a Palais de Justice. The streets were wide and bordered with fine trees. Houses nestled in little gardens with palm trees. They were spick and span with flowers everywhere. There were prisoners with straw hats and pink-and-white striped clothing cleaning the streets and tending the gardens. It seemed that they could go where they liked. The impression was that of an ideal life.

It was an initial impression. After a short walk of several hundred yards the line was turned to the left and was soon confronted with a high wall and a huge gate with a few armed guards in front. Over the gate in large letters, the seemingly unassuming announcement of their new home:

## CAMP DE LA TRANSPORTATION

The unreality of their arrival evaporated with the reality of the destination. Those words in the title spoke the truth of it. This was not a holiday camp, it was not a place of joy. It was a place of punishment. After filing through into the large yard behind the gates, they were addressed by the Commandant of the Penitentiary of St Laurent. It was clearly a speech that had been given many times before and would be again. And again.

Even the tiny minority who might have been unaware of the reputation of this penal establishment would in time reflect on the true meaning of the speech. Nonetheless, at the time it did not seem disingenuous.

"You must behave yourselves, first and foremost, or suffer the consequences. If you follow the regulations and do not cause trouble you may well qualify for a pardon. That is a fact of life in this colony that is given. Its founders had the hope that for you all there would be something positive and productive and that you would contribute in time to the creation of a good society with economic benefits for the inhabitants and your homeland.

I urge you to cast off the iniquities of the life that you have left behind and look forward to rehabilitation and a better future. I am not going to suggest that your time here will be easy, after all there are very good reasons that each one of you has as part of your sentence to join us here. But believe me that if you adapt willingly to the rules of the administration you will be rewarded in a very positive way. Life is not all bad here unless you choose it to be. There are guards here, there are workers in the local community here, that formerly shared your situation. They have thrived, have a satisfactory and productive existence and there is no reason why you cannot be part of this positive process.

We have our responsibilities but so have you. Let us share them in peace.

There are some among you who will wish to escape but I warn those of this disposition that there are formidable obstacles in the way of such temptation. We are no fools here and realise from experience that such is, was and always will be the desire among, in particular, some of the young convicts. It may seem a natural inclination but it is a dangerous one.

Let me warn you that those who attempt to run away from the tasks allotted to them will be shot on sight by the guards. But beyond that is the jungle and the sea containing their own natural guards. And the bullet compared to their realities will seem merciful by comparison. I do not wish to emphasise these dangers, all or any that take them on will find out soon enough.

But allow me to emphasise that in the event that some want to take this route, the sea contains sharks and the river piranha, both of whom will strip a human bare of every last inch of flesh from the body. A slow and horrible end which I am sure the majority of prisoners would want to avoid. But those by chance who avoid this awful death and are returned here will face severe punishment in solitary confinement, which I assure you is far from pleasant.

You may all live in peace with us and your guards; that choice is entirely up to you. All are welcome by the administration and if we all get along then all our lives will be made as accommodating as possible. We do not want your punishment for your crimes to be rendered any more difficult than the deprivation of your freedom. That I assume is more than sufficient for the differing reasons for which you have been brought here.

But in these difficult circumstances, for all of us, let us hope that your stay in French Guiana will be as pleasant as it can and should be. The climate is not the best for us, no more than you, used to the more temperate one of our homeland. But we must all endure that together. It is as demanding for us as it is for you. The Third Republic has decreed fit to support the administration in its best efforts to house you.

Let us all attempt properly to dwell in peace and I hope sincerely that some future prosperity awaits those prisoners who will be returned to their homeland. I wish you all *bon chance*. Your peace and welfare is our first and enduring priority."

After the speech the men were locked into barracks with 60 men in each.

Soon he heard from his fellow-prisoners about the real obstacles to escape that the Commandant had mentioned.

At first, the neighbouring government of Dutch Guiana had provided sanctuary to those who successfully crossed the piranha-infested Maroni River. Later as a result of atrocities committed by *bagnards* the Dutch administration adopted a firm policy of returning all convicts (except, in later years, those of German nationality – a policy instituted by Hitler on his

# The Gouffé Affair

Hanging Gouffé

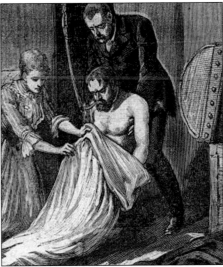
Putting body in sack

Dumping the body

Bompard accuses Eyraud

The infamous Gouffé Trunk – a replica was viewed by 25,000 visitors.
Paris, 1889

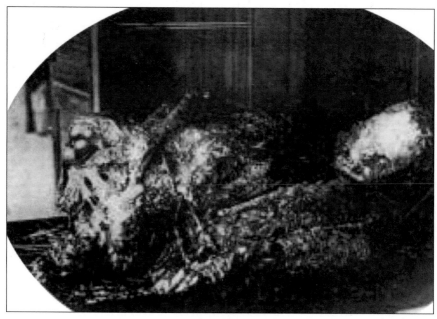

Gouffé's remains, 1889

Gabrielle Bompard, murderess

Michel Eyraud, murderer

Eyraud approaching the guillotine, 1891

Célestin Hennion (1862-1915), Préfet de Police:
father of modern policing

The Tiger: President Georges Clemenceau
(1841-1929)

Professor Alexandre Lacassagne (1843-1924),
criminologist, pioneer in forensic science

Dr Edmond Locard (1877-1966), pioneer in
forensic science, the 'Sherlock Holmes' of France

Irish Open Tennis Championship 1883 (Goold second back right, standing)

Monte Carlo Casino

Vere St Leger Goold (1853-1909)

The Goolds' victim: Emma Erika Levin

Vere St Leger Goold, condemned, Monaco 1908

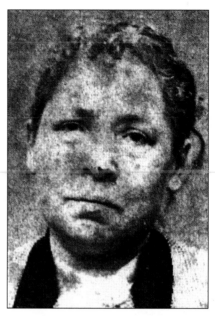

Marie Giraudin Goold, condemned, Monaco 1908

Guillotine on Devil's Island

# Le Petit Journal

| Le Petit Journal | **5** CENTIMES **SUPPLEMENT ILLUSTRE** **5** CENTIMES | ABONNEMENTS |
| --- | --- | --- |
| CHAQUE JOUR — 6 PAGES — 5 CENTIMES | Le Petit Journal Militaire, Maritime, Colonial.... 10 cent. | SIX MOIS  UN AN |
| Administration 61, rue Lafayette | Le Petit Journal agricole, 5 cent. ~ La Mode du Petit Journal, 10 cent. | SEINE et SEINE-ET-OISE.. 2 fr.  3 fr. 50 |
| **Le Supplément illustré** | Le Petit Journal illustré de la Jeunesse, 10 cent. | DÉPARTEMENTS......... 2 fr.  4 fr. » |
| CHAQUE SEMAINE 5 CENTIMES | On s'abonne sans frais dans tous les bureaux de poste | ETRANGER ............ 2 50  5 fr. » |
| | | Les manuscrits ne sont pas rendus |

| Dix-huitième Année | DIMANCHE 25 AOUT 1907 | Numéro 875 |

Violette Goold — Emma Lévin — Vera Goold

## LE CRIME DE MONTE-CARLO. — UNE FEMME COUPÉE EN MORCEAUX
### Portraits de la victime et des coupables

THE MONTE CARLO CRIME – A WOMAN CUT INTO PIECES

accession to power in 1933). Hundreds of the less imaginative convicts persisted in crossing to the Dutch side. This was an attempt to escape down the Moengo Road to Paramaribo, the only passageway through the dense jungle.

Catching them was simple. Dutch soldiers stationed themselves along the road and waited. A soldier guarding a section of the Maroni River once heard horrific screaming after dark and went to investigate. About 25 feet from the bank he saw a convict struggling forward with the water boiling underneath him. Fist-sized chunks of flesh were being torn from the victim's arms, face and chest. The piranhas were making a skeleton of the man before the eyes of the helpless soldier and he sank screaming under the blood-coloured water.

Other escapees were picked clean by army ants in the jungle and there were other spinechilling accounts of starving convicts killing and cannibalising their fellow fugitives. It did not stop some of the more inventive young convicts from attempting to succeed where so many others failed. They resembled all convicts and murderers in particular on that account. But the odds, as always, were stacked against them.

A couple of days after arrival there was a roll call and the prisoners were given their camp numbers and a medical inspection to ascertain whether they were fit for work. Very few if any failed this test. There was no purpose in the examination. Just another farcical ritual.

At the end of the week, all were distributed among the labour camps in the jungle. Whether a convict was young or old, feeble or strong, serving a sentence for life or five years, they were all sent to the same backbreaking task.

Most were accustomed to a city life in temperate zones. Men who had never held an axe in their hand were put to work in the camps, chopping down huge trees in the heart of the tropics. The true message of Camp de la Transportation became obvious. It signalled the first stage of a ghastly routine, full of privation and pain, the occupation of a hell that not even Satan himself could have invented.

The Commandant's speech soon showed the lies at its heart. Nothing he uttered contained the least whit of truth. It was instead a community, built on the concept of slave labour and all that entailed, the very worst of penal settlements the world over.

There was a regime of punishment, as a matter of daily routine, not designed simply to grind the convict into submission but in effect to kill him in a manner which would make the guillotine a merciful option.

In the morning at half past five while it was still dark, the guards roused the prisoners. Tools were distributed and the convicts trooped off in gangs to the jungle. Soon the more troublesome or notorious among them would be transferred to the islands.

There was a specific target given by the administration. One stere, the equivalent of one cubic metre, of lumber for each man per day. The convict had to chop down the tree, cut it up into pieces and pile his stere in a designated spot. This was often hundreds of yards from any place where there was standing timber. He was given four days in which to learn how to do the work; on the fifth day if he had not completed the task, he was given only dry bread when he returned from the jungle.

The convicts worked without the supervision of the guards who showed up at three in the afternoon and visited the spot where the steres were to be stacked to check if the impossible targets were met. Those who had not finished were faced with empty stomachs as a reward. They had been given half a pint of coffee for breakfast and then despatched to carry out a backbreaking monotonous task. Drenched in perspiration, they struck with what strength they could muster at trees so durable that the blade of the axe bounced off the surface.

They worked under a blazing sun, liquid pumping out of every pore, attacked constantly by mosquitoes and other insects, frantically trying to reach the target by the appointed time of the guards' visit. As well as the early morning coffee, they were given at noon 26 ounces of bread and a pint of broth which contained no meat or vegetables. At night, two ounces of rice or dry beans or peas. Even resting they would be in a constant state of hunger. Considering the workload, the food was deliberately rationed with the purpose of quickly destroying the bodies of the toiling men.

They were rapidly ground into the earth and their health broke down. They became ill and those who did not survive the brief hospitalisation finished up in the communal cemetery at St Laurent called the Bamboos. They were effectively murdered by the authorities without the possibility of any official retribution. It was a form of mass extermination.

The convicts laboured under horrendous tropical conditions, burnt by the sun, drenched by the monsoon rain. They were undernourished, badly housed and treated with indifference and cruelty. Men would wake up in the morning, feet soaked in blood having been bitten by vampire bats, full of tiny insects which had burrowed into their skin. They suffered from infection and blood poisoning and a pervading sense of utter despair.

He, like the older men, was soon broken in body and spirit and harboured thoughts of ending it all by suicide. But hope, of what they did not know, kept a vigil and they attempted to soldier on even though melting in despair. He remembered in the midst of desperation that he was born only one year after this colony had been established as an institution of unimagined punishment. In a matter of weeks, many were deranged by all sorts of confused thoughts and emotions.

There was further irony for him, quite apart from the fact it was much harder for men of education than those who had not known anything but squalor, filth or promiscuity in their previous lives. They had no light after 8 o'clock, but using sardine tins, a little oil and a rag they could see enough to play cards. The men gambled furiously for the money that they kept secured in their bodies. They were unscrupulous, ruthless, and rows occurred frequently and were settled with knives.

The morning after, when the dormitory was opened, a body was often found, but no threats, inducements of any kind including extra punishment would lead to a betrayal of the killer.

Every prisoner was worn out from fatigue on top of all the other adversities of the climate and incarceration. Many could not sleep with the anticipation of another day of hellish labour and privation. None were excused work. All were devoured by big black ants as well as all the other bugs. In the barracks they were stifled by the stink of sweat and excrement. Many had to sleep with one eye open in order not to be robbed or killed.

The mental and physical suffering was amplified by the constant threat of illness and the fact of companions perishing all around them. Reduced to a daily struggle for existence, they shut themselves up within themselves for refuge, miserably lonely and full of despair and hopelessness in the knowledge that there would be no escape from or end to this daily hell.

Many suffered from deep depression, haunted by moments when the past surged into their consciousness and their minds were tortured by everything they had lost.

Whatever the nature of their crimes, how could such punishment be justified? Even for the hardened and the recidivists, those supposedly born into and made for evil acts, many of whose social circumstances allowed for no other way of life, this fate was hardly deserved. It engendered hatred and distrust in a community damned from every angle. In the *bagne*, it was every man for himself.

The only liaisons were sexual and forced on younger convicts by older ones who would have been degenerate in any circumstance. They started with rape and then forced submission. The younger men were known as *mômes* (meaning: kid, brat, fool). These were considered the "pets" of the older ones, "pet" being a singularly inappropriate way of describing their role. The *mômes* who did not comply were sometimes murdered so no other degenerate could lay hands on him, or at other times in a fit of jealousy. Here was human behaviour at its most squalid and sickening.

The majority had some trace of decency, but there were those born under a bad sign and whose behaviour and actions added to the stinking pollution of the lives of the prisoners.

For most, their past life was constantly replayed like reels in their minds and there was no outlet for the ultimate anguish such reflections bring as companionship and friendship were almost non-existent in an environment in which survival was paramount. The only collectiveness was for illegal enterprise, gang-fighting and escape. But even then trust between the players was at a premium and suspicion a far greater motivating force. Thus violence and murder was another factor of life as if the regime and climate were not enough in the constant war of attrition on life.

Mutual trust was unattainable and therefore meaningful exchange of confidence or problems was non-existent. The convict withdrew into his shell, deprived of the comfort of any support, and lived a life stripped of all reasonable sentiment.

Any other civilised nation would have given them a chance to mend their ways and remake their lives, instead of sending them on a torturous path to inevitable death. Some of them committed a first crime out of bravado, stupidity or sheer necessity, caught in a cycle of circumstance and influenced by environment as so often happens, and were not in any conventional sense criminals.

They had lost a gamble with the odds stacked against them. Lady Fortune had turned her back on them and they were now locked up like animals in close quarters with assassins, thieves and perverts.

There was a man by the name of Bayard in his 25th year in the prison colony. He had been in the terrible Oraput timber camp about which the well-known anthem of the prison camp had been composed – the poet himself had died there. He was called to sing the song incessantly. Set to the tune of a hymn to the Eucharist it told of the life and the miseries of the convicts who worked and died in the death camp of the jungle.

*There goes the bell! Up all of you! Five o'clock
fellows!
The night mists are still hanging over Oraput,
And foul bats, drunk and heavy with our blood,
Are flapping towards their hiding places for the day.
A fearful awakening for most of us; our spirits
For a little while have been drifting under kinder
skies.
But the infernal bell has called us pitilessly back
To another day's suffering in this Hell.*

There was another, Peploch, condemned to five years' hard labour in 1902. He was given 36 supplementary punishments for escape attempts. He would die in the camp.

The more literate convicts were asked to write letters for those who might be barely able to read but could not write. Very few wrote to relatives or friends, because there was nothing to report other than the misery of their existence. Many poor prisoners, deluding themselves constantly, sent letters to the Ministry for Justice looking for a pardon. They were a waste of time and were always turned down. But maybe the act of writing gave them a glimmer of hope.

The turnkeys were convicts, mostly Arabs, and detailed to help the guards. They opened and locked the doors of the cells. They searched the men at the command of the guards and sometimes took their place when necessary. They were also useful to the convicts as they passed on many forbidden items to them in return for money.

Since 1852, conditions had not changed, nor any aspect of the administration of the penal colony. It was a world removed from France and so did not touch on the public's consciousness or conscience. Apart from Dreyfus's experience there, further publicised in his book *Five Years of My Life: 1894-1899*, the only previous time a spotlight was thrown on the doings of the colony was after the 1894 Cayenne Massacre when the administration, it was alleged, had 'engineered a provocation' in order to rid themselves of a vocal rebellious group of anarchists. One anarchist was killed by a guard, then he himself was killed in retaliation. A man hunt began and some 16 unarmed anarchists were shot down in cold blood and the bodies fed to the sharks.

There was a scandal but nevertheless the death, misery and torture continued unabated through the different generations of the human cargo transported to the nearest thing to hell on earth. The administration stuck steadfastly to their task of maintaining an inhuman and degrading regime without the tiniest trace of care or compassion for the condemned men.

They were either incapable of pity or had suppressed it for the sake of their own survival. Not for the first or last time in history, in the name of justice a system of unremitting cruelty was inflicted. There was no liberty, equality or fraternity for the inhabitants of Devil's Island.

# 8

## LE CRIME

**MARSEILLES, AUGUST 1907**

This was indeed a crime scene, but of course there was the original one, yet to be examined. Dupin instructed Froissart to return to headquarters and acquire a vehicle and two extra policemen to help with the removal of the trunk and inform Dr Dufour of their impending task.

He could interview the porter Beraud who delivered the trunk, but decided to wait. Bad news travels fast and he did not need the press just yet. When Pons returned from the Hôtel du Louvre with the couple, in a cab driven by a man called Bizot, he reported that they had tried to bribe him to avoid coming to the station. Dupin was surprised to see a man and woman in clearly middle age – not what he expected – he introduced himself.

"Charles Dupin, Préfecture, Marseilles. Is this your trunk?"

"Yes," replied the man.

"Your names, please."

"Sir Vere and Lady Goold."

Dupin opened the trunk. The man appeared to faint and was held up by the woman. She seemed to ignore the contents.

The detective paused and put back the top of the trunk.

"I think that we should back go to your hotel. Hôtel du Louvre, I believe?"

"Yes," replied the man.

"To find the rest of the body?"

The man and woman made no reply.

Dupin ordered his team to accompany him with the couple to the Hôtel du Louvre.

But first there was the task of transporting the trunk to the police station. Froissart soon returned with a vehicle. Pons arranged for an entrance at the rear leading into the goods yard off the Boulevard Voltaire to be opened and the vehicle drove in there. The newly arrived policemen then removed the trunk from the rack, wheeled it out and lifted it into the vehicle. They drove off. Pons opened the door to the platforms and it was business as usual.

Dupin, Froissart, Lazare and the Goolds descended the monumental staircase at the front of the station onto the Boulevard D'Athènes, and from there departed for the Hôtel du Louvre.

For Charles Dupin it was the beginning of another long day's journey into night. But he was galvanised and his personal time had no meaning for him. The immediate future had been plotted for him. In this he had no choice and that was the way he liked his life – like the tide, brought on by the flow.

When they entered the suite in the hotel, the brown-haired stout woman became enervated and the man asked if he could have a drink, which was allowed. He raised a glass of whisky to his lips with shaking hands, finished and immediately filled another one.

Dupin requested that they sit down, but not before Lady Goold protested loudly.

"This is outrageous. I don't know why you are here! What are we supposed to have done? We know nothing about the trunk – anyone could have put our name on it."

"Unlikely," replied Dupin, at ease. "Next you will be suggesting that someone murdered a woman and placed her dismembered body in your trunk without your knowledge? I think not."

The man was obviously in a state of distress, gulping whisky down.

"Believe me, it is not as it seems," he said. "We are innocent. It was someone else that –"

"*Shut up!*" screamed his wife.

He looked at her, silent, and slurped down his drink.

Dupin said nothing for a minute and then asked Lazare to search the bedroom and bathroom.

"*You can't, you can't!*" screamed the woman, leaping up from her chair.

Dupin rose slowly. "Yes, I can," he replied firmly.

Her husband buried his head in his hands and sobbed quietly.

The detective could hardly believe that this wreck of a man, obviously the worse for prolonged consumption of alcohol, was capable of murder and then the effort required to dismember a body with instruments not designed for such a task. Indeed, if he had been asked to imagine the perpetrators he could not have come up in his mind's eye with such an unlikely pair.

The woman was rotund, middle-aged and not unattractive. Matronly, but with a hard edge. Pons had said that she had fallen when alighting from the cab after it had pulled up outside the station, but felt that there was something calculated in her action. She would be giving nothing away under questioning. Even so she would have a lot of explaining to do, even if she had concocted some story to cover the awful discovery.

For a small few moments the victim had disappeared from his mental radar, but not for long.

Lazare returned to them with a large valise in his hands. He was as pale as the early morning sun. He laid it down on the floor.

Dupin approached it. The open top revealed the head of a woman with chestnut-brown hair, and beneath that a pair of bloodied legs, cut off at the upper thighs. All underneath what appeared to be a bloodstained sheet or a dress with ragged edges, suggesting that it had been torn.

"Who is this?" he asked firmly.

The woman remained silent. Her eyes were averted from the dreadful partial remains. The man became agitated, folding and unfolding his arms, not knowing what to do with his hands.

"Madame Levin," the man uttered with a croak. "Emma Levin."

"A person known to you both?"

"Yes, yes, yes," he replied.

A silence ensued, broken only by the opening and closing of the shutters of the camera. Froissart finished and moved aside. Dupin allowed the silence to stretch and thus render the couple even more uncomfortable, if that were possible.

"I am detaining you, Sir Goold and Lady Goold, for questioning in relation to the murder of Emma Levin. You will now accompany us to the Préfecture to be examined on the matter."

He gestured to Lazare to close and remove the valise and its ghastly contents. Froissart handcuffed the pair. Dupin went on to the landing and summoned a member of the staff who then brought the party down a back staircase and to an exit at the rear of the hotel.

❧

At the police station Dupin pulled up a chair opposite the couple and sat down. The man was attempting to disguise his shaking hands by wringing them together. He looked in a bad condition. The woman held her head haughtily in the air, but the Inspector could see the small beginnings of her discomfort as she glanced momentarily at his two colleagues, now sentinels in her eyes.

He paused, as was his habit, laid his notebook on the table, took out his pen and asked the couple to confirm their identity.

After an hour of questioning Dupin had received confused

and contradictory explanations for the fate of Madame Levin. They were simply without logic and incredible. There was a suggestion from Mrs Goold that the victim's lover had burst into the room, killed her and left. They merely attempted to get rid of the body to avoid being implicated in the tragedy. He listened patiently, took notes and dismissed such nonsense in his mind.

However, he had established that the victim was Swedish, a widow of a rich stockbroker in Copenhagen and was staying at the Hotel Bristol in Monte Carlo, where the Goolds had been residing from the previous October in the Villa Menesini. He felt that to continue interrogation would be a waste of time, until he had preliminary post-mortem results, so that he could be more specific. They had so far admitted disposal of the body but denied responsibility for murder.

He informed them that they might as well be more frank and forthcoming in the next interview as an examining magistrate would now begin a judicial investigation and the hearings would be in open court.

"Let us say that my judicial counterpart, Monsieur Maliavalle, will be far less tolerant in the surroundings of a court of law. Therefore, given that hunting packs of the press will be slavering at the mouth over the case and will show even less mercy, it would, I humbly suggest, be in your interest to speak the truth as early as possible in the investigation process. The magistrate will of course organise a lawyer to act as your defence. If you have a preference for any member, you can let him know."

Goold thanked him in a low whisper, while his wife maintained an air of silent defiance. They were then removed to their respective cells.

Dupin made his way to what was popularly referred to as "the room of the dead". Despite the connotation it was a particular source of pride to the force. It had been set aside and fitted with the assistance of Lacassagne's department at Lyons University and a grant from the Sûreté, in tandem with the commitment to Locard's laboratory.

Most morgues were makeshift and set up wherever suited the purpose, with no facilities whatsoever. Bodies were thus exposed to changes in the ambient temperature and other organic influences which could frustrate the efforts of the pathologist to come to definitive conclusions about matters such as the time of death, then mistakenly concentrated on body temperature and nothing much else. In this case as well as others, in the absence of witnesses, a reasonably accurate deduction of the time of death could tie the perpetrators to the location of the crime – or not.

In the morgue under Dufour's supervision, the trunk and valise were opened yet again. Everyone present steeled themselves for the sight, even Dupin who had already beheld its horrors. What Dufour, his assistants and the young fresh-faced policeman Carlin were to witness was beyond imagination. Even more shocking were the contents of the valise: the head shrouded by thick brown hair, mouth wide-open and steel-blue eyes staring wide underneath the legs. The full impact of the victim's death was amply illustrated by her facial expression – one of frozen fear, the eyes reflecting the horror.

There had been little effort made to cover the mortal remains of a once beautiful woman. Portions of her clothes were stuffed hurriedly, it appeared, under and around the torso, presumably to remove all traces of her from the original scene of her murder.

For those not used to such sights, the impact does not dissolve for some time. None had experienced dismemberment. There is something intensely sickening about a headless corpse. It speaks of further gratuitous humiliation in death, even when expertly carried out by the executioner. It is hard to look and equally hard to look away. The focus of the sight always returns to the bloody neck.

Dupin released Carlin whose pretty face had been suffused with greenish colour and told him to go back to the main office to rest, and get refreshments if he was so inclined, which he suspected for the moment he would not be. He was to pass a message on to his fellow-policemen not talk to anyone, not their colleagues outside the unit or their nearest and dearest. Utmost secrecy was needed until he decided on his next move. He had earned their loyalty and knew that he could trust them.

He and Dufour paused for some moments.

"Poor Carlin! There is more blush on the victim's face than his, right now," mused Dupin.

"There are two reasons for that – his shock and the physiological impact of the lack of oxygen after death. Funny how a purple blush has never usurped the pale marble representation of the departed," observed the pathologist. Of course, he added, he had the utmost sympathy for the young policeman – after all, he himself had fainted his first time in the anatomy room as a student.

"You get used to anything and everything in time," Dufour said, an uncharacteristic smile creasing his grizzly grey visage. "But I understand there is something more upsetting about dismemberment. It is almost like dealing with two bodies as opposed to one."

Then Dupin signalled for Lazare to begin the pattern of work. The photographer set up his camera and for the next 30 minutes from various angles and heights recorded, again and in more detail than before, the horrific scene within the trunk and the valise.

Dupin noticed not a twitch in his photographer's eye and admired his total dedication and professionalism. He had selected his team with the utmost rigor and now watched in action confirmation of both his reason and instinct in the matter. Lazare's eye was now one of an investigator and yet he had not abandoned his artistry. Dupin had always held the opinion that scientific logic could be enhanced by artistic imagination.

As Dufour was about to effect the removal of the remains from the trunk to the slab, one of his team entered the morgue and informed Dupin that he had received a call from a Madame Castellazi to say that her friend Madame Emma Levin, a widow of a Danish industrialist, had been missing from her hotel, the

Bristol in Monte Carlo, from the previous evening and she had her suspicions of who might be responsible.

She had given him two names, saying she knew they had planned to travel to Marseilles, and their address which was the Villa Menesini in Monte Carlo. She suggested that Madame Levin's jewellery might be in the possession of the couple. She had also left her contact details. He passed the note to Dupin.

"Aha! The British aristocrats who apparently own the trunk. And independently confirmed, the name of the victim." He turned to one of the police team. "Very well, good Bloc, search Mr Goold's other luggage and remove any items of jewellery."

Dufour and his dieners had removed the body parts carefully and placed them on the slab.

In the bottom of the trunk there was a salmon-coloured bodice with a number of bloodstains. It was removed and bagged as evidence.

Quickly the pathologist identified two stab wounds on the torso, which had pierced the site of the heart from the front and the back. These, he established in his external examination, were probably fatal. There was also indication of blunt-force trauma to the head, possibly carried out in advance of the stabbing.

There were numerous contusions on the face, eight wounds on the head, small wounds on the neck, all caused by the same instrument and the two wounds on the back and front caused by the second instrument. The contusions possibly indicated there had been a struggle, more likely than not.

Rigor mortis was no longer present in the limbs and body, indicating that the murder had been committed up to 48 hours previously, fitting into the picture of an effort to get rid of and transport the body away from the original site of the killing but with the interval of perhaps one night.

He also noted that the dismemberment had been carried out with implements that had with most probability been a common saw and knife. There was also a deep incision in the stomach region and a removal of a portion of the intestines.

"For what purpose?" enquired Dupin.

"More likely than not to disguise, rather crudely, the effects of putrefaction. After all, this corpse was supposed to travel to London after a one-night stop in Monte Carlo, and another in Marseilles, not to mind the rest of the journey."

"I am more and more inclined to believe this murder was planned."

"No doubt," replied the doctor.

"Which does not explain what was to happen to the head and legs," proffered the investigator.

"I am assuming – and this is pure speculation which I do not like to indulge in at any time – they were to be disposed of in the sea in this very port. The trunk might attract too much attention."

"And what of the intestines which were removed?" asked Dupin. "There has been no trace of them."

"I would imagine they have already been committed to the sea. Don't you agree?"

"Almost certainly. I will get some of my men to comb the beach, in case by chance the entrails could be washed ashore again."

The cause of death at this stage, in his opinion, was the stabbing. He told Dupin he was confident that his completed post mortem, after internal examination, would confirm the initial finding.

"The question is," the detective posed, "was there more than one person involved in the execution of the crime?"

Dr Dufour replied that he would attempt to establish that fact. And in his opinion there would be remnants of bloodstains at the original location as there would have been little time to properly dispose of that evidence. He presumed that the perpetrators planned to be well away by the time this was discovered.

"It is quite extraordinary how difficult it is to efficiently remove all trace of blood," he said. "There is not yet a cleansing agent that will get it properly out of clothes."

"Thank you, Dufour, I will let you finish your work in peace while I return to the office and consult my team."

Dupin left, glad to be away from the claustrophobic atmosphere of the morgue and the next grim stage of the pathologist's examination.

Back in the central office, he noted the time and quickly set about and received permission from Monsieur Malavialle, the examining magistrate in Marseilles, to arrest and question the suspects. While he would continue the investigation under French law, a magistrate would also be involved and would begin preliminary examination of both suspects and witnesses in a public court.

He contacted his counterpart Inspector Garonne in the Monte Carlo Direction of Public Safety who agreed to conduct a search of the Villa Menesini and, contingent on his findings, seal the crime scene and get back to him. Within an hour he received the call from Garonne. There were bloodstains in the bedroom of the villa and in a wardrobe under some clothing his team had discovered a saw and a large knife with some discolouring, indicating there had been an attempt to clean them but not efficiently. There was no sign of the intestines which had yet to be located.

There was a niece of the couple at the villa, who apparently had been living with them, but in his opinion knew nothing of the murder.

Dupin expressed the desire to travel to Monte Carlo to continue his investigation and interview witnesses, including the Madame Castellazi who had contacted his office. In advance he would send some members of his forensic team to examine the scene and secure evidence. Garonne was more than happy to oblige and offered the services of a Dr Corniglion to assess the medical forensic aspects of the crime scene.

"He is excellent at the interpretation of blood-spatter patterns which I think you will find in this case particularly appropriate."

"Thank you, Garonne, I am indebted to you."

Garonne laughed. "Not at all, Dupin, I will be in your debt

because the trial will take place on my patch. And all the evidence will be of crucial value to the success of the case. *Bonne chance!*"

Indeed, Dupin mused, indeed. But he also knew he would not be erased from the picture. For the moment the investigation was his and when it came to the Principality, all French expertise was welcomed. Crime was no stranger to Monaco but the frequency of murder was low compared to Marseilles.

But, as always, he could not afford to put one foot out of place. All the more so because the eyes of Paris were fixed in the most concentrated way on Marseilles. Having promoted the all-powerful Sûreté over the incompetent municipal cousins, Marseilles principal among them, Hennion would make sure everything about the investigation would go right. And Dupin expected a call from him.

With utter certainty, the detective knew that he must watch his front, his back and every side that the human frame possessed. Like a good athlete, the one he had been in his youth, he would envisage the tape and then count every footfall until he reached the finish line – first. It did not matter who was breathing down his neck. He banished every competitor from his mind. The one most capable of inflicting defeat was himself.

He gathered his team around his desk in the office, having first ordered them to bring in their coffees.

"Lazare, take the next train to Monte Carlo. Carlin will assist you. Here are the details of the address. Consult with Garonne and get the photographs of the scene from him. Froissart and Bloc will stay with me for the interrogation. Then we will take things as they develop. We hope to join you tomorrow morning, all things being equal." He paused and looked intently from one face to another. "For reasons that must be obvious to all of us, this operation needs to be carried out quietly and without fuss and for the moment far from the sniping attention of the newspapers. That will happen, but it is the last thing we need now. Already they could be on the trail, for all we know."

They were. And, in this arena of public discourse, the investigators would have no control. The elements and the facts, as even cursorily gathered would be far too big for anyone to keep under wraps. The Fourth Estate would be soon on the case and as unrelenting in its pursuit of information as the investigators of the crime.

Dupin and Dr Dufour discussed Mr Goold's condition.

The doctor gave his assessment thus: "He is a hopeless alcoholic, completely dependent both physically and mentally, and will without doubt experience delirium tremens. With the help of the medicine he will calm down in a day or two. He is at the moment completely confused and nothing he might say would be acceptable in a court of law." The doctor then prescribed sedatives when necessary to calm the prisoner and lessen the effects of the hallucinations he would inevitably experience.

They analysed the obvious line of defence of insanity, which more than likely would be taken up considering his present condition. The woman? Dufour, conceding that he had not engaged with her, judged from what Dupin had told him from the first interview that she was the stronger of the pair and would continue to deny her part in the crime. It appeared that she might be the dominant partner in the relationship.

"The man," he suggested, "is not only weakened by dissipation but by the very relationship which under normal circumstances should be a source of strength." The doctor then continued, taking the thought straight out of Dupin's mind, "I would, when it comes down to the examination of character, bring Professor Lacassagne into the equation."

"Agreed," replied the investigator. "His experience in the Gouffé case will prove invaluable. Most particularly in the matter of the balance of power between the protagonists. I am convinced that Mrs Goold will be an unwilling person in the process, while her husband will in time co-operate as fully as possible."

They discussed the murder from a number of angles – motive, opportunity and guilt, the last of which they harboured little doubt about. What they found more worthy of debate was the method of the murder and the grisly mechanics of attempting to cover it up. The attempt to transport the body parts to England for disposal was worthy of note. The risks appeared to the medical man to overwhelm such a modus operandi with insurmountable odds.

"However," posited Dupin, "it always seems that way in retrospect. Like the Gouffé case, the method of concealment – which I hold was the inspiration for the Goolds – was attended with great risk. But let us say that if the body of the bailiff and that of Madame Levin had reached their intended destination, who could have predicted the outcome? With more attendance to detail, each case might well have remained a mystery and evaded the scientific process that we rely upon to convict a murderer."

Perhaps, conceded Dufour, but pointed to the more clinical method adopted by Eyraud and Bompard. The mess was left by the passage of time and the process of decomposition. With the Goolds, the mess was created at the beginning in the most savage fashion, in a scene more redolent of an abattoir. The motives were fairly close but the psychological element somewhat different. The reverse, it seemed.

∞

The Inspector telephoned Professor Lacassagne who was more than willing to help. When all was in readiness, he would travel to Marseilles to interview the perpetrators.

He concurred with Dufour's view of Mrs Goold. "She will behave in a hysterical manner when probed about the truth, hide in denial and refuse to co-operate. Mr Goold, I am positive, will be more forthcoming. While considered as monsters, they will initially view themselves as victims. Hard to imagine, Dupin, but true of many of their kind. But there is a grain of truth in that stance and it is that grain that we need to unearth."

Lacassagne then enquired about what background or antecedents of the couple had been established.

"Very little so far," replied Dupin. "Goold said that he is from Waterford in southern Ireland. All we got from his wife so far is that she is originally from Isère." Lacassagne paused. "The latter will be fairly easy to establish. The former might be more difficult but I may be of help. I made the acquaintance of the professor of medical jurisprudence in Cork University in Ireland at a conference. There may well be information about the Goold family in the university archives. I will make enquiries."

Dupin put down the telephone. Not a bad day's work, he thought. But we never know what is around the corner. He was prepared to encounter whatever was thrown his way. One way or another, he knew full well that he would not get off lightly. There were other tasks to undertake.

The detective consulted with the examining magistrate Monsieur Malavialle about the establishment of the judicial process. The prisoners would be transported to separate prisons where the magistrate could interview them when appropriate and set up the impending preliminary court hearings which, under the French inquisitorial system would be exhaustive, before the prisoners were extradited and brought to trial in Monte Carlo. There a similar process would take place under the baton of magistrate Monsieur Savard.

Dupin would take the overnight train to Monte Carlo to continue the investigation with the co-operation of Garonne and the local police authorities. First he had to ring Hennion.

# 9

## LA GUILLOTINE?

The words rang out through the room, transfixing its gathering of amazed and admiring listeners:

> "Danton, you have served the cause of tyranny. You were, it is true, opposed to Lafayette; but Mirabeau, Orleans, Dumouriez were also opposed to him. Dare you deny that you were sold to these three men, the most violent of conspirators against liberty? It was by the protection of Mirabeau that you were named administrator of the department of Paris, at a time when the electoral assembly was decidedly royalist. All the friends of Mirabeau openly boasted that they had shut your mouth. Moreover, as long as that frightful personage lived you remained silent. At that time you charged a rigid patriot in the course of a dinner that he would compromise the good cause by stepping aside from the path along which Barnave

170

and Lameth, who abandoned the popular party, were moving.

Amid the first gleams of the Revolution you displayed a threatening attitude toward the court; you spoke against it with vehemence. Mirabeau, who meditated a change of dynasty, scented the price of your audacity and seized you. Thenceforward you strayed from rigid principles, and you were no longer spoken of until the massacre of the Champs de Mars. Then you supported, at the Jacobin Club, the motion of Laclos, which was a baleful pretext, paid for by the enemies of the people, for the unfurling of the red flag and an attempt at tyranny. The patriots who were not initiated in this conspiracy had ineffectually combated your sanguinary opinion. You were named with Brissot to draw up the petition of the Champs de Mars, and you both escaped the fury of Lafayette, who caused 2,000 patriots to be massacred. Brissot went about peaceably after that in Paris; and you, you passed away happy hours at Arcis-sur-Aube – if a person who conspired against his country could be happy. Is not the calm of your retreat at Arcis-sur-Aube comprehensible? You, one of the authors of the petition; while of those who had signed it some were loaded with chains, others were massacred; Brissot and you, were you not objects of tyranny's gratitude since you were not objects of its hatred and terror? What shall I say of your cowardly and constant abandonment of the public cause in the midst of crises, when you always took the part of retreat?

Mirabeau dead, you conspired with the Lameths and supported them. You remained neutral during the Legislative Assembly, and you held your peace during the sore struggle of the Jacobins against Brissot and the Girondist faction. At first you supported their opinion upon the war. Pressed afterward by the reproaches of the best citizens, you declared that you would observe the two parties, and you retired into silence. Allied with Brissot in the affair of the Champs de Mars you thereafter shared his tranquillity and his liberty-killing principles; then, given over entirely to this victorious party, you said of those who held aloof from it, that since they were alone in their opinion upon the war, and since they wished to ruin themselves, your friends and you must abandon them to their fate. But when you saw the storm of the tenth of August gathering, again you betook yourself to Arcis-sur-Aube. However, urged by shame and reproaches, and when you knew that the fall of tyranny was well prepared and inevitable, you returned to Paris on the 9th of August. You hid yourself during that terrible night. Your section, which had nominated you its president, long awaited you; they dragged you out of a shameful repose. You presided for an hour; you quitted the chair at the moment the tocsin sounded; at the same instant the satellites of tyranny entered and thrust the bayonet through the heart of him who had replaced you. You, you slept!

You detached yourself from the Mountain amid the dangers which it ran. You publicly claimed it as a merit not to have denounced Gensonné, Gaudet, and Brissot; you incessantly held out to them the olive branch, a pledge of your alliance with them against the people and strict republicans. The Girondists made a mock war against you; in order to force you to declare yourself it demanded a reckoning of you; it accused you of ambition. Your far-sighted hypocrisy conciliated all, and contrived to maintain itself in the midst of parties, always ready to dissimulate before the strongest without offending the weakest. During stormy debates, your absence and your silence were commented on with indignation; you, you spoke of the country, of the delights of solitude and idleness, but you could quit your apathy to defend Dumouriez, Westermann, his boasted creature, and his accomplices, the generals.

You knew how to allay the wrath of the patriots; you represented our misfortunes as the result of the feebleness of our armies, and you turned attention from the treachery of the generals to occupy yourself with new levies of men. You were associated in the crimes of Lacroix, a long denounced conspirator of impure soul, with whom one could not be united save by the knot which binds conspirators. Lacroix was always more than suspected, hypocritical and perfidious: he has never spoken with good faith within these precincts; he had the audacity to praise Miranda and to propose the renewing of the Convention; his conduct with Dumouriez was the same as yours. Lacroix has often testified his hatred for the Jacobins. Whence came the pomp with which he was surrounded? But why recall so many horrors when your evident complicity with Orleans and Dumouriez in Belgium suffices for justice to smite you.

Unworthy citizen, you have plotted; false friend, you spoke evil two days ago of Desmoulins, an instrument whom you have lost, and you attributed shameful vices to him. Wicked man, you have compared public opinion to a woman of loose life; you have said that honour was absurd, that glory and posterity were a folly. These maxims were to conciliate you with the aristocracy; they were those of Catiline. If Fabre is innocent, if Orleans, if

Dumouriez were innocent, then doubtless you are innocent. I have said too much: you shall answer to justice."

Clemenceau had stunned his audience with his perfect rendering of Louis Saint-Just's condemnation of Danton delivered before the Convention in March 1794, to which the accused had no opportunity to reply in his own defence.

When the applause died down, the Minister would no doubt have a point to make to the gathering of his Cabinet.

Célestin Hennion was mightily impressed with his mentor's delivery of that age-old speech and wondered with the rest of the assembled company what was going to come next. Clemenceau loved such diversions before he got down to business, but apart from anything else, he already had a captive audience.

"Well, Célestin, what do you think?"

"An example of evil, deceit and betrayal that would make any of the government's allies and indeed enemies appear saintly by comparison."

"Indeed, false accusations, distorted facts, delivered in an atrocious but very effective manner, and left unchallenged. In the interests of justice it is, however, to be recalled that despite the fact that Danton was executed six days later, the deliverer of the speech together with its undoubted author Robespierre four months later were led to the guillotine!"

The Prime Minister had now revealed his reason for using this example: there had been a concerted political effort to get rid of the guillotine which was gathering some credibility.

They were in different times now, Clemenceau remarked, with far different outcomes to the swings and roundabouts of politics, but he emphasised the same swings were still present and the same inclinations for alliances of convenience and betrayal. A brief history of the Third Republic would provide ample evidence for that fact. Just now the radicals and socialists were pushing for legislation for the abolition of capital punishment, a move which he urged his colleagues and allies in government to oppose.

"We are all aware from the history surrounding the speech which I have just hopefully properly recounted, that abuse of capital punishment has unforgivable consequences both for society and individuals. That awful time in the development of the republic provides a classic example of the total breakdown of law and order. We are concerned with the preservation of law and order which we are well aware is under threat from many quarters."

He went on to outline the much-publicised increase in violent crimes and murder in both urban and rural areas and the constant threat of political violence from anarchists and extreme left-wing radicals. The gang terrorism on the streets of Paris and Marseilles could not and would not be tolerated.

Hennion gave an analysis of the situation which he considered serious enough to merit setting up a dozen mobile brigades to respond to serious crime in a quick and effective manner. All present would be derelict in their duty not to recognise the worsening trends that posed great risk, both to the citizens of the country but also to the state itself. In addition to all their best efforts to deal with criminals, it was his opinion that effective deterrents must always be central to a successful policing policy.

"We are privileged to have a reformed and highly motivated force which day by day on a national level is coming under the control of the Sûreté. The mobile brigades will reach every corner of France and destroy the hegemony of the armed gangs and thieves. In Professor Lacassagne and Dr Locard of Lyons we have the two greatest forensic experts, not just in this country, but in the world. Lacassagne is also an accomplished criminologist with a number of important studies completed into the criminal mind and the genesis of criminal behaviour. He is, to be absolutely clear, implacably opposed to the abolition of capital punishment. In surveys he has carried out, in prisons housing the most dangerous and persistent recidivists, he has found a surprisingly high proportion without any remorse or regret for their actions, including murderers who have avoided execution due to extenuating circumstances. In these and many other cases, to remove the deterrent of capital punishment would be an absolute folly. There are irredeemable criminals, who show no regret for the victims of their crimes."

Hennion went on to state that he was a policeman, not a moralist, just as the professor from Lyons was a scientist not a preacher. But both also had broader interests in the arts, music and literature in particular. He mentioned this because all those who shared such interests, including the Prime Minister and much of his Cabinet, would recognise copious reference in literature to the matter of conscience.

"It is supposed to be one of the most powerful agents in human behaviour. Writers tell of the pangs that assail the wicked and vividly express the torture and anguish of a stricken conscience; poisoning all pleasure, inducing nightmares and repeated memory of the event. Punishment by all accounts comes as a welcome relief. This may be largely true but, in my experience and that of others on the front line, there are killers and criminals who have no conscience or remorse and the only pity they possess is for themselves for being caught."

Most of those, he added, would commit the crimes all over again. Determinists without knowing it, they seemed to view the crime as ordained by fate, something over which they had no control. Certainly by all means abolish capital punishment, throw the citizens to the wolves of crime and their parliamentary representatives to the bombers and assassins. The consequences would, in his view, be catastrophic for France.

It was a view that would gain a lot of both parliamentary and popular support and ultimately defeat the efforts of the abolitionists.

Hennion was glad to get back to his office in the Sûreté. He was not entirely comfortable in the company of politicians, but had responded to Clemenceau's entreaty as his boss. It was a small concession for the support his mentor and friend gave him in regard to the operation of the Sûreté.

Some hours later he received a call from Dupin of Marseilles about the discovery that morning of a dismembered body at Gare Saint-Charles.

"It will be all over the newspapers tomorrow, so I just wanted to forewarn you," said Dupin.

"I appreciate your call very much," said Hennion. "It is very timely for a reason that I won't go into – let us say politics – which I know, with respect, will not be of any concern to you. And I agree this will cause a sensation just like the Gouffé case. The newspapers are particularly fond of murder within the higher classes, where it is not supposed to happen. But the method would have attracted considerable attention all the same. It is a tide there will be no point in resisting. Better not leave too much to their imagination. But needless to say there will be details they publish which will surprise us all, whatever the basis in fact. Such is the doubtful, at times, privilege of the press. Concentrate, no matter, on your investigation. *There is nothing covered that shall not be revealed; and hid, that shall not be known.*"

Dupin recognised the last statement from the Gospel of Matthew. Nothing, he thought, has changed since it was written.

"*Bonne guerre,*" concluded Hennion.

⌒⌒⌒

Dupin could not believe his luck.

There was help if he wanted it but the case was his and he should get on with it; and without betraying confidences or prejudicing the trial, there should be reasonable co-operation with the newspapers.

He was back at the Saint-Charles station at eleven that evening to catch the overnight train to Monte Carlo. He got a compartment on his own and settled down to get some much-needed sleep.

# 10

## RENDEZ-VOUS

**MONTE CARLO, AUGUST 1907**

The detective woke just once in the darkened compartment, prompted into wakefulness by a dream of confused signals and forking paths of thought translated into image. Nothing unusual, just part of the subconscious stress that came with his position. Very rarely there was a revealing nugget released by his subconscious in dream form that could be of value. The web of his dream unfolded, and he recalled every detail.

This was a strange one, but on reflection there would certainly prove to be connections with the case.

In his dream he had stopped to look into the waters of a river. Dark shadows of fish moved through the submerged reeds. They parted like the curtains on the stage of the theatre and revealed a kaleidoscope of colour and in the middle a basket with a baby in swaddling clothes.

The baby boy's eyes were wide open and the face began to move to the surface of the water. From its eyes tears mingled with the moving river. There was a most lonely and lost look on his face and his hands emerged from the surface in a pleading embrace.

He was transfixed with fear. If he yielded to the embrace he would be drawn to a watery grave. To limbo with the baby.

He turned away and with leaden legs ran towards a bridge which straddled the rushing, gushing waters of the river. His heart was pounding along with the river current.

His attention was drawn to a clock above the bakery shop No numbers but hands still moved across the face. There wasn't a soul on the street, not a dog, cat or human.

He began to cross the bridge, aware of a deathly silence.

The river made no sound though the waters moved in gigantic flood towards the open sea. His eyes took in the small harbour on the right-hand side of the river where at low tide the swans would eat from the hands of their admirers. Beyond he could see the expanse of the bay, not a ship, a small boat or a seagull in sight. The silence was broken by the toll of the church bell just down from the harbour.

From the direction of the city centre a funeral procession appeared. The hearse was drawn by a pair of white horses with black plumes sticking upright from their heads. The cortege approached, followed by a number of women in black dresses with shawls drawn over their heads so that their faces could not be seen. The undertaker sat on his seat above the horses' rumps. Under his tall black hat he wore dark glasses and in his right hand he held a white stick. He wore a butcher's apron, covered in blood.

As the hearse approached, the detective saw the coffin which like the windows of the hearse was made of transparent glass. In the distance he could see the corpse was a young woman with long dark hair. As the hearse drew abreast, the woman's eyes opened and she turned toward him, her arms rising, beckoning. It was Emma Levin. He recoiled in shock.

Splashes of blood from the undertaker's apron dripped on his hands.

He was dragged into a darkening void, an eternal tunnel. He felt his breath taken from his throat, making a sound like a rattle. With all his strength he resisted. The church bell rang louder and louder and he felt the ice-cold grip of the corpse's hands.

That had been enough to jolt him out of the nightmare. Nothing much in the subconscious could match the horrors of reality. There were parts of such dreamy rumination where it would be quite pleasant to halt an event or image for more pleasure or thought. But dreams do not work that way. The images follow one another like the waves coming in to the shore, they allow no pause for contemplation. More's the pity, he often thought to himself.

A shaft of sunlight penetrated the slit in the blinds and Dupin raised them, with the broken webs of the dream still clinging to his mind. Sunlight flooded the compartment. He briefly considered some logical interpretation of his dream. The victim looking for help and justice? That much was clear. But the rest?

Certainly this woman would get justice, but he still needed to know more about her and in particular her relation with the Goolds.

In particular the wife – Marie. Dr Dufour's assessment of Goold had given him much pause for thought. The man was a physical and mental wreck, incapable of planning and carrying out the crime on his own. On the other hand there was little doubt, he knew from experience, that a drink-and-drug-fuelled rage can produce extraordinary violence. But the man that he had seen, he suspected, did not fit that category. Then again evil often gets weak men to do its bidding.

The detective was convinced, however, as Goron was in the Gouffé case, of the identity of the architect, the person that planned and without doubt both orchestrated and participated in the last minutes of the victim's life. One of his main priorities then was to find out as much as possible about the former Marie Giroudin, to provide support for this theory.

The expanse of the sparkling Mediterranean stretched

181

towards the infinity of the horizon. It was beautiful but sometimes made him sad, in the way days at the beach are not always a joy for children. But he had plenty to distract him from the views and the attractions of Monte Carlo which held no real fascination for him. He shared with the professor and Dr Locard a love of the arts. Monte Carlo was not a place any of them would have felt comfortable in, not even in a policing role.

Inspector Garonne, a man of imposing presence, being over six feet in height and of typical Mediterranean good looks, was waiting for him at the station and they proceeded to the villa where the Goolds had stayed, to examine the crime scene. On the way the Monte Carlo chief told him that he had tracked down a number of witnesses who had made useful statements which he would provide. He had, of course, also found the implements probably used in the commission of the crime.

"You will find that the perpetrators were in such a hurry that they literally abandoned the most importance of evidence, hoping that it would not be discovered," said Garonne. "It appears that Isobel Giroudin, the niece, knew nothing of the crime and was hoodwinked by the Goolds into believing that bloodstains were as a result of a nosebleed suffered by Mr Goold. You may examine her yourself on that matter."

During the course of the conversation Dupin expressed his desire to establish which of the apparent accomplices had planned the awful crime and what the respective physical involvement was. The motive well might have been robbery but that, he posited, was the tip of the iceberg.

Garonne agreed. "I believe that, as far as this is concerned, the witness Madame Castellazi could be of vital importance. I will arrange for an interview on the subject with her."

Dupin thanked him profusely but Garonne deflected his good manners. They were on the same side. The eyes of the world would be brought to bear on the crime and it was in the interests of the investigation both in the Principality and France to get everything right.

"You know, Garonne," Dupin mused, "the sum of what we learn often refuses to add up too neatly."

He was greeted with a large laugh. "Too true, Dupin, too true. On the other hand, the thing in plain sight is the last thing you see."

The detectives hit the same reaction at the same time.

"Rarely is anything as it seems."

"*Touché.*"

The inspectors concurred that witness evidence must be looked upon with scepticism; there were too many factors involved quite apart from self-interest and mistaken interpretation. They would approach all with as fresh eyes and objectivity as possible. And they also concurred that the examining magistrates, after the investigation was complete, would take all the glory as if they were responsible for all.

"Glory means nothing to me," observed Dupin. "The truth means all. They are welcome to the glory, if that is all they seek."

"It is, believe me. The lawyers love the open stage. We will get on working at the coal face!"

Dupin laughed. "We are but servants of the law, we will get on with it. After all, they will just retrace our steps."

The Monte Carlo detective had not been idle. He had established that the victim was Emma Erika Levin from Stockholm, a brilliant hostess and owner of a magnificent set of jewels. Born in Malmo, she married Leopold Levin, a wealthy Danish company director. The couple lived in Stockholm in splendid style and entertained in their flat in the Noble Institute in North Railway Square. Her priceless rings were celebrated in the city. Her older husband died in 1905, leaving a smaller fortune than expected – he was always thought to be immensely wealthy. The widow was left an annuity by her husband's company more than sufficient for her needs.

In May 1907 she went to Monte Carlo. Many residents of Stockholm met her during the summer there. Her mother lived in Copenhagen. Inspector Garonne stated that Madame Castellazi had been the source of this information and she knew a lot more about Marie Goold, having met an acquaintance of hers in the casino whose information she had passed on to Madame Levin. And she now felt that this information had the opposite effect to that which she had intended.

The rooms on the fourth floor of the Menesini provided plenty of objective evidence. The servants of the law got on with their business. Dupin observed the bloodstains on the carpet on the living room and on the floor and walls of the bathroom. In the box room there was bloodstained linen, a large stain on the floor and splashes on the wall. In addition, there was the saw and the knife, though that knife was clearly not the one that had produced the stab-wounds.

The doctor told Dupin that the initial attack had taken place in the living room, the body then dragged to the bathroom, dismembered, and moved to the box room before being placed in the trunk and valise. The bloodstain patterns proved that without doubt.

In a drawer in the bedroom they found letters of demand from the victim for money owed by the Goolds to her, signed by her. One on a card bearing the name of Goold read: *"I await payment of money borrowed. Send it by telegraph. I need it."* The signature was somewhat illegible.

Dupin said he would need confirmation of the signature and handwriting. Garonne assured him that Madame Castellazi would provide that and much more.

The niece was then interviewed and could add little to what was already established. She was, noted Dupin, a lovely-looking young woman with a naturally delicate disposition. She had been sent out by the Goolds at the time to walk to Cap Martin and the bloodstains were explained to her by a medical problem attributed to Mr Goold, namely nosebleeds.

"Who told you of this?" enquired Dupin,

"Mrs Goold," she answered.

That was sufficient for the detective. He would not put her under more pressure than she was already experiencing. She voluntarily offered some facts about how and when she had been engaged by the Goolds as a form of housekeeper. This young woman was totally innocent, in his view, and had been exploited by the perpetrators. He requested Garonne to somehow find her employment to save her from the worst consequences of an act that she had had nothing to do with. The Inspector assured him that this would happen.

The next stop was the Hotel Bristol where the victim had stayed during her time in Monte Carlo. It was a modest place with nothing of the so-called graces of the other habitations in this place of excess. Madame Levin's room was small and neat. There was nothing out of place. Her dresses were in the wardrobe, all in a line to be taken out when necessary, the underwear nicely stacked in a drawer.

In another drawer there was discovered a sum of 140 dollars in cash and a number of items of jewellery.

On a bureau, a small photographic album, a record of family life. There was a wedding photograph of a young attractive woman and a rather older stooped man.

Madame Levin. What initial compromise of comfortable prospects with an old man should deserve such a fate? Dupin held the album in his hand and wondered about how simple turns of mind lead to such horrific consequences. What decisions had she made, as a relatively young widow, that had brought her to such a den of iniquity and her ultimate demise?

He felt he already knew the answer. But he needed a lot more answers to complete that puzzle to his satisfaction. Perhaps Madame Castellazi of that flamboyant name might be of assistance.

They met the said madame in the Café de Paris but Dupin was loath to interview anyone in their natural habitat. After cursory conversation, she agreed rather enthusiastically to go to Inspector Garonne's office on the strict understanding that there would be no other witnesses to their meeting.

The woman, he reckoned, was in her late forties and had seen better days which was only emphasised by an over-enthusiastic application of rouge on the cheeks and clothes that might have better befitted some girl twenty years her junior. One makes judgments based on such details, thought Dupin, which can prove to be totally off the mark. He suspended such judgement until he heard what might come from the heavy lips, obscured as they might be by a deep blood-red application.

The story that she told was quite astounding. She spoke rapidly and Dupin had great difficulty in keeping up with his notes.

She was a habitué of the casino and had very rarely lost much money, being prudent about her betting as well as being somewhat dependent for her living on the winnings. She had seen people win and lose fortunes, being catapulted from great heights of euphoria to great depths of despair. She became immune to such extremes during her time in Monte Carlo. That was essential to survival in the gaming rooms of the casino, as well as possessing an ability to identify 'chancers' abundant in the rooms as opposed to the more naïve players affected too deeply by the seductions of chance. She became, she claimed, somewhat expert in recognising the two categories. She was not an innocent herself in these matters and not proud of some things she had done but did not wish to implicate herself in shady dealings. She wanted to help and give information of use to the investigation which would prove of no benefit to herself. Yet she wanted her past left with the indignities of memory and her own pangs of conscience.

The detectives had no problem with that but Dupin emphasised that any criminal behaviour found in her case would not be beyond the appropriate punishment. If she had useful information that would be of benefit in the case, they would be glad to hear it, but without fear or favour. Otherwise she could just walk away.

He bared his white teeth with a radiant smile; she looked into the pools of his deep brown twinkling eyes. His expression would have melted the resolve of younger and better women. Dupin was not beyond using his charm, without conceding anything.

Madame decided not to take the option of walking away. She decided to take her chances, something which for her, by her own admission, was familiar territory.

"The most important information I can give," she said, "apart from my knowledge of the parties involved, was given to me by a person I met a week before the crime and who was at one time, some years ago, intimately involved with and a subsequent victim of Marie Goold. A pecuniary matter, I hasten to add. She is very much alive and may or may not want to confirm what I am telling you. As a result of her monetary loss, she hired a private detective to enquire into Mrs Goold's background. It was to no avail. Mrs Goold threatened a suit for slander and defamation. My friend had no appetite for scandal and withdrew. But, as you know, we all reap what we sow and here we are. I have no doubt whatsoever that this background will be of help to your investigation, particularly in relation to the character of Marie, or as she would prefer to be known 'Lady Goold'."

Madame Castellazi's comprehensive account followed.

Marie Giroudin was never a beauty. As a young woman, she was considered plain-looking with a rather nasty and aggressive manner. She did not make friends easily. But what she lacked in looks and social graces she compensated for with a clever and resourceful character. She was driven by a desire above her station to mix in fashionable circles and get rich quickly but without much effort on her part. But she had a dominating and overwhelming presence which all men are not averse to, as was proved by three marriages. All by outward signs should have been to her profit.

Her first marriage was to a young man who fell in love with her despite her obvious lack of charm. He proposed but was rejected which was interpreted by his family as an insult which they repaid in kind. This had the unfortunate result of reversing her decision and she married him but later left him as she could see no material profit forthcoming. He was miserable but took her back after a long absence. She had been in Paris and London while away and only remained at home for three months.

Then her husband died suddenly and she was off again. This time into the arms of an English army officer by the name of Captain Wilkinson. She was however very fond of the high life and spending money, which put a strain on the family finances. At one time she took off on a tour of the Continent, staying a couple of days at Nice, and when leaving relieved some trusting woman of £2,000 worth of jewellery. There was no proof of her guilt, so she got away with robbery.

Her tastes were not to her husband's liking, among them her lack of thrift and love of the high life, but it did not matter in the end because he pre-deceased her. Whatever money he left, which was not a lot by all accounts, would not last long in her hands, but she did have a collection of jewellery to stave off the rainy day until she could target another man of means. She was pushing thirty, not very attractive in the first place and not helped by the passage of time.

But she still had a silver tongue. She was given to fantasy and name-dropping, but was persuasive to some gullible enough to be taken in. She inferred rather than baldly stated her high-society connections. She had no problem when it came to impressing people, but a good talker without work cannot produce money and Marie began to feel the want of it. So she flattered an old well-off Englishwoman to give her a position as secretary-companion.

Marie refused to accept a salary, giving the impression that she did not need the money and only wanted the companionship. The Englishwoman was naturally delighted with the arrangement but some weeks later was relieved of the considerable sum of £600 while she and her secretary had gone on a trip to San Sebastian. Her employee then informed her that she had been summoned to Paris to consult with her lawyers about some property she had been left in her husband's will.

She in fact travelled to Marseilles, booking into the Hôtel du Louvre, the most expensive in the port, and lived the high life on the money she had stolen from the gullible old woman. But the money soon ran out and Marie was left without any liquid assets but still holding on to the jewellery. A few swindles she embarked upon came to nothing and, feeling the pressure, she moved on again – this time to London. There she could not get credit in hotels and was forced to work and eventually cash in the last assets she had.

With the proceeds she leased a small shop in the West End and began a dressmaking business. It could well have been a success but she was not inclined to hard work and began to extract money on account from wealthy clients, women whom she flattered with false promises about keeping them looking young, and who came to regard her as a friend and confidante.

What on the surface seemed to be a thriving business was anything but. One day a middle-aged client came into the shop and found the proprietor in tears. She said that the bailiffs were about to close her down and managed to extract the sum she said was owing from the sympathetic woman. She had also taken to gambling and losing and started again to look out for a man to take up some of the financial slack.

It was then that she picked out Vere Goold, an Irishman of achievement and education who had fallen foul of drink, drugs and gambling and had been sent to London by friends and relatives, anxious for him to get away from his Dublin haunts to reform in a better environment. He had been given a small allowance with the hope that he would get employment and straighten out his life.

His life had not been transformed. He frequented bars and restaurants in the West End and Soho. He was generally considered an ineffectual and well-meaning drunk who on occasion paid small fines at police stations for being drunk and disorderly. At no stage during this time did violence play any part in his antics, more redolent of an overgrown student. The only damage he was capable of doing was to himself.

And so he fell prey to Marie Giroudin, and married her – a marriage made in hell, his dissolute behaviour offset by a scheming, dominating partner determined to become a personage of importance without any effort on her part, and attain a social standing without the means to support it. And she had chosen someone of some former substance and lineage but in every sense now but a man of straw.

Her dream was pursued over a number of years in various locations and countries that Madame Castellazi said the police would establish in time. But some incidents were instructive of all. The honeymoon took place in Paris with clothes on the bride's back that had been obtained from wholesale sources without payment. The money ran out and bride subjected the groom to abuse about his inability to provide funds. He would wander the boulevards in despair looking for someone to borrow a few francs from.

They were turned out of several hotels and boarding houses. This set the pattern of their lives right up to and including their stay in Monte Carlo.

Then, most recently, again in Paris, Marie Goold had conned money from people she had met in a hotel. She'd also got a 24-hour approval from a jeweller's shop on a diamond ring and instantly pawned it. Then she and Goold took a train to Monte Carlo with the proceeds of both scams.

On arrival in October they took an apartment in the Villa Menesini with their niece acting as "housekeeper" to keep up appearances. They then set about making their fortune in the casino where she and Madame Levin had the misfortune to make each other's acquaintance.

At this point Madame Castellazi paused, hand to throat, and asked for a drink. Garonne poured her some water and then ordered coffee for all. He urged Madame Castellazi to take a small break before coming to the vital last stage of the very valuable statement she was offering to the investigating team. The coffee arrived and they drank it, exchanging only desultory remarks. When they finished Dupin gestured to the witness to continue.

"Let me tell you about the cunning manner in which Marie Goold first met my poor friend," she said. "It was about six weeks ago, in the Café de Paris, as I remember. Emma was beautifully dressed as usual, wearing her finest jewellery, and this woman 'bumped' into her. And after the apology and small talk, she introduced her to her husband Sir Vere Goold. Despite being titled, they came across as humble and genuine people and Emma was impressed. It was later that we met them again in the casino and, I have to say, knowing nothing of what I have related to you as I was just recently told all that by my informant, I took an instant dislike to the so-called Lady Goold and I am certain that the feeling was mutual. My suspicion did not take long to be proved. Emma informed me that Lady Goold had asked her for a loan of forty pounds and I urged her against it. But she eventually gave in. I was disappointed but more so because it established a connection that would become embarrassing and much more."

Madame Castellazi recounted that her friend had one night in the casino brought up the matter and Marie Goold had been dismissive, almost rude to her.

"I objected about this uncalled-for attitude and I am sorry to say that, with more provocation, a screaming match ensued between myself and Mrs Goold which transpired to be extremely embarrassing when the casino security were called to intervene. It was the next morning that Emma told me she was determined to leave Monte Carlo and return home to Copenhagen but was not going to go without her money being paid back. It wasn't so much the money that motivated her, but the scandal that Mrs Goold had caused that night by her vehemence and aggressiveness. She wrote letters to the Goolds about the matter several times without reply."

She said that this ultimately led to the invitation by the Goolds to their apartment to settle the debt. To this very moment she reproved herself for not being more forthright and preventing Emma Levin from having anything to do with the Goolds. She relived that moment of weakness ten times a day and ten times a night, every day and night.

Dupin put down his notebook. "There was nothing you could do any more than you did. There were other forces at play over which you had no control, namely in the life, circumstances and minds of the Goolds. You have been of great assistance to the investigation, madame. No doubt the examining magistrate will be needing your help in more straightforward manner."

He referred to one more thing which, he added, was not part of the investigation but would no doubt be a subject of press speculation.

"I will try to put this as delicately as possible. The matter of Madame Levin's, let us say, moral behaviour here?"

Her friend explained that she had led a closeted life during her marriage to an older man and was somewhat like a bird that escaped the cage when she arrived in Monte Carlo. She was intoxicated by the atmosphere, but was not alone in that. There were one or two unsuitable liaisons which she was warned off and did eventually recognise that the men were motivated by anything but romance.

"Not an unfamiliar tale in Monte Carlo," she added, addressing Inspector Garonne.

"Indeed not, madame, far too common I would say."

"But she then seemed to have settled down to simply enjoy herself – until of course she met the Goolds."

Her statement completed, Madame Castellazi left, having impressed Dupin despite his initial wariness.

Then the detectives, with Lazare and Froissart and a member of the local force had a quick conference. Copies of the statements of other witnesses were handed over to the French force. All agreed to continue the very satisfactory level of co-operation.

It was time for Dupin and his men to think about returning to Marseilles.

The Inspector looked upwards toward the clock on the wall. Unlike in his dream, both numbers and hands were there. Time was moving on and so should he.

∽≀∾

Back at Gare Saint-Charles in Marseilles, Dupin and the team were met by what seemed a massive army of reporters from local, national and English newspapers and a large contingent from the wire services. The detective, as Hennion suggested, was open without giving too much away. The basic details of the events were communicated and then the team moved on to the Préfecture.

They were happy because they would be now well out of the public eye as the very next day the examining magistrate, Monsieur Malavialle, would begin his work at the first of a long line of preliminary hearings where the press would be literally hanging from the rafters. Their reports would go all over the world.

# 11

## LE QUATRIÈME POUVOIR

The newspapers, as Dupin's team expected and feared, had a veritable field day at the first hearing – with other such days to follow. The newspapers of the English-speaking world reported the crime with great gusto but little accuracy, as evident from the contradictory versions the different newspapers published – on occasion even contradicting themselves within the same report. Indeed, one wonders whether much was lost in translation. Nevertheless they got the essential story over to the public and made sensational reading, which was their aim.

The following are samples from the great deluge of reportage that reached the English-speaking public.

### MONTE CARLO MURDER
### THRILLING DETAILS

*Reuters Reports*
August 9th, 1907

An elderly lady accompanied by a middle-aged man arrived at Marseilles by the 5.40 train last Tuesday from Monte Carlo. The gentleman gave porter Berard a luggage ticket telling him it was for a trunk which he desired to have forwarded by goods train to Charing Cross in London, to be left till called for.

After giving instructions, the gentleman told the cabman to drive to the Hotel du Louvre. When the cab had driven away, Berard called an out-porter named Pons, gave him the ticket with the necessary instructions and thought no more about the matter. At ten o'clock, Pons went to the luggage office, took over the trunk, placed it on a truck and started for the goods station.

On the way he noted, to his horror, that blood was trickling through a corner of the trunk. He ran to the Station Commissaire who ordered the trunk to be forced open. When the lid was forced a gruesome spectacle met the eye. A woman's body without the head or legs. To trace the owners was an easy matter as Berard had heard the name of the hotel. Without loss of time, the police proceeded to the Hotel du Louvre and arrested the gentleman and lady and seized their other luggage.

The arrested couple proved to be Vere Goold, a moneylender residing at Monte Carlo, and his wife. Taken before a Judge d'Instruction they denied responsibility for the murder but admitted that they were responsible for the dismembering of the corpse. The victim, it appears, was Emma Levin, widow of a wealthy Danish company director, possessor of a valuable collection of jewellery which she was in the habit of carrying about with her.

The theory of the police is that Goold and his wife enticed the woman to their villa and there murdered her for the sake of her valuables. The Goolds, however, deny that they are guilty of the crime and tell a peculiar story. Levin, they say, came to their villa to borrow money. Goold was out but, whilst his wife was in conversation with Mme Levin, a young man burst suddenly in upon them.

Addressing Levin, he cried: "Wretched woman, you have ruined me", then stabbed her with a knife. Mme Goold alleges that she fainted and remembers no more. When she recovered the young man had gone and Emma Levin was lying dead before her. She and her husband, who had returned home, feared the responsibility and, dreading they might be accused of the crime, cut up the body, placed part in the trunk and the remainder in a handbag and took a train to Marseilles in order to dispose of the remains.

The story by the pair is by no means in agreement. Goold stated that Mme Levin was killed at his villa in Monte Carlo by a man named Burker while he and Mrs Goold were absent. It was only on their return that they found the body, so they put "the head and legs in their portmanteau". Mrs Goold, on the other hand, asserted they were at home when the tragedy occurred and Mme Levin was paying a visit when the young man entered the villa. Seeing Mme Levin, he said: "You wretched woman, you have ruined me, now I am going to kill you." He then dealt her severe blows on the head with a heavy stick, immediately afterwards leaving the villa. Neither of these statements are supported by the result of enquiries, for no trace of the man named Burker has been found.

At a post mortem examination, the doctors diagnosed severe blows with a dagger to the chest and wounds on the head. They are of the opinion that a struggle took place with the victim and her assailants. In the Goold suite has been found a twisted dagger, stained with blood, a chopper and a saw. The sunshade of the victim was found in a box.

When the magistrate paid a visit to the Goolds' villa at Monte Carlo, Mme Isabel Giraudin, their niece aged 24, was there. She was not at home on Sunday afternoon when Mme Levin was supposed to have been murdered and she professed absolute ignorance of the crime and astonishment at the magistrate's visit.

The walls of the dining room in which the crime was supposed to have been committed are splashed with blood and there are also blood-stains on the carpet. A young girl in the service of the concierge of the villa states that about 5 o'clock on Sunday evening, she heard sounds of a struggle going on in the residence and someone cried: "Let me alone." But thinking it was just a domestic squabble, the girl paid no attention.

The victim's name is now given as Mme Emma Levin. Contrary to previous reports received here, she is described by those who knew her of a woman of high respectability, the widow of an engineer who died two years ago. She possessed fine diamonds, her jewellery being estimated as worth more than £2,000 and on Sunday evening she left the Hotel Bristol where she was staying, wearing the greater part of them.

Some time ago Mme Levin lent £40 to someone and she was heard to complain that she could not get her money back. In the course of a search made in the rooms occupied by Mme Levin at the Hotel Bristol, the magistrate found a card bearing the name of Goold on which she had written: "I await repayment of the money borrowed. Send it by telegraph, I need it." The signature is illegible but it is believed to be that of the murdered woman.

The crime has caused the greatest sensation in the Riviera. The victim, a beautiful woman, was the widow of a businessman and always wore magnificent jewels. She was extremely well known at the Casino. Mme Levin belonged to Stockholm, where her mother still lives at 13 Nebrogatan. She has stayed for the last two months at the Hotel Bristol.

Here she formed an acquaintance with the Goolds at the Casino. Mr and Mrs Goold have for three years occupied a charming suite on the first floor of the Villa Menesini, situated in the Boulevard des Moulins. In appearance, they were most respectable. They have with them their niece Mme Giraudin. Although numbering many acquaintances among the cosmopolitan society of the place, they received very little, and indeed rarely at home.

Mrs Goold was born at Isere, France. Her name was Maria Violette Giraudin (or Girodon). Twenty-five years ago she was a milliner at Montreal, Canada. There she became acquainted with Vere Goold from Clonmel, Ireland, aged 54. He was at Montreal in the silk trade but his business was unsuccessful. Mr Goold insists on calling himself a baronet.

The murder, most experts think, has been committed by at least two persons. First Mme Levin was knocked down and then she was stabbed to the heart. Her head and legs were cut off and forced into the small portmanteau which

Mr Goold was carrying in his hands. The body was put into the trunk, a pillow being placed underneath it. The abdomen had been opened and the intestines removed to prevent putrefaction.

As to the story that Mme Levin's lover had pursued her, no confirmation has been obtained of the existence of any such person.

### *Liverpool Friends Amazed*

It seems that cards found in the Goold's luggage, as telegraphed by a Marseilles correspondent yesterday were addressed 18 Adelaide Terrace, Waterloo, Liverpool, not London, as the French police, naturally assumed. Some of the cards bore the title Lady Goold. Our Liverpool correspondent ascertains that a husband and wife known as Sir Vere and Lady Goold did live at that address up to 18 months ago. Waterloo is a better class suburb of Liverpool and Adelaide Terrace is a row of large houses with long gardens in front, the promenade facing the Mersey.

By a section of society in Waterloo, Sir Vere and Lady Goold were received as thorough gentlefolk of high degree but according to their acquaintances they had a rather adventurous and chequered career. One lady, moving in the highest circle, who had been an intimate friend, indignantly put down the idea yesterday that anything of unworthy conduct could possibly be attributed to her friends. They were, she said, of the highest respectability and perfectly correct in all of their behaviour.

Sir Vere was described as an amiable and clever gentleman whose title was old Irish. They were in very good circumstances and spent much of their time in France. Their stay in Waterloo was merely temporary, as they did not want England as a permanent residence, having a great fondness for the South of France. Lady Goold she described as a thorough genteel woman and French lady to her fingertips, accomplished, amiable, most generous and good mannered. She possessed certain landed property in France.

Sir Vere Goold was said to be a gifted amateur photographer. It was especially noted that they were both strict teetotallers and there was nothing mysterious about their conduct before departing for Monte Carlo and in advance made a round of adieu calls.

## The Baronetcy Claim

How Goold unsuccessfully claimed his title to his brother's baronetcy, though Sir James Stephen Goold is still alive, forms a curious narrative. Even if Sir James was dead, Vere Goold would not be justified in using the title of Sir Vere, as there are three sons and one grandson of his brother who would take precedence before him.

The family of the brother are all residing in Australia but are not in a position to keep up the title. In 1900 a paragraph appeared in Canadian and Australian newspapers stating that, in consequence of the death of the titleholder, Mr Vere St Leger Goold of Montreal had succeeded to it. The only foundation for the story was the fact that a brother named Frederick Edward Michael Goold, who came between James Stephen and Vere St Leger, died in hospital in Australia, leaving no heirs.

Vere St Leger seems to have fastened on to this fact and circulated a statement that it was the elder brother, holder of the title, who had died without family.

In May 1901 he wrote to the editors of leading

books of reference, telling them of his brother's death. While not wanting to use the title "until proofs came to hand" he said he would like to establish his position as a baronet "for my wife's sake." He also informed the editors that he had no children and that he travelled a good deal.

His friends, he explained, wished to call him "Sir Vere" but he told everyone that it would be "somewhat premature" to do so. He wound up by disingenuously stating that he had not seen or heard of anything of his brother James Stephen Goold since 1863.

That statement was denounced the following year by the real baronet as a falsehood. He had seen the newspaper paragraphs and had written to the editors to inform them that while he was not in a position to keep up the title, he wished to preserve the rights of his three sons and the children that they might have.

In relation to the matter that Vere had not seen or heard of him since 1863, he settled the question by proving he had frequent communication with him on the matter of the use of the title since 1897. In subsequent letters, Sir James Stephen Goold said that Vere St Leger wrote to him offering him £100 if he would sign a document waiving his and his children's claim to the title. The money was never sent and either way it was not in anyone's power to abandon a title in that manner.

One of those letters from Vere was written from 18 Adelaide Terrace, Waterloo, Liverpool. Other letters had been written from Montreal.

## *Irish Times*

Friday, August 9th

## MONTE CARLO MURDER
## GOOLDS CROSS-EXAMINED
## ANTECEDENTS OF THE PRISONERS

The newspapers state that the British consul has asked that the trunk mystery be withdrawn from the French courts and placed before those of Monaco. The Goolds will be removed from Marseilles to Monte Carlo as soon as their extradition has been obtained.

The depths of the wounds on the corpse and the strength necessary for their infliction make it appear unlikely that Mme Goold could have actually committed the crime.

Nevertheless, the instruments used have been found in her apartment. At the present moment, the authorities are endeavouring to trace the real means of existence of the Goolds and the manner in which they became acquainted with Emma Levin. It has been ascertained that Mme Goold sent away her niece on Saturday and had informed the people that her husband was subject to blood-spitting. A note signed by Emma Levin has been found in a notebook in which she states that she lent 1,000 francs to the Goolds.

### *Marseilles, Thursday*
The Goolds were subjected to a searching cross-examination today by the examining magistrate. He put it to them that they first stunned the woman Levin with a blunt instrument, and after killing her

with a dagger, dismembered the body and removed the intestines. In accordance with French legal usage, the magistrate then urged the Goolds to confess that they were guilty. The man simply hung his head, without replying while the woman who was seized with a violent fit of hysterics and had to be treated at the ambulance station at the court-house.

The prosecution contends that the Goolds also took jewels to the value of 80,000 francs from Miss Levin.

*Evening*

This afternoon, the examining magistrate heard the depositions of various witnesses concerned in the arrest of the Goolds. The witnesses were the porter who carried the Goolds' luggage to the cloakroom, the Commissionaire Pons, the cabman who drove the Goolds to the Station Hotel and the police who arrested them. All witnesses confirmed the statements previously made to the railway police. The two prisoners today addressed a request to the public prosecutor asking that they may be defended by Maître Granier of the Marseilles bar. They will not be subjected to further cross-examination here and will be removed to Monte Carlo.

*London*

A remarkable story of the prisoners was told to a Star reporter by Mr T. J. Reilly, the Monte Carlo chemist who is spending a holiday in London. According to him Mr and Mrs Goold arrived in Monte Carlo last October, giving their names as Sir Vere and Lady Goold. They remained at Monte Carlo throughout the whole of the season and when

Mr Reilly left at the end of May they were still residing with their niece at Villa Menesini.

He said: "Mr Goold was an exceedingly quiet, unassuming, well spoken man and they let it be known that they were well off and had taken the villa for the whole season. His wife was French and spoke English fluently. They had living with them a very pretty girl who they gave people to understand was their niece. Sir Vere called in at my shop several times a week and his niece often accompanied him.

They mixed with the best society and were frequently seen at the tables in the Casino. The villa they lived in is close to the Carlton, the celebrated night restaurant along the new road which runs parallel with but below the Boulevards des Moulins. The villa is a huge building let out in ten suites and they lived on the fourth floor for which they would have paid about £100 for the season. Vere was always well spoken of and his niece was quite one of the belles of the season. She was about 25 and friendly with daughters of English doctors who practise in Monte Carlo."

Mr Reilly said the couple were on visiting terms with people of note in the resort, were always well dressed and paid their bills regularly.

∽◦∾

## Weekly Irish Times
### Saturday August 10th

*Marseilles, Tuesday Evening.*
The inquiry as to the trunk tragedy shows that the victim was a woman aged 37 of Swedish origin. All the indications point to the crime as a result of a

love affair. A man named Bucker, aged 24, is now under arrest at Monte Carlo. Bucker is alleged to have thrown human remains down the toilet of a hotel in Monte Carlo, so as to prevent the body from decomposing too rapidly. It is further asserted that the man and woman Goold dismembered the corpse. It is expected that an application for extradition will be made so that Bucker can be brought to Marseilles and confronted with the Goolds.

~∽~

## Irish Times
Saturday, August 10th, 1907
*Reuters telegrams*

In connection with the Monte Carlo trunk mystery, the Matin gives a list of jewels handed to the police as belonging to the murdered woman and says that some pieces have been discovered in a bag belonging to Madame Goold. It seems more than ever confirmed, therefore, that the object of the murder was robbery.

A police expert today estimated that the value of the jewels found in possession of Madame Goold was 15,000 francs. Goold's niece states that on Sunday evening she went by the box-room which was locked and her aunt said: "You have nothing to do here." This is where the body remained during Sunday night. This crime was perpetrated at two different moments.

It was on Monday that the body was cut to pieces. On that day Madame Goold had told her niece not to come home before six in the evening, owing to her husband's illness. After this statement by Mlle Girodin, the magistrate had the box-room searched. It was found to contain linen and a large stain of blood was found on the floor and splashes of red on the walls. The Journal has opened a subscription list on behalf of the man Pons who brought about the arrest of the Goolds. The Journal heads the list with 1,000 francs.

## Monte Carlo, Friday

The Monte Carlo Court has applied for the extradition of the Goolds. The police are actively pursuing their investigations but are experiencing much difficulty in piecing together the evidence at their disposal. M. Savard, examining magistrate, today took an inventory of the victim's room at the hotel. He afterwards proceeded to the house where the crime was committed and examined Mlle Girondin, supposed to be the niece of the Goolds, who declared she knew nothing whatever about the alleged murder.

The next examination of the two prisoners will take place on Monday, when they will be asked to give precise information concerning the statement as to their identity, already furnished by them. No actual proceedings can be taken until the authorities have exact and certain knowledge of the nationality of the accused.

It is believed that the person who describes herself as Mr Goold's real wife, is in fact a sister of the late Mrs Goold who is understood to have died some years ago.

# New York Times
August 10th, 1907

## LIGHT ON THE LIVES OF THE VERE GOOLDS

### A FORMER EMPLOYEE, NOW AT SHEEPSHEAD BAY, TALKS OF PAIR ACCUSED OF MURDER. GOOLD A GAMBLER, SHE SAYS.

### WHEN INCOME FROM MILLINERY BUSINESS GAVE OUT, HE WORKED ON A SYSTEM TO BREAK THE BANK AT MONTE CARLO.

Light on the characters and careers of the persons concerned in the discovery of the body of Emma Levin, a wealthy Swedish woman, in the trunk and valise of Vere St Leger Goold, an Englishman, was obtained by a Times reporter in as unlikely a spot as Sheepshead Bay, in this city. Spending the summer at a hotel there is Miss Charlotte Shranz of Ottawa, who knew the Goolds well and managed Mrs Goold's dressmaking establishment at 56, Drummond Street, Montreal, for two years.

Goold, it seems, is not a baronet, but the younger brother of one, but he and his wife had been travelling all over Europe for the past five years, posing as "Sir and Lady Goold" on the slim revenue of this practically bankrupt dressmaking-business in Montreal.

Miss Shranz says that the couple were last seen in Canada three years ago, after an absence of two years, and that the firm is still in existence, under the management of a Frenchwoman, but is heavily in debt.

Miss Shranz says Goold was always a hard drinker and a heavy gambler. He lost large sums of money in different business ventures, including the big failure of the Thomas Fay Company, importers of millinery in Montreal, several years ago.

Goold, says Miss Shranz, is the sixth son of Sir Henry Valentine Goold of Cork, the third baronet of the name, which is one of the oldest and most respected in Ireland. After a stormy youthful career, he married a London dressmaker, two years his senior in 1901.

Three years later they went from London to Montreal, where the woman established a fashionable dressmaking shop. Goold continued his dissolute life, and was soon a familiar figure in the gambling houses and other resorts of Montreal. It was understood that his wife accompanied him on many of his escapades, and what part of the revenue of the business, which prospered, they did not spend in this way, Goold frittered away at the gambling table or sunk into unprofitable business ventures.

While in his cups, Goold was accustomed to boast of his titled lineage and informed his associates that he was next in line for the baronetcy. In the fall of 1902 he announced that his brother was killed suddenly by a fall from his horse in London, and leaving Miss Shranz in charge of the business, the couple departed for London, ostensibly to straighten out the brother's affairs and take over the title. They were gone two years, and in that time travelled all over Europe, using the profits of the concern, which were forwarded to them by Miss Shranz.

After two years' absence, they returned to

Montreal but only remained a few weeks. It was during this time that Miss Shranz severed her connection with the Goolds, realising that it was impossible to keep the business going in face of the drains they were making on it. During the short stay in Montreal, she says Goold devoted his entire time to working over a roulette system by means of which he was going to 'break the bank' at Monte Carlo.

After their return to England, the business began to fall off, and large unpaid bills piled up. No collections could be made from the French-woman who was only an employee and all efforts to locate "Sir and Lady Goold" failed. After they were away for a year, word was received from Algiers that 'Lady Goold' had died of fever while at a resort at the coast. Miss Shranz says that was the last she ever heard of the pair. Miss Shranz says that Isabelle Girodin, Mrs Goold's pretty 20-year-old niece lived with the couple for several years in Montreal.

⌒⌒⌒

## *New York Times*
August 11th, 1907

## PORTER DISCOVERED MONTE CARLO CRIME

Blood oozing from a trunk at the Marseilles railroad station on Monday brought about the detection of a terrible crime. The trunk belonged to a highly respectable looking English couple who had just arrived from Monte Carlo. They left the trunk to be registered for London while they went to a hotel for breakfast, taking their hand baggage with them.

A porter, named Pons, who handled the trunk, noticed some blood on it, followed the couple to the hotel and found that they had already started to drive back to the station. Pons ran after the hack and insisted on getting in the box. The woman offered him sixty francs to go away. This merely confirmed his suspicions and when the cab reached the station, he informed the police.

The trunk was opened and a woman's body without the head and lower part of the legs was discovered. The missing parts of the victim were found in a gripsack carried by the Englishman. The owners of the baggage gave their names as Mr and Mrs Goold. They were immediately arrested and told an incredible story. They said that the dead woman had been stabbed in the heart in their apartment in Monte Carlo by a man named Burker, who ran away immediately after committing the crime.

The victim proved to be a Swedish woman, Emma Levin, widow of a rich Jewish trader of Stockholm. About a month ago, she made the acquaintance of the Goolds who had lived there for the last three years in fairly good style. She had remarked to a friend that the Goolds had paid her unusual attention and seemed anxious to cultivate her; also they offered to advance her money on her jewellery when she was temporarily short of funds.

At the Goolds' invitation she went to their apartment on Sunday afternoon at 5 o'clock and was never seen alive again. A neighbour heard a woman's voice exclaim "Leave me alone" but paid no attention, thinking that it was merely a domestic quarrel. Mrs Goold's niece who lived with the Goolds was sent out the same morning with special instructions not to return until the evening.

She came home at 9 o'clock, when her aunt informed her that her uncle was ill and would have to go to Marseilles immediately to consult a doctor, a specialist. The trunk was already packed and the girl sat on it and talked to Goold for a few minutes. In the three hours that elapsed between the woman's cry and the niece's return, Emma Levin's body had been cut up in the bath and the remains had been stored away in the trunk and the bag. The girl noticed nothing unusual except a strong smell of lavender water which her aunt accounted for by saying she had accidentally upset the bottle.

The Goolds admit cutting up the body, but it is doubtful whether two elderly persons could have accomplished the ghastly work unaided in such a short time. So it is likely that a third person participated, especially as the immediate cause of death was a stab through the heart, delivered with great force, of which the Goolds seem incapable.

The police are trying to ascertain whether Burker is merely fictitious or one of the dead woman's acquaintances. Robbery is the only motive for the crime. The Goolds were always pressed for money and had no regular income, whereas Emma Levin lived well and had a quantity of valuable jewels. When arrested, the Goold woman had some of the jewelry in her handbag.

Until three years ago, the Goolds lived in Montreal, Canada, where the woman ran a dressmaking business, which the couple sold. At Monte Carlo, they were supposed to be persons of independent means. Goold is the brother of an English baronet, living in Australia. The woman is French.

There is reason to doubt that the couple were married, and should this prove justified, the woman will be tried in Marseilles, as France does not surrender its citizens for trial abroad, whereas Goold will be extradited to Monaco, where the crime was committed. The case thus presents the possibilities of curious complications, involving the laws of France, England and the Principality of Monaco.

The man and woman are now in prison in Marseilles and are being subject to the process, known in French slang as "cooking". Other selected prisoners are left night and day in the cells with the alleged culprits in the hope that the latter may confide in their companions and thus give useful clues, which are immediately reported to the investigating magistrate. The leading spirit of the Goold family was undoubtedly the woman, who ruled the man and the girl with an iron hand and allowed them very little freedom of action.

She frequently gambled at the tables in the Monte Carlo casino, but never permitted her supposed husband to enter the place. Ever since her arrest, she has been questioning the prison warders and the police with a view to ascertaining what Goold said, and she has also repeatedly urged them to give him plenty of whisky. Goold is plunged into abject depression, from which he arouses himself occasionally only to clamour for drink.

The crime has excited as much interest as the Guldensuppe case did in America. M. Jaume one of the detectives who solved the celebrated Gouffé murder case in which a body was also concealed in a trunk, said to me today with great professional contempt: "The English are mere children in crime and are generally found out very quickly. The Goolds acted like novices. Any of the criminals I have had to deal with would have contrived the affair more artistically. If you ever cut up a body and put it in a trunk, never entrust that trunk to anybody."

The Goolds were photographed today by the police operator. The woman broke down and shed tears copiously but the man maintained an air of dignified composure and merely remarked: "I am sorry I didn't commit suicide before I got into this trouble." Death is the punishment for a premeditated murder under the law of Monte Carlo. France provides the guillotine and the executioner at the expense of the principality.

～∞～

## Irish Times

Monday, August 12th, 1907

A ship's steward named Alquist, living at West Hartlepool, has come forward as brother of Emma Levin, the victim of the Monte Carlo trunk murder. He states that he has no knowledge of the Goolds but he imagines his sister met them casually at Monte Carlo. She was the widow of a wealthy Jewish stockbroker, Leopold Levin, and was in receipt of an income from the firm.

～∞～

## Reuters telegrams

Paris, Saturday 10th

Yesterday Goold wrote a letter to his niece, who is believed to be still living at the villa. The letter was delivered to the chief warden, with instruction to deliver it to Monte Carlo. The writing was indistinctly in English. Goold who addresses his niece "Dear kid", compliments her on her attitude, saying she has shown great courage and he had admired her for it.

### Sunday 11th

The Matin has received information from Marcellin, Isere, representing Mrs Goold as an adventuress of great energy and with complete authority over her weak husband. She is looked upon as the instigator and actual author of the crime.

Fond of luxury and extravagant, she needed money for the fulfilment of her desires and was always prepared to procure it, by any means. In all her doings her husband was merely a slave of his wife. This is also the opinion of Mlle Girodin, the niece who lived with them for 15 years.

A Spaniard named Fausto Echeverria who had declared he could make sensational revelations, was examined by the magistrate yesterday. He said nothing new, and appears not even to have known the Goolds. The Petit Journal, likewise, looks upon Mrs Goold as the moving spirit in the crime.

꧁꧂

# *The Times*

August 12th, 1907

## THE MONTE CARLO MURDER

*Monte Carlo, August 10th*

M. Savard, examining magistrate, this morning interrogated the servant and charwoman who were dismissed by the Goolds sometime before the alleged crime. According to their evidence the woman Goold dominated the household and had absolute power over her husband. It appears certain that the Goold's niece Mlle Girodin, knew nothing of the murder until she was interrogated by the magistrate.

*August 11th*

The police authorities of Monaco were informed last night that what appeared to be human entrails had been found attached to an iron steel [rod?] some yards from the edge of the Larvotto beach. At 10 o'clock today, the examining magistrate accompanied by Dr Corniglion proceeded to the beach where they were joined by the Deputy Prosecutor. As the state of the supposed entrails did not permit the doctor's giving a definite decision as to whether they were of a human being, they were placed in spirits and taken charge of by the authorities until they can be thoroughly examined.

The preliminary investigation is still proceeding but there will be some slight delay owing to the extradition formalities which have to be gone through and which may take a fortnight. When they are brought to Monaco, the Goolds will be confronted with witnesses. Mr Goold is alleged to have been of intemperate habits.

It is not yet known whether the prisoners will be tried in France or Monaco.

## Marseilles, August 10th

It is stated that Goold, who has been suffering from profound depression since his arrest, last night violently attacked two other men confined in the same cell. He was overpowered by the warders, and the Public Prosecutor, on being informed of the matter, ordered that Goold should be examined by a doctor.

This afternoon, Goold again attacked his fellow prisoners and threw himself at the door of the cell, crying loudly to be let out. In view of the prisoner's state of mind, the examining magistrate, after consulting with counsel for the defence, decided to postpone the resumption of the cross examination until Tuesday or Wednesday, when it is hoped that Goold will have calmed down.

This afternoon, the judicial authorities received communication of a letter written by Goold to his niece, Mlle Girodin, who is still living at Monte Carlo in the house where the crime is believed to have been committed. The letter, which was somewhat incoherent in terms and was written in an almost illegible hand, was placed among the documents relating to the case, and was not sent to Mlle Girodin.

This afternoon the examining magistrate received a communication from the chief warder of the prison, stating that during a fainting fit which Mrs Goold had, a fellow prisoner had noticed bruises and injuries which had been recently sustained. The examining magistrate immediately requested Dr Dufour to examine Mrs Goold. The injuries are regarded by the authorities as strengthening the presumption that Mrs Goold took an active part in carrying out the crime.

In the effects contained in a trunk belonging to the Goolds, a dagger with a jagged blade and bearing suspicious stains has been handed to the judicial authorities.

*Paris, August 10th*

The Matin has received information from Saint-Marcellin (Isère) concerning Mrs Goold. Marie Girodin who lived with her father and mother was first married to a young man of Saint-Marcellin contrary to her parents' wishes. A week after the wedding, the young woman left her new house with a little money. She went to Geneva where she worked for some time as a dressmaker and then she proceeded to London.

She became a companion to an English lady and went with her to India two years later. There she met Capt Wilkinson, whom she married, her first husband having died in the meantime. After three years, she once more became a widow, and penniless was forced to sell her jewels. She then returned to London, where with the money raised from the sale of her jewellery she opened a dressmaking establishment. It was at this period that she became acquainted with Mr Goold and married him.

∾∾

# *The Times*

Tuesday, August 13th

*Monte Carlo, August 12th*

M. Savard, the examining magistrate, this morning again questioned the Spaniard, Fausto Etcheveria, an acquaintance of Mme Levin. His examination brought no new facts to light, but when the jewels forwarded by the Marseilles authorities were shown to the witness, he recognised several of the items as having belonged to Mme Levin. The inquiry here is now finished, and the conclusion of formalities for extradition or provisional transfer of the prisoners are being awaited.

## Marseilles, August 12th

Dr Durfour who was entrusted with the examination of Mrs Goold in consequence of the discovery of injuries, supposed to have been caused in a struggle, has placed his report in the hands of the examining magistrate. The report shows that Mrs Goold has 13 bruises on her body, most of them being on her arms and legs. Mrs Goold explained that these injuries were a result of a fall when getting out of the carriage, when she was being brought back to the station with her husband after the discovery of the crime.

According to the doctor, however, this explanation is not sufficient to account for the bruises, which he states might well date from the time of the murder. Dr Durfour declares that it is impossible that one and not very serious fall could have caused the injuries both on the right and left side of the prisoner. Some of the bruises might, he says, have been due to a fall, but the others must have been caused in some other way, which can only be determined by judicial inquiry.

This morning, the examining magistrate had an interview with the Danish consul, who communicated to him the following telegram which he had just received from Copenhagen: "Please inform the proper authorities that the murdered widow, Emma Levin, a Danish subject, made a will here of which

I am the executor. It provided that the bequests contained in it shall be made here." This telegram comes from a lawyer in Copenhagen.

The examining magistrate intimated to the Consul that the identity of the victim of the Monte Carlo crime had not been established, and that he would not say whether she was really the same Mme Levin who was mentioned in the telegram. The Swedish Consul interrogated Mrs Goold today concerning the identity of Mme Levin. Mrs Goold declared that she had a slight acquaintance with her, having been introduced to her two months ago and received only three visits from her. Mrs Goold admitted that she had in her possession the greater part of Mme Levin's jewellery and intended to get rid of it, by throwing it into the sea.

~~~

## *The Times*
August 15th, Thursday

## MONTE CARLO MURDER

In his confession to the examining magistrate, Goold stated that on the day before the murder, he met Mme Levin who asked him to lend her 500 francs. She came to the villa the following afternoon, whereupon she asked him for another 500 francs in order to give it to Edward Barker. The prisoner refused, harsh words followed and in an access of rage, accentuated by drink, he stabbed her in the back. There was, he claimed, only one blow. His wife had no share in the murder, and it was he, unaided, cut up the body and placed the dismembered parts in the trunk and a valise where they were discovered. Robbery was not the motive, as he had ample means to live on.

In the concluding portion of the interrogation, which turned on the prisoner's identity, Goold stated that his grandfather was created a baronet. His father was a magistrate in an Irish town, and he, Vere Goold, and one brother, who was at present in Australia, were his only surviving sons. He, himself had been in the public service in Dublin and London. He made the acquaintance of his present wife in London and they married in Bayswater.

He and his wife went to Montreal and afterwards settled in Waterloo, near Liverpool. There he started a laundry business, in which he lost a considerable amount of money, and he afterwards went to Monte Carlo to try his luck by means of a system.

~~~

## Irish Times
Wednesday August 14th, 1907

## MONTE CARLO MURDER
## CONFESSION BY THE GOOLDS
## HOW MADAME LEVIN WAS KILLED

*Press Association Foreign Special*

*Marseilles, August 13*
The examining magistrate, M. Malavialle attended the Prison des Presentines, where Mrs Goold is incarcerated, for the purpose of interrogating her in

reference to the crime with which she and her husband Vere Goold are charged. The magistrate was accompanied by his clerk and Maître Gravier, the advocate, who has been retained by the female prisoner to conduct her defence.

The interrogation, which lasted four hours, took place in the room known as Parloir des Avocats whither Mrs Goold was conducted as soon as M. Malavialle arrived. In reply to the first question, addressed to her, Mrs Goold stated that down to the present she had not told the truth, so as not to incriminate her husband; but she had decided to make a full confession.

She thereupon commenced a fresh recital of the murder in the Villa Menesini, in which she strove to minimise her own share of responsibility.

"Yes," said Mrs Goold, "I confess that it was my husband who killed Emma Levin. I have not said so hitherto, in order to screen him, but I now prefer to tell the whole truth.

"It was on Saturday at 5.30 that the murder was committed. At that hour the villa bell was rung. The visitor was Emma Levin, who came to see my husband about certain business matters. She was temporarily short of cash and my husband had promised to lend her 1,000 francs (£40). Naturally, I thought it right to leave them alone while they discussed the transaction. Suddenly I heard piercing cries and the sounds of a struggle.

"Terrified, I hurried from my room to the drawing room where I had left Emma Levin and my husband. I had a presentiment that something dreadful had happened. Then I saw a terrible sight. Emma Levin was lying dead on the floor and beside her was my husband, covered in blood. I received such a shock that I fainted. When I recovered consciousness, my first impulse was to go and tell the police, but my husband implored me not to do so, but rather help to conceal his crime.

"My husband, however, was so drunk that it was out of the question for him to begin cutting up the body, as we had decided to do. We dragged the body to the bathroom, and it was not until the next day that my husband proceeded to cut it up. Part of Mme Levin's clothes were burned, the remainder were put away in a trunk. All of this happened in the absence of my niece, who on her return, noticed nothing, except, perhaps that we were upset.

"To explain this, I said that my husband had a sudden attack and had vomited a quantity of blood. During these two days, I was quite beside myself and did not know what I was doing. It was with an Indian knife, which was in the dining room, that my husband killed Mme Levin."

Answering a question by the examining magistrate, as to whether she had not invited Mme Levin to the villa that day, Mrs Goold said that she had not anyone home for a long time. "Our means did not permit of our entertaining. Emma Levin only came for the purpose of borrowing money from my husband." The examining magistrate called the prisoner's attention to the fact that most of Mme Levin's jewellery was found in possession of herself and her husband.

She replied: "That is true but we had only one desire and that was to get rid of it, so that we should not be suspected of the crime. Our intention was to get rid of the body into the sea."

In the concluding portion of the examination, Mrs Goold furnished the magistrate with the following particulars of her life:

"I was born at Saone in the Department of the Isere, where my father was in the grain trade. There were five children. Three sons and two daughters but they are all dead except myself and a brother named Hyppolite. It is four years since my other brothers and sister died. My first marriage took place in 1869, when I married M. Borrulier. He died three years later at La Saone. I then left my native country and settled in Geneva where I found employment in a dressmaking establishment in the Rue du Rhone. I afterwards worked in two similar situations as a dressmaker with M. Ricard and M. Wolf.

"Together with another dressmaker of whom I had made an acquaintance, I went to England and after four years in London as a modiste's employee, I set up in business for myself and had a dressmaking establishment in Abbey Street and Hereford Road. I was married to Vere Goold in 1891 at The Church of St Marys of the Angels, but I did not wish him to know that my previous husband was a Frenchman.

∽∾∾

# New York Times
## August 14th

### August 13th, Marseilles

Vere St Leger Goold confessed here today that he was the murderer of Emma Levin, a wealthy Swedish woman, whose dismembered body was found in the baggage of Mr Goold and his wife on their arrival on August 6 from Monte Carlo. This trunk mystery created much excitement, especially as it was

learned that the Goolds, who are English, were of
good family. Their explanation of how the body
came to be in their baggage was unconvincing, and
the confession of today does not come as a surprise.

Goold made his confession to the Examining
Magistrate. He related coolly all the details of the
crime. He alone had slain the woman, he declared,
and it was he who cut up the body, although his
wife helped him pack it away in their baggage. After
this had been done, they both agreed to journey to
Marseilles where they planned to cast the body into
the sea.

Mrs Goold, whose first name is Violet, confessed
her part in the crime. He said her husband had
promised to give Mrs Levin $100 dollars for a
certain reason, but she wanted to give it to a man
friend. To this Mr Goold objected, saying he would
not pay the extra hundred. Referring to what
happened next, Goold said in his confession: "I had
been drinking and becoming angry I seized a
hunting knife and buried it in Emma's back. She fell
dead. The next day I dismembered the body with
a saw and a knife and placed the torso in a trunk
and the head and legs in a valise. I only stabbed
the woman once. The other wounds on her body
must have been caused by shaking around in the
trunk."

Goold said they carried off Emma's jewels, not
for their value but to prevent their discovery in his
apartment. Referring to his family, Goold said his
grandfather was a baronet and his father an Irish
magistrate. He said he had at one time served
secretly on the Land Commission in Dublin. In
1893 he moved to Montreal, where he said he made
a fortune. He then went to Holland and later moved

to Monte Carlo. Mrs Goold corroborated all her husband said.

The discovery that a crime had been committed was made by a railway porter on August 6. He noticed blood oozing from the trunk in which the torso was later found. Goold and his wife had gone to a hotel for breakfast. They hurried back and got their luggage into a hack but the porter ran after them and took a seat on the box with a driver. Mrs Goold offered him 60 francs to go away but he stuck to his seat and called attention of the police to the luggage. The arrests followed.

At the time of the discovery, the couple told a story about Mrs Levin, having been murdered in their apartment by a man named Burker, saying they had simply started for England to bury the body in order to avoid any complications with the Monte Carlo authorities. The explanation was not believed and the Goolds were locked up. Up to yesterday, the police were not able to get anything but falsehoods out of the two prisoners, though they subjected the couple to the process which is called in French slang "cooking".

The murder created a great deal of talk all over Europe. Its developments here have been followed with as much interest as the Guldensuppe murder in this country. The London papers learned that Goold's brother Sir James Stephen Goold, Bart, lived at Gladstone in Australia, and though he is a real baronet he is working as a labourer on a railway train.

The baronet tried to conceal his identity by burying himself in South Australia, saying as he did not have the means to support his title, he didn't care to claim it. Sir Vere Goold as the aged murderer called himself in London and elsewhere was well thought of in England. He studied at Trinity University, Dublin, and was known as a man of breeding and country manners.

❧

## Irish Times
August 15th, 1907

## MONTE CARLO MURDER
## GOOLD'S CONFESSION
## HOW THE CRIME WAS COMMITTED
## THE ALLEGED MOTIVE
*Press Association Foreign Special*

*Marseilles, Tuesday*

The examination of the prisoner Vere Goold by the Judge D'Instruction lasted for five hours from 3 till 8. The accused whose statement was translated by an interpreter, made the following avowals: "I do not remember what I said at my first examination. Here is the whole truth. On Saturday, August 3rd, I met Mme Levin at the Casino. She asked me to lend her 50 francs. I agreed and told her to come for the money the following day, Sunday at about 5 o clock. She came in and I handed her the sum as arranged.

"She then asked me for 500 more and I said for what purpose?"

"I want to give them to Edward Barker," she replied.

"Very well," I rejoined, "if the money is for him, I will see him hanged first."

226

"Madame Levin then became very abusive calling me an old beast of a *souteneur*. I had been drinking a little and these insults incited me to such a point that I seized a hunting knife which was on the table and stabbed her in the back, and she fell down dead. It was the only blow that I struck. At the sounds of the struggle and the shrieks of Mme Levin, my wife came running in. "*A Mon Dieu!*" she cried. "What have you done? How often have I told you drinking would be your undoing?" Then in a hysterical fit, she fainted.

"I took advantage of her unconsciousness to carry the body to an adjoining room. My niece who had gone for a walk to Cap Martin, noticed nothing unusual on her return. My wife helped me to conceal the corpse and we agreed to go to Marseilles. On Monday August 5th I started cutting up the body by means of a knife and a saw. It was I alone who dismembered the remains of Mme Levin and placed part of the body in a trunk and the rest in a travelling bag."

"Did you not invite her to come to your house?" asked the examining magistrate.

"No," replied the prisoner. "I repeat that on the previous day, she asked me for 500 francs and that she came on the Sunday for the money which I promised her."

With regard to the jewellery of the murdered woman which was found in the baggage of the accused, Goold declared that he took it with him, not to turn it into account for himself but simply to avoid being accused of the murder, if it was discovered in his house.

The concluding part of the interrogation turned on the prisoner's identity. He stated that his grandfather was created a baronet. His father was a magistrate in an Irish town and head of a family composed of seven children, six sons and a daughter.

"All my brothers are dead," said the accused, "with the exception of George Charles who is at present in Australia and who was born in 1847. One of my brothers was a captain in the Post Office service. Brother Ernest was an engineer in London. Another brother William died of smallpox in Dublin as did my sister who succumbed in hospital. I was settled in Dublin where I was appointed secretary of The Municipal Boundaries Commission of Inquiry into the Land Act.

"I got the appointment as an Inspector of Civil Service in 1891. It was in London that I made the acquaintance of my present wife at the house of a friend who lived in a square. We were married in August of the same year in the parish of Bayswater. My marriage certificate was in the handbag which contained the head and limbs of Madame Levin. At that time I had an income of £400 a year which I received from the Earl of Cork.

"As to my wife, she continued to manage her dressmaking shop which brought her £1,500 a year. Four years later we went to Montreal where we lived at 56 Drummond Street. After having made out fortune we returned to England and settled at Adelaide, Waterloo, near Liverpool. I started a laundry in which I lost a considerable amount of money. A friend then advised me to liquidate my affairs and to go to Monte Carlo and try my luck by means of a system which he said was infallible.

"I did not lose, my winnings and losings about balancing themselves. I at present possess 10,500 $1 shares and 1,500 £1 shares. I also receive from my tenant an annual rent which is sufficient to live on. I did not kill Madame Levin in order to rob her. I acted in a fit of passion and under the influence of drink."

In terminating this extraordinary recital Goold repeated that his wife had nothing to do with the crime.

## Identification of the Jewellery

### Monte Carlo, Tuesday

At 11 o'clock, M. Savard, the Examining Magistrate, took the evidence of Mme Giroudin, niece of the prisoner Goold. The jewellery sent here by the Marseilles police was shown to her and she recognised several of the trinkets as property of her relatives. Madame Castellazi was next examined and stated unhesitatingly that apart from the jewels identified by Mlle Giroudin belonging to her aunt and uncle, all the others belonged to the deceased Madame Levin.

The report on what are supposed to be the human remains found at Larvotto has not yet been received. Dr Corniglion, to whom they were sent for examination is waiting until the alcohol in which they have been placed has produced the effect necessary to permit conclusive analysis to be carried out. No further announcement has been made concerning the application for the extradition of the prisoners or their proposed temporary removal to Monaco for a "confrontation" and the reconstitution of the crime.

This afternoon the examining magistrate with the assistance of an expert went through the letters and other documents found at the Villa Menesini, where the Goolds lived, and which was the scene of the murder. For the most part they were love letters exchanged by the prisoners when they were in London. Mlle Giroudin communicated to the magistrate various letters which she has received since the murder which contain all sorts of suggestions.

∽∾✄∾

## Grey River Argus
August 16th 1907

## THE MONTE CARLO TRAGEDY
## THE REPORTED SUICIDE OF GOOLD
## THE GOOLDS CONFESS

*Paris, August 15th*
The Goolds ordered a Marseilles hotel waiter to provide them with a deal box. It is surmised that they intended to transfer the head and legs from the bag.

Madame Levin lost heavily while gambling at Monte Carlo. She told a chambermaid that she was unable to resist the attraction.

Mrs Goold, replying to an examining magistrate, confessed that her husband murdered Madame Levin with an Indian knife. She was not present when the deed was done. On entering the room she saw Madame Levin dead on the floor and her husband covered with blood. He implored her to help him so to avert all suspicion. He was too drunk to begin cleaning up the remains and this was done the next day. Mrs Goold was unable to explain why her husband had killed Madame Levin.

Goold explained to the magistrate that the day before the murder, Madame Levin had asked him to lend her 500 francs. When she came to his villa she asked him for another 500 francs, explaining that she wanted to give it to her banker. Goold refused and heated words followed and in a fit of rage, accentuated by drink, he stabbed her in the back but only dealt one blow. His wife did not participate in the deed and he alone had cut up the body and placed the dismembered body in the trunk and the valise. Robbery was not the motive and he had ample means to live on.

## London August 15th
The **Daily Telegraph**'s Marseilles correspondent reports that after the magistrate's departure, Goold hanged himself in prison.

## Paris, August 15th
Nobody believes Goold's statement that he possessed ample means and that his motive for the crime was not robbery. The Marseilles newspapers deny that Goold has committed suicide.

## Paris, August 15th
The examining magistrate found in the ante-room of Goolds' villa at Monte Carlo, a tray containing two used glasses and a third upside down on the tray which was bloodstained. This is inferred to mean that Madame Levin was attacked soon after she entered the house, the third unused glass having been placed for her to drink from. The French magistrate is enquiring into the antecedents of the prisoners in England, Lasone and Montreal.

*Irish Times*
Saturday, August 17th, 1907

## TRUNK MURDER MYSTERY
## DISCOVERIES IN THE MONTE CARLO
## CRIME

Not for years has any crime possessed so much interest for so many places widely apart as the Monte Carlo tragedy. Even Canada and Australia are dragged into the grim story. For the accused couple, Mr and Mrs Goold, charged with murdering and mutilating Mme Levin in their flat in the gambling Mecca, sojourned in Canada in their chequered career and the male prisoner's brother, Sir Stephen Goold, a baronet of Irish blood made his home in Australia many years ago.

In Liverpool and London the Goolds also lived, and many remember him with respect and esteem. They were married at the Roman Catholic Church of St Mary of the Angels, Paddington. They were equally well known in Ireland, Paris and the Riviera. Their alleged victim Mme Levin was a native of Malmo in Sweden, the widow of a prosperous merchant of Stockholm and Copenhagen. Thus the tentacles of tragedy spread far and near commanding worldwide attention.

Mr Goold, for years assumed the title of Sir Vere Goold, presuming his brother's death in the Antipodes, while his wife passed as Lady Goold. From the latest facts disclosed, there seems little doubt that gambling, borrowing and debt were the motive springs of the tragedy. Mme Levin, the victim, had lent the Goolds £40 and was pressing for repayment. She was known to possess valuable jewels and a large quantity of these were discovered in the possession of the accused couple.

In a box room where it is believed the body was put into a trunk, blood splashes told of the grim tragedy enacted there. Four names stand out in the appalling drama. They are: Emma Eriken Levin, a Swedish woman aged 37, widow of M. Levin, merchant of Stockholm, a Dane, frequented Monte Carlo and fond of jewellery; Vere St Leger Goold, born October 2nd, 1853, brother of Sir James Goold Baronet of Adelaide, South Australia; Mrs Goold, Violet, daughter of Hippolyte Giroudin of Isère, France; Mlle Giroudin, niece of the accused, aged 24, daughter of Mrs Goold's brother who was taken charge of by her aunt and uncle when her father died some years ago, but not implicated in the crime.

The crime was committed on Sunday August 4th at the Goold's house and the mangled remains of the victim were found in the trunk at Marseilles station the next day. Mrs and Mrs Goold were arrested there. A dagger and evidences from the murder were afterwards found in their rooms at Monte Carlo. A servant girl says that she heard noise and a struggle on Sunday. Splashes of blood were in the drawing room and box room.

## Mrs Goold Goes Into Hysterics In Court

After passing through many stages in rapid succession the case now goes to Monte Carlo from Marseilles where the trunk and its gruesome contents were discovered and opened. All the evidence will be sent to Monte Carlo with the prisoners as soon as the extradition formalities are completed. The examination of the accused couple in Marseilles was dramatic in the extreme. In accordance with French criminal procedure, the commissioner of police informed the accused of the results of the post mortem and the discoveries made by the police in the Villa Menesini at Monte Carlo where the murder is alleged to have been committed and asked them to explain the circumstantial evidence obtained by the gendarmes.

Their replies were unsatisfactory and suddenly the magistrate with a stern voice and accusing gesture said: "You stunned your victim with a heavy instrument and then stabbed her to the heart with a knife. You cut her to pieces and dismembered her. She has jewels worth £3,200 upon her when you killed her and you made away with them. You are a pair of murderers, confess your crime.

*"Confess your crime!"* he roared bringing his clenched fist down on the desk.

The woman began to answer him and the magistrate, pointing a finger at her, shouted, "You are a murderer and you know it, come confess."

Goold's face paled and he hung his head but the effect on his wife was more startling. She uttered a shriek and fell into a violent fit of hysteria. All efforts to compose her proved in vain and she had to be removed to the infirmary.

When asked where the jewellery found in his wife's possession came from. Goold replied that it was given to his wife a few days before her death by Mme Levin, who was in financial straits and wished Lady Goold to 'dispose of it.' Goold repeated that he had no hand in the abominable murder of which he is suspected. He admits doing wrong in cutting up the body but says he only did it in order to get rid of it so as to avoid a scandal.

When the prisoners left the Palais De Justice, and

angry mob surged around with cries of "Lynch him, lynch him".

## Method Of The Murder

The prosecution seems to have come to the conclusion that Mme Levin was suddenly stunned and then simultaneously stabbed in two places, either wound being instantaneously fatal. The dismemberment was performed in the bath. A search in the Villa Menesini resulted in the finding of two handsaws and a dagger lying on a blood-stained box with a large revolver. There was also a parasol belonging to Mme Levin.

The post mortem found that there were two stabs through the heart, from front and behind, and the victim had been first stunned with a blunt instrument.

A correspondent reports that it has been confirmed that Goold sent a letter to a family of his acquaintance in Ballina looking for money to ease his financial difficulties the day before the murder.

## Monday, August 19th
### Marseilles

Despite efforts of the defence counsel to make it appear that Goold because of his erratic behaviour is insane, he is reported to have quietened down and had a good night's sleep. Prison authorities do not plan to send him to an asylum. This morning Goold who has since his incarceration been restricted to a milk diet told warders he was hungry and begged for roast beef. As a favour he was allowed to have it and ate it with a healthy appetite. Mrs Goold was reported to be in good health.

The victim has been identified to the satisfaction of the examining magistrate as Emma Levin, a widow (née Alquist) 48 years of age. A few days ago Marseilles police received a letter from Cambridge signed Frederick Alquist and believed the murdered woman to be his sister. He enclosed a photograph of the late Mme Levin and his brother in law Leopold Levin, a moneychanger in Copenhagen who died two and a half years ago. He begged the police to show the photograph to persons who had known the deceased to establish her identity beyond doubt.

The letter and photograph were forwarded to M. Malavialle, the examining magistrate, who in turn communicated it to M. Savard, examining magistrate at Monte Carlo. Her features were immediately recognised by those who knew her.

Dr Corniglion who has been analysing the intestines found at Larvotto has now made his report which shows conclusively that the remains in question are portions of human viscera, but in such a state of advanced decomposition that it is impossible to say what they may have contained. M. Savard yesterday summoned Madame Castellazi and another witness acquainted with Mme Levin in order to obtain identification of shred of clothing found in the Villa Menesini as those belonging to the murder victim.

*New York Times*
Sunday, August 18th 1907

*Paris, August 17th*
Dramatic stories of the Monte Carlo Trunk Murder have been told to the examining magistrate at Marseilles by Vere St Leger Goold and his wife.

Withdrawing his assertion that the murder was committed by a third person, Goold confessed that Emma Levin died by his hand alone. The substance of the confession is that she asked Goold to lend her 100 dollars to accommodate a young man to whom she had taken a fancy. When he refused, she abused him; he lost his temper, seized a dagger and killed her in a fit of blind fury.

This version is considered unconvincing. The first improbability is in the assertion of Goold's wife, that she being in a negligée costume and not expecting visitors, left Emma Levin with Goold; whereas the victim came to the house at 5 o'clock in the afternoon in consequence of an invitation to tea. She did not make a casual call.

The Goold woman also asserted that she became insensible when she saw the body. But the neighbours say she appeared on the balcony of the house and remained there a few minutes immediately after the Levin woman's voice was heard for the last time. A further fact tending to disprove Goold's assertion that his victim needed money, is that she paid her hotel bill the day before her death and left 140 dollars in cash and valuable jewellery in a drawer; whereas the Goolds possessed hardly any money and had considerable debts. Their portable property was hardly worth 300 dollars.

The murder and motive thus being established, the only point remaining for elucidation is the relative degree of guilt. All the evidence tends to show that Goold was entirely under his companion's influence. He never displayed the least initiative. No one ever saw him in the state of alcoholic fury, to which the accused attributes his crime. The theory of the prosecution is that the murder was thought out by the woman, who persuaded the man that the only way out of their money difficulties was to kill Emma Levin, dispose of her body and obtain her valuables.

The victim was known as an easy-going woman, always ready to make friends, somewhat vain, and fond of display. The Goolds knew that if she accepted an invitation to their house, she would be certain to wear plenty of jewellery. One theory is that the Goolds tried to make her sign a promissory note and killed her on her refusal in order to obtain the jewellery she wore. What she wore was valued at 5,000 dollars and afterwards found in their possession. The investigation of these points is likely to occupy the Marseilles magistrates for a considerable time. The question of the transfer of the prisoners to Monaco is still undecided, owing to the difficulty of ascertaining the Goold woman's nationality and whether the Goolds were ever married.

A further obstacle is the unwillingness of those who knew the parties at Monte Carlo to give evidence. All betray a strong desire not to be mixed up in the case. The victim herself was one of the most singular personalities in the affair. She belonged to a class of women who, though quite respectable, love to be regarded as demi-mondaines. She gambled at the Monte Carlo casino, beyond her means and often remained in a well known café until 2 o'clock in the morning. Friends repeatedly warned her against making promiscuous acquaintances but the attraction of appearing to live a dissipated life proved too strong for her.

Late last night, Goold suddenly jumped out of bed, hammered frantically at the door and clamoured for help against imaginary enemies, who he said, were trying to cut off his legs and put them in a sack.

This morning when he was allowed see his lawyer, he was seized with another fit of fury and attacked his visitor with his fists. The lawyer now declines to see his client again. Goold's condition will be used in his trial in support of a plea that he is a madman.

### An Idea For Roosevelt.
*London, August 17th*

The sensation caused by the trunk murder case has induced a correspondent of the *London Times* to suggest yet another field of activity for President Roosevelt – nothing more or less than the suppression of Monte Carlo. The correspondent says: "Before the hideous Monte Carlo tragedy ceases to be a nine-day wonder, I would suggest that it's time for attention to be drawn to the *fons et origo mali* – the gambling rooms in that notorious place."

The correspondent goes on to say that the Goolds are merely two among many victims of the vicious circumstances engendered by the place, and urges that the nations combine to wipe out such a plague spot. "President Roosevelt," he adds, "might well assume the initiative of this righteous crusade for American plutocrats are as prominent at the tables as the aristocracy of Europe."

∽∾✐∾

## Irish Times

Wednesday, August 21st 1907

*Monte Carlo, August 20th*
The jeweller who was called into value the trinkets found in Mme Levin's room at the Hotel Bristol had

declared them to be worth 2,300 francs (£92). The examining magistrate had before him today the street porter Gratta Gaetan who took the trunk containing the murdered woman's remains to the railway station and the commissaire who opened it. Their evidence served to corroborate the original statement of the concierge that she was entirely ignorant of the contents. Both witnesses spoke of having noticed the agitated condition of the Goolds.

A copy of Mlle Giroudin's birth cert was received today by the examining magistrate. It proves that she is the niece, not the daughter of the prisoners and shows her to be 27 years of age. The magistrate has intimated that the present position of the case makes it incumbent on him to be much more reserved in his communications with the press.

～～

## *Irish Times*
Thursday, August 22nd 1907

## MONTE CARLO MURDER
## WHAT THE TRUNK CONTAINED

*Press Association Foreign Special*
*Marseilles August 21st*

M. Hwas, an advocate of the Copenhagen Bar, as executor of the late Madame Levin's estate arrived here this morning and, accompanied by the Danish consul, attended the Palace Of Justice, placing himself at the disposal of the examining magistrate, and volunteering all the information in his power as to the affairs and relationships of the murdered lady. The magistrate enquired of the extent of Mme Levin's fortune.

M. Hwas replied that she had an income of 8,000 kroner (£445) a year and besides this she had money on deposit in a Copenhagen bank. Therefore if she was in want of cash, she had only to telegraph for it. There was no need for her to borrow cash from the Goolds. With regard to disposal of Mme Levin's remains, M. Hwas said he had received no instructions on that point from the family. In the circumstances, the body would remain, for the present, in the communal grave in the cemetery of St Pierre where it had been interred.

The Examining Magistrate made an inventory of the articles found in the trunk containing the mutilated remains, the particular purpose being to discover whether among them was a salmon-coloured bodice belonging to Mrs Goold and which she was wearing when Mme Levin called at the villa on the fatal afternoon and it is supposed to have been taken off after the crime.

It is slightly stained with blood but seeing that it had been placed in the trunk along with the recently dismembered corpse, the blood spots do not necessarily prove that bodice was bespattered while the crime was actually being committed. The inventory also includes a broken fan, which is believed to have belonged to the deceased woman, with a dress and another bodice belonging to Mrs Goold and various other articles of apparel belonging to the accused including a man's shirt, with the cuffs cut off.

M. Hwas left tonight for Monte Carlo to confer with the examining magistrate there on behalf of the victim's family. Mme Levin's jewellery will not be given up until after the trial.

*Monte Carlo, August 21st*

A gentleman named Halo at present residing here is reported to have made a statement to the effect that he was acquainted with Madame Levin and had a conversation with her at about 11 o'clock the night before the crime, when she mentioned she had 500 francs (£20) in her possession at that moment. It is presumed if she still had that sum the following day and if the prisoners took it, then this would account for the money found on them when they were arrested at Marseilles. Thanks to the good offices of the examining magistrate, Mlle Giroudin has obtained a post as a governess in a respectable family residing in the Principality.

❧

*Feilding Star*
August 24th 1907

## BARONET GANGER
## SIR JAMES GOOLD'S HUMBLE
## WORK IN AUSTRALIA

*London Express correspondent cables*
*from Adelaide.*

I have succeeded in tracing Sir James Stephen Goold, the brother calling himself Vere Goold now accused of the grisly crime at Monte Carlo. He is a

permanent repairer on the State railways at
Gladstone, a township on the Spencer Gulf in South
Australia. The baronet lives in a four-roomed cottage
with nothing but the stamp of birth to mark him
above the ordinary type of working man.

I found him in charge of a repairing gang at
work on one of the lines of railways which intersect
at Gladstone. He is an old man of sixty, now bent
with years of manual toil. His face is deeply lined,
and his hands are hard and rough. When I showed
him the cabled messages related to the arrest of his
alleged brother Vere St Leger Goold, he was much
distressed, but made no concealment of the
relationship.

"I am the baronet," he said, "my father was
George Ignatius Goold, second son of Sir George
Goold, the second baronet. Sir Henry, the third
baronet was my uncle, but he never married, and
when he died at the age of 90, the title came to me, all
my elder brothers having pre-deceased him. I have
always, however, endeavoured to conceal my rank.
What is the use of being a baronet, if you have no
means to keep up the title or maintain an appearance
which will enable you to mix with your equals?"

"When did you come to Australia?" I asked.

"In 1863," he replied. "During the gold rush I
was a midshipman on the sailing vessel *Murray* and
when we reached Australia I thought there were
possibilities, so I remained. I have not seen my
brother Vere since childhood and heard little of his
life either in England or abroad. I cannot bring
myself to believe that he committed such a crime as
imputed to him in such messages. There is some
dreadful mistake, which I am sure will be cleared up
as the inquiry proceeds."

"Have you any other near relatives in England?" I asked.

"Only one that I know about who lives in London," was the reply. "I married ten years after I came out here, but am now a widower. I have three sons and a daughter. My eldest son is married and has a little boy." In Gladstone the Goolds are held in high respect. Mr Goold is known as a silent, reserved old man, who is believed to have seen better days.

The Goold family were settled in Cork for centuries.

The present head of the house is described in Lodge's and Debrett's Peerage as 'Sir James Stephen Goold of Oldcourt, Co Cork, who succeeded his uncle in 1893 and married Mary daughter of Patrick of Adelaide in 1873, has three sons, one married and one daughter and now lives in Gladstone, South Australia'.

If his last statement is correct, the man who has been living in Monte Carlo as Sir Vere Goold is a brother of Sir James and has a perfect right to the title he uses. He is the fifth son of George Ignatius Goold a resident magistrate in Co Waterford and daughter of Major General Webber Smith. His grandmother was a daughter of the Earl of Kenmare. He was born in 1853 and is described in the peerages as having married on August 2nd 1891 Violet, daughter of Hippolyte Girondin of Château de la Sône, Saint-Marcellin, Isére. As a single man, Goold was well known in the West End as a genial man who spent money freely and had claims to a baronetcy.

Those who knew him then described him a man of perfect breeding and of courtly, charming manners, cultured and generous. He was wont when coming home late from the club or theatre to collect stray cats and bring them in to share his supper.

Mrs Goold before her marriage conducted a highly successful business as a milliner and costumier under the trade name of 'Madame Giroudin' in Hereford Rd, Paddington. Mrs Violet Wilkinson, widow of a British army officer was a stoutish woman, with dark hair who had very high class clientele. She carried on her business at that address for over ten years and left not long after her marriage. After marrying, the couple took a large house in the West End, where they gave numerous dinners and lived extravagantly.

Early in 1902, the couple found themselves in debt and disappeared from the rented mansion. When the landlord visited the premises a fortnight later he found that all the furniture had been removed and presumably sold.

From London the Goolds went to Canada in 1904 where she resumed her dressmaking career at an address 56 Drummond St, Montreal for two years. Goold according to an employee was a hard drinker and heavy gambler and lost sums of money including the failure of the Thomas Fay Company importers of millinery in the city. Her business was prosperous but the profits were lost through the gambling sprees and poor business investments. Goold went to Liverpool and set up a steam laundry business and bought out several other laundry businesses in the city.

Their movements in that city were somewhat mysterious. They were both known as 'Sir Vere and Lady Goold'. Both were distinguished looking and attracted attention from their neighbours. They established a laundry at Seacombe on the Mersey and did so well that several more were set up as a limited liability company.

They returned briefly to Montreal where the business was left in charge of a Miss Charlotte Shranz. Goold spent his time there working on a scheme to break the bank at Monte Carlo. They then returned to Liverpool. They had of course in typical fashion left the business awaiting a large amount of incoming bills, which they were conveniently absent to settle. At some stage word was sent from Algiers that Lady Goold had died there from fever. It was of course far from the truth.

The Goolds left Liverpool for Monte Carlo.

*Irish Times*
August 27th

*Reuters Telegraph*
*Monte Carlo August 26th.*

It having been decided to extradite Mr and Mrs Goold from Marseilles to Monaco, final formalities to this end will be carried out and prisoners will be shortly transferred. The Superior Court which will try them will be composed of a President and two judges to be named for the occasion. The court will be changed to one of criminal nature and according to the law of the Principality, three additional judges will be added. The penal code provides for the death penalty in the case of murder.

246

Friday, August 30th, 1907

## MONTE CARLO MURDER
## TRUNK NEARLY DESTROYED BY FIRE

*Press Association Special*
*Marseilles, August 29th*

A fire broke out in the vaults of the Law Courts here today and nearly destroyed the trunk in which Mr and Mrs Goold are alleged to have placed the remains of Mme Levin. The trunk forms one of the most important pieces of evidence in connection with the Monte Carlo crime.

The court attendants, having noticed smoke coming out of the vaults, were able to master the fire at an early stage with little trouble. The extradition of Mr and Mrs Goold is now merely a matter of hours. The Marseilles judicial authorities are awaiting the arrival of various documents establishing Mr Goold's identity and furnishing proofs of his marriage to Marie Giroudin. If the papers arrive tomorrow, the prisoners will be taken to Monaco in the evening.

∽⌒∾

## Irish Times

September 15th

*Marseilles*

The Goolds were taken from St Pierre and Presentines prisons and conveyed to St Charles Station where they were put into a prison car, in separate cells under the charge of three warders. The car was then attached to a train which left Marseilles at 7.45 a.m. Vere Goold seemed to be in a state of collapse and unconscious of his surroundings. Mrs Goold had more self-possession.

As the prisoners were conveyed across the station, several angry voices were raised by the passengers on the platform. The crowd gradually grew until when the train started the prison car was surrounded by several hundred persons.

## Monte Carlo, Saturday

The transfer of the Goolds today created extraordinary interest along the coast. When the news spread by telegraph that the prisoners would travel on the 7.45 a.m. train, large crowds assembled at the stations along the line, particularly between Toulon and Nice. At the Station des Ancs a number of people climbed onto the steps and buffers of the prison car in the hope of seeing the prisoners.

Soup was served to the prisoners on the journey. Goold was still in a dazed condition and Mrs Goold remained absorbed in some illustrated papers until the train was approaching Nice when she had become somewhat nervous. A huge crowd pressed around the car at Nice station and blinds had to be lowered. When the train arrived at Monte Carlo, shouts of "Death to Them" were raised by the immense crowd.

❧

## *The Times*
Thursday September 25th

## THE MONTE CARLO MURDER

This morning, the Goolds were photographed by the detective anthropometric service. Fresh light may be thrown on the crime by a communication addressed to the magistrate by Vere Goold. This communication alleges that the crime was premeditated, having been arranged between Goold and his wife, who took the leading part in the murder. In order to verify those assertions, the magistrate intends to subject the prisoners to further interrogation.

∼∽

## *Irish Times*
Saturday, September 28th, 1907

## THE TRUNK TRAGEDY
## JEWEL RECOVERED

There have been some strange and startling developments in connection with the Monte Carlo trunk tragedy; but in one instance at least they should be accepted with reserve.

'The Daily Telegraph' Paris correspondent says:

One of these facts is concerned with the alleged theft of jewellery; another with a similar theft of money and a third seems to be further evidence that Mr Goold told the truth when he says that his wife

249

had a share in the murder. It should be remembered that at the beginning the Goolds frequently mentioned a certain young man by the name of Barker as having been implicated in the crime. No trace of a young man of that name could be found. Now, however, it turns out, according to despatches from Monte Carlo that a Mr and Mrs Barker have a villa at Cap Martin and the Goolds occasionally visited them. They returned to their villa recently and M. Savard was informed that they had something to tell him. The magistrate invited them to pay him a visit and they made the following statement:

"We occasionally met the Goolds last June and one day after Mr and Mrs Goold had paid us a visit we found that a locket worth 300 francs had disappeared." As this statement was calculated to throw new light on the case, M. Savard had the jewels of the Goolds brought to him for inspection and Mrs Barker picked out the locket that had belonged to her. She added that she had thought it strange that Mrs Goold at the time of her visit had counselled her to deposit her jewels in her safekeeping.

The Goolds were at once confronted with the witnesses. Mrs Goold energetically denied having stolen the locket. When asked by the magistrate how it had come into her possession she replied that she had found it on the beach.

## Monte Carlo, September 26th

Vere Goold was re-examined by M. Savard the examining magistrate today and he made a fresh confession, in which he admitted that he and his wife had determined to rob someone, as they were at the end of their resources. They had not intended to murder Mme Levin, but merely to stun her, and it was her unexpected resistance which led her to being stabbed by him after he had tried to fell her with a kitchen pestle. Mrs Goold, on being confronted with her husband, said she had nothing to say in reply to his confession. She fainted and had to be carried back to her cell.

## October 10th

The usual formal preliminaries to the trial of the Goolds for the murder of Mme Levin were gone through today and the prisoners were remitted to the criminal court. The date for the trial will be fixed by the President of the Court.

∾◠◡◠∾

# 12

## LA HISTOIRE

**MARSEILLES, SEPTEMBER 1907**

Professor Lacassagne, Dr Grasset, Dr Dufour, Inspectors Dupin and Garonne and examining magistrates Malavialle and Savard met to consider the documents received from archive material and newspaper reports elicited from the professor's contact in University College, Cork, Ireland. Dr Grasset would interview Goold with the assistance of Dr Dufour on the basis of what they had been presented. The purpose of the exercise was to find some reason why the prisoner Goold had embarked on such a horrendous crime. Notwithstanding his obvious state of financial desperation at the time, something else in his history must have led to such an appalling result.

Professor Lacassagne in particular but in fact all participants in the inquiry were concerned with not just the crime but the criminal mind. The professor, in all the cases he had been involved in, most notably that of Vacher and the Gouffé Affair, had established from the backgrounds of the perpetrators facts which would be of primary interest and evidence in the trials that followed. Not alone that, such facts were valuable contributions to the growing body of knowledge and expertise in the field of psychological profiling. The Monte Carlo murder, they all knew, was more than a suitable case for such treatment.

Professor Lacassagne noted that one aspect of the information in the files had eluded the close attention of the press, which was quite extraordinary. This was the prisoner's impressive sporting achievements.

"This history is quite extraordinary," he said, "and I can say that in my long experience I have not come across a perpetrator of such a monstrous crime from such a distinguished family line. A man who on the surface, it would seem, was presented, as a result of his privilege, with every opportunity in life. Education at the famous Trinity College and secure employment in Dublin . . . a city with large municipal financial problems and areas of dire poverty, side by side as always with power and wealth. It can justifiably be observed that Vere St Leger Goold had it all."

The professor suggested that they quickly review the assembled antecedent history and then go on to an open debate. The material at the gathering's disposal included archive material, newspaper reports and photographs.

They began to look through an abstract prepared most helpfully by the professor's contact in Cork which presented what he judged to be the most pertinent sections of the archival material.

## *Brief History of the Goold Family*
### *(Various Sources)*

### Item 1:

Goold is one variant of a surname which has had several in the course of its history: Gould, Golde, Gold.

## Item 2:

Records find the Goold family in Cork, Ireland, from the time of the Norman Invasion in 1172.

## Item 3:

John Golde, the Crusader, was a soldier from Somerset who distinguished himself at the siege of Damietta in the Holy Land and as a reward granted an estate at Seaborough in 1229. He is believed to be related to the Goolds of Ireland.

## Item 4:

The Goold family were at an early period established in the County Of Cork. In 1356, Nicholas Gold was one of those influential persons commissioned to allot a state subsidy of that county as was David Gold a few years after. With the municipal history of the city, they were, during the years previous to the first civil war, intimately connected, Golds having been Mayors of Cork from 1442 to 1640, no less than thirty times; but afterwards ceased to fill any corporate office there.

Queen Elizabeth's instruction to her Lord President Of Munster, Sir George Carew, in 1600 directed that "William Saxey, Chief Justice, and James Golde, Second Justice of the said province, being of special trust appointed to be of his council, shall give their continual attendance thereat, and shall not depart at any time without the special licence of the said Lord President." The salary of the chief was fixed at £100 and that of James Golde at one hundred marks, subject to deductions in case of their absence from the duties so imposed upon them. A manuscript Book of Obits in Trinity College, Dublin, supplies some links with the family of William Goold, Mayor of Cork in 1618, and who died in 1634.

The attainders of 1642 include the names of Garrett Goold of Castletown and of James and John FitzRichard-Goold of Tower-Bridge, merchants. James Goold was the only member of the family who attended the Supreme Council in 1647. The attainder of 1691 include the names of James and Ignatius Goold described as of Cork, esquires; John Goold, of Kinsale esq; Richard of Cork, merchant; Patrick of the said city; James Goold of Galway and Eileen Bagot, otherwise Goold, wife of John Bagot of Cork.

## Item 5:

Ignatius Goold was a supporter of King James and was Jacobite Mayor of Cork in 1687. He and his family forfeited estates in Ireland after the defeat of James.

## Item 6 :

*Vanderplas Cork Deeds, 1598, 1610-1677, 1694.*

By the end of the 16th century the area and population of Cork City was not much greater than that of medieval times. It was largely in the hands of the merchant princes of Old English descent. Despite some advances by the Reformation, by the end of the 17th century the merchant rulers were again predominantly Roman Catholic.

The English authorities regarded Cork's merchant classes with suspicion due to their religion and thought that they were in league with Gaelic and Catholic forces in Cork County. On the death of Queen Elisabeth in 1603, the leading Catholic families in Cork refused to proclaim James I as king. Lord Mountjoy soon put down what was termed the Recusant Revolt, which was mirrored in other Irish cities.

The 17th century was a turbulent period in the history of Cork and Ireland. It was characterised by the re-establishment of the power of the Crown, a power aligned with the Protestantism of the Reformation.

While the civic government of Cork City remained in the hands of the merchant classes, tensions with Crown officials continued to simmer. Members of the leading Catholic families such as the Meades, Tirrys, Goolds and others were fined for non-attendance at formal religious ceremonies conducted according to Anglican rite. The James I charter of 1608, while it created the County Of Cork and the City Of Cork which covered a much larger area than the old medieval walled city and suburbs, also retained for the Crown the right to poundage, tonnage and customs in the port of Cork.

This was a severe financial blow to the merchants of the city including the Goolds.

Cork City was under military governance from 1644-1656 when Cromwell granted a municipal charter to the Protestants of Cork City. Further orders expelling Catholics were made in 1651 and 1656. The municipal government of the city was to remain firmly in Protestant hands until the return of the Corporation in the 1840s, apart from a brief period during the reign of Catholic James II (1685-1690) when the Old English rallied to the cause of the

Jacobites and regained control of the city, which was then besieged and taken by Williamite forces in September 1690. Some of the Old English had properties in Cork returned after the restoration of the monarchy in 1660, but the dominance of the City by the Old English merchant elite, which had lasted for centuries, was at an end.

Despite the political turbulence, the economic fortunes of Cork began to improve in the first half of the 17th century after two centuries of relative decline.

## Item 7 :

Two items [in the *Vanderplas Cork Deeds, 1598, 1610-1677, 1694*] relate to debts owed by James Gould, gentleman, to William Penn (1644-1718), founder of the State Of Pennsylvania, who was sent to Ireland in 1667 by his father Admiral Sir William Penn to manage extensive estates in Cork.

## Item 8 :

A number of items from the 1660's and 1670's appear to relate to the recovery of property by Catholic families following the restoration of the monarchy with the accession of Charles II in 1660 including a decree of innocency for Mary and Anstance Goold, relating to the 1641 estate of their father Alderman Thomas Gould and signed by court commissioners.

## Item 9 :

In La Rochelle, in 1705, James Nagle of Annakissy, County Cork (b. January 21, 1679, d. March 26, 1773) married Elisabeth Goold, daughter of Alderman

Stephen Goold of Cork and his wife Helen. Mrs Helen Goold in a will dated 1725 and proved on November 6th, 1746 left her son-in law (J. Nagle) 14,600 livres tournois. She had a house in Paris.

James Nagle gave a grand ball in 1768 at Annakissy which had to be stopped in the middle on the news of the death of his grandniece Marion, wife of Charles Howard (afterwards 11th Duke Of Norfolk).

## Item 10:

Amongst those who were taken at sea in 1746, volunteering to aid the cause of Prince Charles-Edward, was Captain Gould, Ultonia Regiment, Spanish service.

## Item 11:

In the Church of St Giles at Bruges is a burial place of William Goold "of ancient and venerable lineage in Cork" as inscribed upon a white marble flag inserted in the flag of the Chapel of the Blessed Virgin. There were strong mercantile links between Cork and Bruges in the 18th century.

## Item 12:

*Goolds, of Old Court, Co. Cork, Ireland*

The Goold baronetcy of Old Court in Cork is a title in the baronetage of the United Kingdom. It was created on August 8th 1801 for Francis Goold with remainder to his heirs, male, in recognition of his father who gave valuable service to the government of King George III.

*Coat of Arms of the Goold Family*

*Arms:* azure on a fess or, between five goldfinches, three in chief, and two in base, proper, three mullets, gules.

*Crest:* a demi-lion, rampant, or.

*Motto:* Deus mihi providebit.

*Seat:* Old Court, Co Cork.

Sir Francis' father George Goold of Old Court, Co Cork, esq, married Mary-Ann, eldest daughter of James Galway, esq (a lineal descendent from Sir Jeffrey Galway, bart,) and had the following issue:

1. Sir Francis, 1st bart.

2. Henry-Michael married 27th May 1778, Catherine daughter of Donatt O'Callaghan of Kilgoorey, Co Clare, and had the following issue:

    1) Sir George, 2nd bart, (1778-1870).

    2) Henry.

    3) Marcella.

    4) Mary.

3. William.

4. George.

5. Anne *m.* John Dunellan of Nutgrove, esq, cousin to the Countess of Fingal.

6. Margaret.

Sir George Goold, 2nd bart, succeeded his uncle Sir Francis who died unmarried in 1818; married 13th May 1802 Lady Charlotte Browne, only child of Valentine, Earl of Kenmare, by the Hon. Charlotte Dillon, 3d daughter of Henry, 11th Viscount Dillon; and had the following issue:

1. Sir Henry-Valentine, 3rd bart, b. 7th July 1803, died 8th June 1893 unmarried.

2. George Ignatius, b. 7th Sept 1805, d. 6th Nov 1879.

3. Edward, in the service of the Emperor of Austria.

4. William-Bedingfield.

5. Charlotte.

6. Ellen-Frances.

7. Georgina.

8. Marcella.

9. Frances.

George Ignatius Goold married Clara Smith, daughter of Major-General James Webber Smith on 3rd November 1840. Clara died 9th March 1870. They had the following issue:

1. Frances Mary Goold.

2. Frederick Edward Michael Goold.

3. Ernest.

4. William.

5. George Charles b. 1847.

6. Sir James Stephen Goold 4th Bt
   b. 2nd Oct 1848.

7. Vere Thomas St Leger Goold
   b. 2nd October 1853.

Sir James Stephen Goold, 4th baronet, succeeded his uncle Henry-Valentine who died unmarried in 1893.

# Item 13:

*George Ignatius Goold, Resident Magistrate of Waterford, and the Fenian Movement.*

There was strong suspicion of arms being illegally imported through the port of Waterford. The Fenian rebels had started an uprising in early March 1867 in Tallaght, Co Dublin. Albeit with disastrous results for themselves. The County Dublin Rising was followed by a number of smaller outbreaks in the Munster area. In order to cope with the disorder in Munster, the Government set up army 'flying columns' to scout the country for rebels. These flying columns were to be under the command of a resident magistrate. These groups included a Waterford 'flying column'.

In such a situation panic and rumour abounded. The Dublin Metropolitan Police received a report on March 8th warning that a rising involving 1,800 men was about to take place in Waterford. The insurgents were said to concentrate their attacks on the police. Contact with the army was to be avoided (since many soldiers were said to be secretly sworn members of the Fenian Brotherhood).

The memorandum regarding arms smuggling was the work of George Ignatius Goold, resident magistrate of Waterford. Goold was the second son of Sir George Goold 2nd Bt of Old Court, County Cork by his wife Lady Charlotte Browne, daughter of the 1st Earl Of Kenmare. His son James Stephen was to become 4th baronet in 1893. His youngest child Vere St Leger Goold was born in 1853. George Goold, who was born on September 7th 1805, held the post of resident magistrate from 1840-1878.

During the eventful month of March 1867, Goold had already been in correspondence with the government regarding the Fenian movement on two occasions. He had forwarded a newspaper cutting of a letter from the Fenian chief Thomas Kelly. This cutting had been smuggled into a prisoner in Waterford gaol, Capt Burke. Also he had countered a charge by a Mr Spencer that spirit licences had been granted in Waterford to two known Fenians.

In this latter memorandum he had made some interesting observations regarding the composition of the magistracy in Ireland. The Irish Government in the persons of Lord Naas, Chief Secretary and his under secretary Sir Thomas Lancome swiftly passed Goold's complaint concerning arm imports to the chairman of the Board Of Customs in London, Sir Thomas Freemantle, early in April.

*County Of Waterford*
*March 28th, 1867*

*The Under Secretary,*
*Dublin Castle*

*I would wish to call your attention to the question of the importation of arms in aid of the Fenian movement into the ports of this country and to the difficulty that now exists of exercising any effectual supervision over it.*

*I presume that few believe we have seen the end of that movement. I would go further and say I am firmly of the opinion that we have not seen the real beginning and that, notwithstanding the late spurt and its failure, the agents are working actively and silently, to prepare for a renewal of the attempt when they think circumstances are more favourable to them.*

*Among those preparations, I have reason to think the importation of arms occupies a prominent place and that, probably, they are passing under our eyes along the quays of Waterford, continually. The large iron-bound cases of hardware, large bales of soft goods, and the like, may convey any quantities of them, without detection.*

*I have spoken to the Custom officers, but they have neither a staff nor authority to intervene effectually. Their instructions are to follow anything they may suspect to its destination, but as this is principally a port of transit from Glasgow and Liverpool to the interior, this instruction is practically nugatory.*

*Again they cannot (will not at their own peril even if they had force or staff to do it) stop and examine the most likely packages, which could occupy a considerable time, and leave them liable to the consequences, in the extent of a failure, for the delay and injury to the goods.*

*The police, are of course in the same position so that unless on positive and sworn information, the smuggling of arms cam continue under our very noses.*

*It is not for me to suggest a remedy, but I cannot help calling attention to the subject, because I think it of much importance, and it is forced upon my notice, from more quarters than one, in hope that some greater powers may be devised which will, to some extent, meet the requirements of the time.*

### George I. Goold

Sir Thomas Freemantle replied from the Custom House in Dublin on 9th April, 1867, and noted that within a package two gun cases and ammunition, a machine for making cartridges and some other gun furniture was discovered in a shipment to Waterford and handed over to the local constabulary.

Freemantle dispatched Frederick Trevor, the Collector of Customs at Dublin, to Waterford in order that he might confer with the collector there on the subject. Trevor also included the Port of Cork on his itinerary. A copy of his report was duly forwarded to Lord Naas and remains among his papers.

In June 1867 there was an unsuccessful Fenian landing on the Waterford coast, at Ballinagoul near Helvic.

∽◦◦∾

When Lacassagne and his colleagues had examined these documents at length, with growing wonder, they turned to another sheaf even more pertinent to their present investigation.

### Vere St Leger Goold – Tennis Champion

In November 1877, a group of tennis enthusiasts decided to establish the Dublin Lawn Tennis Club. The plan was to have 30 members who would pay a subscription of £3 a year. The committee decided at the subsequent gathering later in the same month to lease ground in Upper Pembroke Street for £25 a year over a ten-year period. At the next meeting on December 6th a member of the committee Arnold Graves proposed a new name "Fitzwilliam Lawn Tennis Club" which was adopted.

The group was composed of Anglo-Irish stock, Protestant, all of the Dublin professional classes. It would, as newspapers revealed, maintain close connections with the British Army and a special effort would be made to bring officers into the fold. In December 1879 a motion was passed admitting army officers at a subscription of £1 a year. At tournament, bands from the Welsh Regiment or the King's Own Regiment entertained the spectators during breaks in the play.

Tennis it was made quite clear was a sporting pursuit of the privileged classes: the gentry, professions and in the case of one of the leading lights that would emerge on the court, the old aristocracy.

At this time there was a tennis boom in Britain and Ireland. The All England club had been founded in 1877 and clubs began to proliferate throughout the isles. Tennis was the ideal middle-to-upper-class game, expensive to maintain, which meant it kept out the ordinary man and woman on the street, but not so expensive as to be available only to the very rich. Each year the cream of English players would come over to compete in Fitzwilliam Week, usually held in early June.

Although the year was marked by a severe economic depression in the country, caused by bad harvests, foreign agricultural competition and the drying up of the usual seasonal employment in Britain, as in all such events certain privileged sections of society appeared unaffected by the consequences.

On March 11th 1879, a note was published in sporting newspaper, *The Field*:

*It is proposed to hold the Championship of Ireland open to all comers under the auspices of The Fitzwilliam Lawn Tennis Club in Dublin on Monday the 2nd of June and the following days.*

At the same time that this then-expensive sport was gaining popularity, the finances of the capital Dublin were in disarray. In May the Municipal Boundaries Commission, of whom a highly accomplished tennis player Vere Goold was a secretary, was conducting an inquiry into the question of the annexation of the outlying townships to the municipality of Dublin. On behalf of the Rathmines Commissioners, Mr Walker QC sought to show that the population of the district, now under this government of that body would have little if nothing to gain, and a great deal to lose by incorporation with the city.

With the character borne by the present Corporation of Dublin, it was not difficult for Mr Walker to make out a plausible case. Rathmines may not be perfection; but what is Dublin? Is it not notorious that its death rate is among the highest in Europe; that its streets are ill-kept, that its finances are mismanaged; that the members of the Corporation spend their time in speech making, to the neglect of public business and that the Municipal Council has been reported upon with extreme severity by Select Parliamentary Committee?

After many years and protracted enquires, the suburbs would be annexed but the proceedings underlined the financial shortcomings of the administration of the city and the dire poverty that existed in the heart of Dublin. As the counsel observed, the highest death rate in Europe, no doubt largely among the poorly nourished inhabitants of the tenements. Such matters were of little concern to the thriving tennis club or its well-heeled members.

The tennis club committee had applied to the Commissioners of the nearby Fitzwilliam Square and the grounds were to be leased for a week to hold the inaugural championships there.

The square was a magnificent example of Dublin Georgian architecture. Surrounded by beautiful red-bricked houses which could not have provided a more sumptuous backdrop, the smaller windows at the top of the houses were calculated correctly to give an impression of even greater height.

The first All Ireland Open championship was played in the square on Wednesday 4th June, 1879. Rain had delayed the beginning of the tournament and the committee had to extend it to the following Tuesday. There was a Gentlemen's and Ladies' singles and men's doubles and doubles for a lady and gentleman as partners.

A display advertisement in the *Irish Times* two days before the start of the competition announced the event. The gentlemen's doubles admission was one shilling, combined with the ladies' doubles it was two shillings and on the final day, the Friday, gentleman's singles, one shilling again. Three-day tickets were two shillings and sixpence and tickets could be obtained through a number of retail outlets including the famous Elverys shops in Dawson St and Sackville Street.

The ladies' singles was the first competition of its kind to be played anywhere. It would be five years before the All England Club would include a ladies' championship.

The ladies' matches were played in the club premises, admission by members' vouchers only. Their comely ankles, the only parts of their legs exposed were not, apparently, suitable for the gaze of the marketplace.

From the start there was a sparkling social life surrounding the competition, more redolent of race meetings. During the season, the debutantes came to Dublin to be presented to the Viceroy, the King's representative. They stayed in the Shelbourne Hotel or in the Georgian mansions in Fitzwilliam and Merrion squares. The Viceroy and Lady Aberdeen were to be frequent visitors to the Fitzwilliam Tournament.

A number of small reports in the *Irish Times* gave notice of the upcoming All Ireland championship and one correspondent noted in advance of the superseding by tennis of the hitherto hugely popular game of croquet. "Croquet and its great and successful rival lawn tennis are to be seen on the lawn, the former seldom and the latter very frequently – so often as to prove inconsiderably that the mallet and ball are altogether out of favour. Not long ago a very enjoyable lawn tennis fete was brought off with much pleasantness and success at the Earlsfort Terrace rink."

A further report which appeared in the newspaper on Thursday, June 5th, affirmed this view:

"The contest for the Championship Lawn Tennis in this country has obtained a considerable degree of popularity during the comparatively short time that has elapsed since its introduction among our summer sports and to the once universally favourite game of croquet it has established, at least for the present, a formidable rivalship.

Possessing though, in a different form, all the attractions of the latter pastime, the more animated exercise it demands and the consequently closer continuous attention that it requires, constitute in the consideration of many one of its direct charms, whilst to the unquestionable advantage it has in not rendering necessary that absence of all inequality in the ground, so desirable in croquet, may perhaps be ascribed some of the success with which it has been attended.

Both as a means of gentle exercise, and in its more social character, it has become extremely fashionable; and that is probably in some measure owing to the fact that, while it affords a pleasing open air amusement, combined with physical exertion sufficiently gentle for the participation of ladies, it can be conducted with all the rapidity and vigour that can satisfy the most enthusiastic player of the rougher sex.

Were a proof of the popularity it enjoys wanting, the large and fashionable assemblage yesterday present in the green of Fitzwilliam Square, when the contest commenced for the Lawn Tennis Championship Of Ireland, would have amply supplied it to the most sceptical mind. Around the whole line that surrounds the greensward upon which the play took place, there was a dense unbroken circle of persons, or standing throughout the whole of the games, the utmost interest evinced by the spectators.

The wavering fortunes of the day were watched with the greatest attention and wherever a brilliant stroke of play was made it was greeted with loud applause. The weather during the greater part of the afternoon was beautifully fine, and beside the attractions afforded by the contests, many appeared to appreciate those of the promenade during the intervals that succeeded each game. The band of the 77th Regiment, by permission of Colonel Kent, attended and excellently played a selection of music, which considerably added to the pleasantness of the occasion.

The play being confined to gentleman's doubles, no ladies took part in this, the commencing portion of the contest. As from bat to bat the ball was struck, caught again and on the bat of the antagonist, and again came the whistling through the air, to be eagerly watched and as quickly followed with a ready and skilful blow, the scene presented by the players was animated and extremely interesting. Beside the ball and the simple bats used, there are no other artificial adjuncts to this play, with the exception of a red-topped netting stretched across between the divisions, chalked in white on the soft green grass-grown ground.

Considered as a means of affording the beautiful open-air exercise without even a suspicion of danger or a temptation for injurious over-exertion, the game of lawn tennis must unquestionably meet with the approval of all. The play yesterday continued to the fall of evening and had not concluded until after 8 o'clock. Three rounds of doubles were played and the first prize was won by Messrs Elliot and Kellie of the 82nd Regiment."

One of the players involved in the doubles was Vere St Leger Goold partnered by Phillips who progressed to the third round where they were defeated by CD Barry and Aungier 6-4, 2-6, 6-2. Their victorious opponents were defeated by Elliot and Kellie in the final round 2-6, 6-3, 8-7. But there would be glory waiting for Goold in the men's singles final which he won defeating CD Barry in straight sets 8-6, 8-6.

He was the star of Fitzwilliam in this period. His name was so prominent that when the colours of the club were changed to chocolate and maize, the second colour was more often referred to as 'gold' in honour of the club champion. As another outstanding player was E de S.H. Browne, the club colours became to be known as Brown and Gold.

A man with the world at his feet it seemed. In the very same year as he took the inaugural Irish Open championship title, he would go on to reach the Wimbledon final and his opponent Rev J.T. Hartley would say of him later: "At that time he was a happy impetuous Irishman, the champion of his own country and all in all a fine player. He was given to volley more than any of the rest would but there must have been something amiss with his game, for after a good night's sleep I would beat him easily in three sets."

J.G. Heathcote had been defeated by Rev Hartley in the quarter finals. A large proportion of the competitors in 1879 adopted a very safe style of play, introduced by the previous year's champion and Hartley was pre-eminent in that style. Over a thousand spectators watched him defeat Goold in the All Comers Final. Hartley was renowned as a steady basecourt player, with a persistent return of serve.

He did not expect to reach the final which was being played on Monday and had arranged to cover for Sunday service back in his Yorkshire parish. He made a 500-mile round trip by train to fulfil his ecclesiastical duties. He was the only clergyman ever to win a Wimbledon final. The format in those years was that the All Comers winner would play the defending champion in a one-off challenge to decide the championship.

But in that year Patrick Hadow did not defend his title, so Hartley was awarded the championship on a walk over. He took prize money of 12 guineas and a silver cup worth 25 guineas. As defending champion the following year he defeated the All Comers winner Fortescue Lawford over four sets 6-3, 6-2, 2-6, 6-3.

How good Goold was considered as a tennis player of his time was not in doubt. The great player J.G. Heathcote and an equally good commentator put him up with the best. In the matter of the hugely popular game of the time, his subsequent switching to gambling had no part in his game of tennis.

That there is little luck in tennis, Heathcote maintained, may be inferred from the fact that a "bisque" taken or received will materially alter the chances of success, while the odds of "half-fifteen" or approximately one stroke in eight, would make an issue of a match between two equal players nearly a certainty. The surest key therefore to success, is practice, aided by an ambition and encouraged by elation consequent on well earned victory.

In this year, 1879, Heathcote recalled, was also inaugurated the Championship of Ireland played in Dublin and repeated with ever increasing prestige every year. The prize was won by Mr V. Goold at the time better known by the name of St Leger under which he played. The meeting was further remarkable as being the first occasion in which ladies competed for a championship, on this occasion, secured by Miss P. Langrishe, whose name occurs frequently in lawn tennis annals.

A proof of the increasing popularity of the game, as well as the general possibility of success not at that time limited, as now is the case, to three or four well known players, is furnished by the fact that there were forty-five competitors for the All England Championship of 1879, of whom nine had taken part in previous contests at Wimbledon. Mr P. F. Hadow the holder, being in Ceylon, could not defend his title but the list in addition to Messrs Erskine and Lawford, the second and third prize winners of the previous year, included Messrs W. Renshaw, E. Renshaw, A.J. Mulholland, O.E. Wodehouse, E. Lubbock, C.F. Parr, V. Goold, the Irish champion, C.D. Barry who had taken second honours in Dublin and J.T. Hartley, of whom the last, though quite unknown at Wimbledon came from Yorkshire with a great reputation.

Of these, the two Renshaws were prevented from putting in an appearance, but the absence of two men of 18 years of age was hardly noticed at the time amid the host of competitors; and no forecast could at that time be made of their coming greatness. At the end of six rounds, made necessary by the large number of entries, Mr J.T. Hartley emerged as the winner, like his predecessor an old Harrovian, but unlike him a tennis player that had represented Oxford in 1870.

His closest struggle was in the second round against Mr L.P. Erskine, but the practice he had in the earlier matches was of the highest value to him and when on the final day he met and vanquished Mr V. Goold, he was undoubtedly a much stronger player than he had been on the occasion of his first match on the All England ground, a week before. The result of the play was summed up by a writer in a daily paper: "Safety is the first requisite in lawn tennis and brilliancy the second" and this remark, from which as a general proposition large deductions should be made, was certainly true of the tournament of 1879.

The showy and attractive style of Mr Goold, with all its brilliancy, could achieve no success against the unfailing judgement which was the most conspicuous characteristic of Mr Hartley's game. The French proverb, *"La belle recherche, le bon joueur"* might indeed be applied to the lawn tennis championship of 1879. It was not so much he who went after the ball as the ball went after him. The accuracy of his return, too, was equal to that of his judgement, and though tested, by modern standards, he might not be classed as a hard hitter, he nevertheless made the ball travel at a good pace. Seldom volleying himself, he would repeatedly defeat the tactics of a volleyer by passing him in the most dexterous manner.

In short, he was more accurate than hard hitters, and hit harder than the accurate players of his day, and this combination of qualities secured for him victory, which was as popular as it was unexpected. Mr V. Goold took the second and Mr Parr the third prize.

It may have been accidental circumstances or due to the prevailing type of play, that service in this tournament more than maintained its old supremacy, the analysis showing that, with the service line unaltered and excluding hollow matches and those played on one day when the wind was excessive, service won 352 games and lost 295, a proportion of about eleven to nine, while the strokes won by the server were to those won by the striker out, in the proportion of twenty-four to twenty-three.

One more open tournament was played in Cheltenham in October, partly outdoor on asphalt and partly on a covered court and was won by Mr W. Renshaw who defeated Mr V. Goold. It was a hard-fought and close contest all the way going to five sets, 6-4, 6-3, 5-6, 5-6, 6-4, Goold having been up 4-1 in the final set.

The future achievements of his opponent Renshaw would only serve to underline the undoubted talents of the Irish player who could mix it with an opponent who would go on to create Wimbledon history. A reporter summed up the winner: "With more experience he will trouble the best players in the Kingdom. He is most active in the court and seldom misses a return."

It was an accurate prediction. The following year, W. Renshaw won the Irish Championship, defeating successively R.T. Richardson, H.F. Lawford, M.G. McNamara, E. S. de Browne and V. Goold, the previous year's champion. He was only 19 and considered amongst the strongest players in England and Ireland.

In dealing with the encroaching monotony of the game it was remarked that some originality had been given to it by the versatile genius of Gore, the unerring judgement of Hartley and the unstudied grace of Goold – the opposite of mechanical precision.

In 1881, W. Renshaw retained the Irish title, won the Princes tournament and won Wimbledon at the age of 20. He also won the doubles title with his brother Ernest at Oxford and Dublin. He won all Wimbledon titles from that year until 1887 after which he retired as a result of tennis elbow.

Goold just once again displayed the talent which, if disciplined and honed, would have led to even greater heights when in an international doubles game he and his partner W.H. Daly defeated the number one English duo of H. Lawford and A.J. Mulholland.

But by the end of 1883 his tennis career was effectively finished. Other infinitely less healthy pursuits had replaced the racket and the ball.

∽◠◡◠∾

Professor Lacassagne summed up:
"It would seem to me, gentlemen, that quite apart from the well-established facts of M. Gould's recent history, addiction to

gambling and alcohol, he was a man of seemingly impeccable family history and an athlete in his youth of great promise. He had, as the saying goes, everything in life going for him. He has during his incarceration achieved with the help of chaplains and reading, something of what could be described as a process of rehabilitation. Yet the enormity of the crime seems to overwhelm all his past and present situation." He paused. "I open the forum."

Dr Dufour posited that his addictions to gambling and alcohol had got the better of any of his best instincts and that his relationship with a dominating woman imbued with fantasies bred from a relatively modest background had added to these acquired weaknesses. She, he added, was determined to acquire a status of life that would prove continually beyond both of their means, and an ambition that defied her husband's innate weakness of character.

Goold, when he first examined him showed signs of hopeless addiction to alcohol. He had to treat him for the effects of delirium tremens. Such a man was open to suggestion of a stronger more effective partner in a relationship. He would literally do anything to please this woman, including the fantastical act of coming to Monte Carlo, to beat a bank that, despite well-publicised acts of this nature could not in the end of the day be beaten.

Magistrate Savard, with the benefit of plenty experience of this kind in the Principality, agreed. The streets of Monaco were paved with such hopeless ambitions, not much publicised because it did not suit the ambitions of the administration. The Graveyard of the Suicides provided enough evidence of such destroyed fantasy. This case, he felt, was a form of suicide by any other name. Unfortunately the victim was not given that option; the perpetrators took that route by their crazy action, which in his opinion had no chance of success.

But then again, the professor interjected, chance intervened and without that element, the outcome could have been quite different. Also he acknowledged there was a certain incompetence involved, but this is the risk all murderers take – no more than the habitués of the casino. Hindsight is all too fickle in its own way.

Magistrate Malavialle concurred with the professor. It was on appearance an act of incompetence. How could the Goolds hope to escape from the consequences of their action? Sure, it was planned but there was evidence of unrestrained rage. The battering of the head of Madame Levin and the stab wounds to the front and back. The crude cutting of the body and the evidence of bloodstains that could not be effectively cleaned at the site.

Dr Grasset said that it was beyond his imagination that a man of Goold's lineage, privilege and opportunities had chosen the path that had led him to this pass. It demonstrated that there was an innate weakness in his character, a self-destructive impulse which had driven him to the most desperate measures of survival, aided by attempted obliteration of his circumstances by drink.

"I would not entirely agree with M. Malavialle in the use of the word *incompetent*. That can too easily seem to be the case after the event. The curious aspect for me was the removal of a portion of the intestines. This displayed some basic medical knowledge of the process of bodily decomposition. The soft organs decomposing first. So where did this come from? I can only guess that Goold may have had a medical student for a friend or tennis partner while an undergraduate at Trinity College. Such a decision was hardly taken during the process of dismemberment. However crude the crime may appear to professionals, it might well have succeeded had the trunk been sufficiently insulated with packing material to prevent any leakage. However much he was dominated by his wife, there was a fatal chink in the character of Goold that allowed him to participate in the ghastly act. Its provenance is not obvious to me from the material we have at our disposal."

Dupin kept, as did Garonne, his counsel. They were police investigators, they would leave the psychology to the doctors and legal matters to the magistrates but when and if called would give their views. They felt that whatever transpired from the conversation, it would be their role to corroborate the scientific facts.

The Marseilles chief investigator, when asked his opinion, referred briefly to Dr Grasset's assessment of the matter of the entrails.

"There is little doubt in my mind that the removal during the commission of the crime proved intent in advance. That is allowing that Dr Corniglion could not connect them directly, those found on Larvotto beach, to the victim. But the discovery is beyond coincidence. Where such knowledge came from I could not comment upon with any degree of accuracy. But I would concur that the effort failed on the basis of poor concealment in the aftermath. That undoubtedly led to the discovery of the victim."

The professor, on the basis of Goold's biological background, could only deduce in a speculative manner from the evidence that his father was a strong man and probably dominating in the manner of a magistrate who regarded his professional life as far more important than his family life. The elder son Sir Stephen had fled the family coop to Australia where he worked in a position that might be viewed as well below his station but was more than happy in that role. He had wanted to get away.

"We have among the files," noted the professor, "a letter from Goold's father to the authorities in relation to an aborted Irish uprising of the time which reveals a lot about his character. It might, considering the religion of the family within the context of its history, be seen as a form of betrayal. He certainly was joined to an English administration which had little to offer the Irish native population in their aspirations towards some sense of freedom. A tough self-serving character, by all accounts.

Vere Goold's mother died when he was only 17 years of age and his father towards the end of 1879, the year of his greatest achievements. There is not a lot to deduce from that, other than the speculation that he may well have, in his earlier life, as the youngest of seven children, lacked a maternal comfort and perhaps suffered from an overbearing paternal presence. Many, if one was to attempt to take this into account, have suffered worse familial experience without resorting to dubious practices in later life, not to mind serious crime.

Goold seemed to have more regard for the family lineage than his brother but only when it suited his purpose in the extremities of financial need. His abandonment of his very promising tennis career displayed a weakness of character, not wishing to put in the sweat of practice and sacrifice that brought his rival Renshaw to heights which Goold's talent could also have brought him. He then married a woman who by her nature played more the role of mother than wife, but with all the expectations of privilege, on her part, which that marriage did not provide. She could and did exploit her husband's weakness but largely to no avail.

"The accounts provided by the investigators and the examining magistrates suggest to me, along with the utter denial of Mrs Goold of her dominant role in the murder and her propensity to feigned hysteria, that her husband was more her instrument in the crime. He carried out her wishes, as he always did. His deranged behaviour in the commission of the crime urges me to conclude that at no stage in his sociological and psychological development did Goold display any character-istics of the killers that I have had the dubious fortune to study."

The professor pointed to two photographs of Goold as a young tennis player, one in the Wimbledon championships and another at a tournament some five years later at Fitzwilliam Tennis Club, his alma mater. He noted in the earlier one a man of quiet, handsome demeanour, determined of expression. The latter, he pointed out, placed at the back of a group of which in the front row sat one of the Renshaw brothers, his facial character was much diminished, jaw drawn and his eyes staring in no particular direction. The sense of determination had for some reason vanished.

It appeared that he had abandoned the game of skill to one of chance, a great pity, given his innate ability. And thus forfeit some basic hold over his destiny.

"He is to some extent analogous of the murderer as victim which of course in no way exculpates his responsibility for the foul crime that he carried out, most likely at the behest of his wife. He must suffer the consequences but I am bound to say that it will be held by his defence that there were, as in the case of Bompard in the Gouffé murder, extenuating circumstances. Whatever the difficulties of his youth, I see nothing that would constitute the genesis of a killer. He had clearly lost the plot of his life and disappointment of expectations. Not enough, in my opinion, to initiate the crime and lead him to this misfortune of circumstance."

He pointed to the investigation file and the extensive account of Mrs Goold's previous history prior to her marriage to Vere Goold, which proved her to a person of devious personality and behaviour, bordering and exceeding criminality at times. It described a woman without any moral compass who was determined to exploit any opportunity and person who came her way, but little aptitude to maintain that advantage or sustain any course of action to the point where it brought any lasting success.

"This," he said, "was one simple example, but not alone of her character. Fortune for this woman was a matter of chance and not to be gained by hard work and sweat of the brow. She, not born of riches, was devoted to attaining the status of wealth by any means available to her at any time. Worse still, she has not to this juncture expressed any remorse for or any responsibility for her actions. She has in my view both sociopathic and psychotic tendencies, but I will allow the court to determine that matter."

The professor then finished his summing up, finding general

approval of the group which then retired for coffee and further discussions on the subject. Time was marching on towards the trial, which it was generally agreed would happen sometime in December with even more intense scrutiny from the local and world press – though most of the facts had already been ventilated in the preliminary hearings. For the accused the shadow of the guillotine loomed large.

# 13

## LE DERNIER SET

By the same law of periodical repetition, everything that has happened once must happen again and again – and not capriciously, but at regular periods – and each thing is in its own period not another's, and each obeying its own law. The same nature which delights in period repetition in the skies is the nature which orders the affairs of the earth. Let us not underrate the value of that hint.

~ MARK TWAIN ~

**MONTE CARLO, 1907**

In October of 1907 the Goolds awaited their upcoming trial in Monte Carlo as had some years before the killers of Gouffé, Eyraud and Bompard, in Paris. Both murderous couples linked inextricably by the use of a trunk to dispose the bodies of the victims. The very horror of the crimes was defined by an inanimate object designed to carry luggage, not the remains of a human. The trunk was the object, fuelled by media reports in both cases, that most captured the imagination of the public.

Both sets of killers, a man and woman in each event, were almost superseded in the public consciousness by that pragmatic but of course entirely dramatic method of carriage: *the trunk*. Both killings were inspired by an overwhelming need and desire for quick money to sort out financial difficulties. A gamble by perpetrators whose very existence had been dependent on such an activity.

No different in essence than the motive that drives speculation in any arena, the casino and its apparently more legitimate counterpart, the stock exchange. Gamblers are exposed to the same risks in both houses, for stocks and shares forever and a day before this year were subject to the Wheel of Fortune, the spins of which were not a lot removed from the action of the roulette wheel.

Schemes were the stock-in-trade of the players, and so it was in that month that a gamble would induce a financial panic centred on the New York Stock Exchange. It was started by a stock manipulation scheme to corner the market in F. August Heinze's United Copper Company. Heinze formed a close relationship with a notorious Wall Street banker Charles W. Morse, who had once successfully cornered New York's ice market, and the couple gained control of many banks.

Suffice it to say that the activities of these two who embarked on a somewhat criminal enterprise brought the banking system to its knees ('The Panic of 1907') and required the expertise of the famous financier J.P. Morgan to save the banking system by a form of recapitalisation.

Morgan, when questioned by a congressional committee in the aftermath, got to the heart of the matter of speculation of all kinds. And by more unusual analogy, the gambling of murder although the latter was clearly not in his mind at the time. The following exchange between him and Samuel Untermyer, corporate lawyer, has become famous as an astute perception of the psychological nature of banking.

Untermyer: Is not commercial credit based primarily
upon money or property?

Morgan:     No sir, the first thing is character.

Untermyer: Before money or property?

Morgan:     Before money or anything else. Money
cannot buy it. A man I do not trust could
not get money from me on all the bonds
in Christendom.

Trust indeed is everything – that trust which Gouffé and
Levin inevitably displayed to their killers and lost the gamble
that they had taken without knowledge of the gamble of the
killers. But inevitably there was for them, like the speculators in
New York, a price to pay. That is also an innate part of periodical
repetition.

The investigative teams gathered in Monte Carlo at the
beginning of December, not expecting failure, but careful
nonetheless, of the outcome. The die in relation to the Goolds
was well cast.

Dupin was confident but just shrugged his shoulders when
asked. "We'll see. The evidence is all there, we have nothing
more to do. What more can you do?"

"Indeed," replied Garonne, "that is true. It is all left now to
the legal team."

But the confession of Goold made the verdict beyond any
doubt guilty. The trial, under the French system in which an
extensive examination in court precedes it, would prove somewhat
of an anti-climax.

The first day was uneventful, occupied as it was by
preliminary judicial matters. Some basic facts to which all
parties were familiar were ventilated. A number of witnesses
gave evidence which added little to the already well-known facts.

The male prisoner's antecedents were established. In 1866
Goold's brother James Stephen emigrated to South Australia

where for many years he led a somewhat hermetic existence as a railway ganger at Gladstone. On the death of his uncle Sir Henry Goold Bt in 1893, he became fourth baronet. There was a sister Frances who never married. There were a number of other male siblings who according to Goold's earlier evidence had died.

Mrs Goold, born Marie Violet, a daughter of Hippolyte Girodin of Château de la Sône, near Saint-Marcellin, Isère, France. Against her parents' wishes, she married a local young man. But this did not work out and a week after the wedding she left him and went to Geneva to work as a dressmaker. In 1870 she travelled to London and became a companion to an English lady. Sometime afterwards she accompanied her to India where, her husband having died in the interim, she married a Captain Wilkinson who subsequently died. Three years later in 1886, a widow again, she returned to London. She sold her jewellery and with the proceeds set herself up as a court dressmaker at 22 Hereford Road. Around this time she became acquainted with Goold and they married at the church of St Mary of the Angels, Paddington, London, on August 22nd 1891. Both gave their ages as 38.

After much interrogation Goold confessed the murder but his wife protested her innocence.

The previous October, Maître Kuneman, Vere Goold's counsel, had applied to the magistracy for an expert to examine his client's mental condition. Goold occupied himself by reading a number of religious books. He asked for a priest to be sent, so that he could make his confession. Evidence was offered of remorse on the prisoner's part.

The British consul at Marseilles requested that the case be transferred to Monte Carlo and this was agreed after the authorities established that Mrs Goold had lost her French nationality.

News travelled before them and when they arrived at Monte Carlo station they were greeted by a hostile crowd chanting "Death to them!" The trial commenced on December 2nd 1907 before Presiding Judge Baron de Rolland, assisted by two assessors and three other judges. There was a large public attendance and approaches to the court were guarded by carabinieri and police.

Among the 30 witnesses called was Mlle Isobel Girodin, the niece of the wife, who had been living with them in Monte Carlo. She stated that Goold often drank and quarrelled with his wife. Goold claimed that his wife had been an accomplice, but she strenuously denied any involvement in the actual killing.

The murdered woman was a Danish subject, Emma Levin. She had visited the Goolds to reclaim a loan but, during a furious argument, tempers rose and the woman was struck. The prosecutor Maître Allain said that the crime took place on the 4th of August at the Goold's flat in the Villa Menesini, where they had led a hand-to-mouth existence, while frequently gambling at the casino. He added that the couple sank from borrowing to stealing to murder. He produced evidence that the crime could have not been committed by one person and called for both to receive the death penalty.

❧

*Irish Times*
Wednesday, December 4th, 1907

## MONTE CARLO MURDER.
## SECOND DAY OF THE TRIAL.

*Press Association Foreign Special*

*Monte Carlo, December 3rd.*
The first part of today's sitting in the Goold case was taken up by the medical evidence. Dr Dufour, who made the post mortem examination of the remains of the murdered woman, gave the court

a catalogue of the wounds he discovered. There were, he stated, numerous contusions on the face, eight wounds on the head, four small wounds on the neck, all caused by the same instrument, and finally two deep wounds on the back. He adhered to his deduction that more than one person had taken part in the murder.

Dr Grasset who had examined Goold to ascertain his mental condition described him as intellectually degenerate and a drunkard who at times would be obstinate and at other times vacillating. What he needed was a controlling influence of a stronger mind and this he found in his wife. The witness considered Goold's responsibility for his acts slightly diminished.

A porter named Berard employed at the Marseilles railway station deposed that he was engaged by the Goolds to send off a trunk, the stench from which aroused his suspicion. A hotel waiter named Vincent gave evidence of having been requested by Goold to find him a flat in Marseilles. The prisoner also asked for packing paper.

The station commissionaire Pons who was engaged to forward the trunk also spoke of the gruesome discovery. When he noticed coagulated blood on the trunk, he reported the matter to the police and, acting on their instructions, he went to Hotel du Louvre and told Goold he must come to the railway station to register the trunk himself. Goold called a cab and forbade the witness to accompany him, offering him a bribe of 20 francs. This only confirmed his suspicions and, jumping up beside the driver, he told him to drive to the station which he did and there the fugitives were arrested.

The President of the court complimented the witness on the intelligent manner in which he had furthered the ends of justice.

The cab driver, Bizot, told how he was hailed by the prisoners in front of the hotel and engaged to drive them to the station. He confirmed the evidence of the previous witness and added that Goold told him to drive fast and gave contradictory directions as to the route he wanted to take. When he was ordered to stop, he noticed that Mrs Goold while getting out of the cab fell. Her husband seemed completely upset, but the witness could not say if he was intoxicated.

～∞～

On December 5th the *Daily Globe*, New York, boasting of scooping the *New York Times*, triumphantly published the following:

## MARIE GOOLD MUST DIE BY GUILLOTINE.

## CONVICTED AT MONTE CARLO OF MURDERING EMMA LEVIN, HER GUEST.

Lady Macbeth Reborn – Husband, Her Helper, Gets Life Sentence.

After a speedy trial at the Superior Court of Monaco, Vere St Leger Goold and his wife Marie were convicted of the murder of Emma Levin here last summer. The court found that Mrs Goold was the chief instigator of the crime and

sentenced her to death by the guillotine and that
Goold was less responsible by reason of being
under the influence of liquor at the time of the
murder. He was sentenced to imprisonment for
life.

Great crowds within and without the building
received the announcement with excitement and
applause following the rendering of the verdict.
The trial of the Goolds consumed less than three
days. It attracted attention from all over the
world. The news out of Monte Carlo is huge.

~~~

The *New York Times* treated the story with a lot more restraint,
something which of course had been entirely absent during the
whole case. A dismembered body in a trunk in the fabulous but
shady surroundings of Monte Carlo was not a murder scenario
that would exercise restraint in any age.

On the very same day as the Goold verdict was carried, the
*New York Times* reprinted an article from *The Outlook
Magazine* that placed the newspapers at the forefront of the
communications world.

> The affairs of the whole world are now spread
> before us at a moment of rapid and dramatic
> change. Nowhere has the story of real life been
> more dramatic, fuller of surprises, more
> commanding in its interest than in this country
> where the newspapers are as interesting as the
> novels . . .
>
> Sooner or later, such a tide of vitality will find
> its way into literature, but for the immediate
> spending of its energy, the newspaper offers the
> most available channel. Sooner or later, the

permanent record will take the place of the vivid, partial, inartistic but vital report of the comedy and tragedy of life; but would it not be surprising if it should appear that for the moment men are more interested in fact than fiction, more interested in the serial story told by the newspaper than in that told by the novelist?

ᴄᴗᴄᴗ

## Hawera & Normanby Star

### THE TRUNK TRAGEDY.
### GOOLDS TRIED AT MONTE CARLO.

The trial at Monte Carlo of those callous creatures Vere Goold and his wife for the cold-blooded murder of Madame Levin has ended, as it could only end, in the conviction of both. But whilst the death sentence has been passed on Madame Goold, it is not in the least likely to be carried into effect – the husband's punishment is penal servitude for life. Though condemned by her own confessions and those of her husband and by the evidence piled up remorselessly against her by the prosecution, Madame Goold seems to have been quite confident that she would be acquitted and confided to her counsel her plans for her future as a free woman.

These included an action against the court interpreter for inaccurately translating evidence and a trip to America or Australia where she intended to open up a business as a dressmaker.

During the trial, though obviously depressed,

the female Goold never once betrayed any signs of remorse, until there was talk of the death sentence. Then she broke down and sobbed aloud and later indulged in hysterical screams of "C'est terrible."

The Advocate-General, after recapitulating the unworthy lives of the prisoners, and "reconstructing" with a wealth of gory details the crime for which she was arraigned, proceeded to a dramatic denunciation of the vile woman in the dock.

"If," he cried with terrible earnestness, "crime could be punished with two deaths, you would deserve them both. You have horrified the public conscience, not only with your crime, but by your callous behaviour and cynicism." Concerning Vere Goold, the Advocate-General spoke of him with more or less contemptuous pity, as a drink and drug debauched creature, completely under the control of his wife. But he made no distinction between the prisoners when he called upon the court to sentence them.

He asked that the death penalty be passed on both. The conclusion of the prosecutor's speech elicited loud applause! This demonstration of popular feeling elicited from the President a mild rebuke. He reminded the audience that the accused were in the hands of the law and dubbed the demonstration "unseemly".

Maître Kuneman made a brave attempt to mitigate the enormity of Vere Goold's crime, expiating on his efforts to clear his wife of all responsibility for the murder. Maître Kuneman proceeded to describe the tragedy, making special point of the look Mrs Goold gave her husband at the critical moment, and the commanding effect of it, which impelled him to go into the kitchen, bring the pestle and strike the victim.

Premeditation, he urged, was not established. If Goold had wished to kill Madame Levin, a single blow would have sufficed. His only object was to stun her. Passing next to the male prisoner's mental condition, Maître Kuneman said Dr Grasset had diagnosed premature senile decay. Goold was a curious mixture of physical contrasts. He appeared to have no proper sense of the enormity of this crime and yet he was moved to tears when speaking of his wife.

After quoting several other contradictory traits of his client's character, counsel pointed out how his will had been enfeebled and his mind debased by excessive alcoholic indulgence. The medical reports were to the effect that Goold's responsibility for his acts had been "seriously attenuated" and counsel begged the judges to bear that in mind.

Maître Barbarin, Mrs Goold's counsel, admitted that the position of the prisoners was desperate. With regard to Goold's confession counsel submitted that those facts which were personal were admissible for himself but not for his wife, who denied all participation in the crime. There was no proof against her; but only presumptive evidence. He maintained, further, that there had been no premeditation.

Counsel, in conclusion, protested against the application of the death sentence, and asked the court to impose a term of imprisonment.

The Advocate-General, replying, said he neither hoped for or desired the death penalty, but a study of the dossier had convinced him of the imperious necessity, in the interests of justice, of demanding the supreme punishment in this case.

After careful examination of Dr Grasset's report, he denied that extenuating circumstances could be found. He had sought in vain for a trace of remorse in the female prisoner, and had only found selfishness. The only signs she had given was when she realised the peril in which she stood.

After two hours deliberation, the judge sentenced Goold, in whose case extenuating circumstances had been found, to penal servitude for life, and Mrs Goold to death.

In reply to Mrs Goold's cries that she was innocent, the President informed her that she had three days in which to appeal.

As the public were retiring, the condemned woman had another hysterical attack, during which she declared that she was "going to die."

∽∾

The jewellery of Madame Levin, who was murdered by the Goolds has now been sold for the benefit of her heirs. It has realised a sum of £880. The famous diamond and ruby necklace, which was broken in the struggle with her assassins fetched £640. Madame Levin, the beautiful widow of a Swedish broker had an income of £1,500 a year and much valuable jewellery which she always wore. The post mortem showed ten wounds inflicted, one pierced the heart.

∽∾

In January 1908, both of the Goolds appealed unsuccessfully against the verdict. A month later Mrs Goold's sentence was commuted to life. During April 1908 they were transferred back to Marseilles. Mrs Goold was sent to Montpellier prison while her husband was placed in the Central Prison. He was later transferred to the Île de Ré and put on a convict ship to French Guiana on July 19th 1908.

# 14

## LA MAISON DU DÉFUNT

**FRENCH GUIANA, SEPTEMBER 1909**

The tentacles of fever spread over and gripped the aching bones of his body. The memories of his earlier incarceration, so vivid at the time, had faded into a mixture of confusion and wanton forgetfulness. It was too painful, oppressive and dangerous to commit to memory. The escape was the past, also a source of suffering, but anything to escape from the present.

Within a year he was stripped of honour and friends and his background, with death hanging over him. All the worst results of his downfall in his face and in his mind. In a state of exile that no one that ever knew him could imagine. Nothing left, not even the reward of a good conscience. Worst of all, reputation is the first thing to abandon the unfortunate.

He had no reputation left as he faced death. The awful cut of what he would be remembered for. That haunted his feverish consciousness. Not the whack of his racquet over the net, putting his opponent off, running to the return and failing.

Those glorious days in Fitzwilliam and Wimbledon and Cheltenham, those sunny days of his youth.

Days when the sun seemed to shine forever, life and especially hope stretching into an infinity, when nothing of your existence would ever end. Those times you should never forget. Where fortune crowned the head without any sense of recompense. Where audacity and evil had no place to dwell, and the unhappy deserved their fate.

Grief and suffering was his fate, and probably in his case well justified. Nonetheless he sought redemption as any condemned man would. The click-clack of the roulette wheel ran through his head, a constant reminder of his love of the blind woman, the one with the veil and the inconstant wheel at her feet, his addiction to the perfidious Wheel of Fortune.

He loved her, this wife that had brought him to living hell, this house of the dead.

Boethius came back to him on this matter. With analogy.

"Thou hast found out how changeful is the face of the blind goddess; she who still veils herself from others hath discovered to thee her whole character. If thou likest her, take her as she is and do not complain. If thou abhorrest her perfidy, turn from her in disdain, renounce her, for baneful are her delusions. The very thing which is now the cause of thy great grief ought to have brought thee tranquillity."

His perfidy was beyond even his own imagination. But even after the awful event when he was gripped with tremens it never left his mind. There were men whom he was imprisoned with who displayed on the surface no sense of the consequences of the crimes they had committed. One had killed a wife, another a lover, another a father. But all had dreams and nightmares. Shouting out from their subconscious the confused details of their crimes.

He was no different. Emma Levin's deathless eyes came back

to him again and again. Staring at him. Not letting him escape. The closer he came to death, the nearer she came. *"Cut the head off, cut the head off!"* His wife's voice came into his mind. She was far away in Montpellier prison and he missed her beyond his own belief.

He cut the legs away, he cut the head away. Blood spattered everywhere. He cut, he cleaned, she cleaned but nothing would clean. It was all crazy, he felt mad in its stupid execution. Her eyes stared at him, they wouldn't close. He was drowning in her blood. He wanted to scream and his voice was silent. There was nothing. Her staring, unrelenting staring. Nothing. He screamed, nothing, nothing. The bloodstained walls said nothing.

*Other than his fate.*

*He felt the wall of darkness descending. At last. Final relief from this hell on earth. Nothing afterwards could possibly match it. His body was for the sharks. It didn't matter anymore. Nothing mattered anymore. Eternal darkness, sleep forever.*

*Or was it?*

*Click, clack, click, clack, the wheel rolled and stopped. Zero.*

Vere St Leger Goold died on 8th September 1909 in Devil's Island. The same day a telegraph was sent and received in Paris to announce the fact. His wife Marie Goold died in Montpellier prison in 1914.

# SELECTED BIBLIOGRAPHY

Belbenoit, R:
  *Dry Guillotine, Fifteen Years Among the Living Dead*
  (EF Dutton & Co, 1938)

Berlière, J-M:
  "Professionalism of the Police Under The Third Republic
  in France" 1875-1914 (in C. Emsley and B. Weinberger, eds.,
  *Policing Western Europe: Politics, Professionalism, and
  Public Order, 1850-1940*, London: Greenwood Press,
  1991)

Cohen, WB:
  *Urban Government and the Rise of the French City*
  (Palgrave Macmillan 1998)

Dostoevsky F:
  "The Gambler"

Foucault M:
  *Surveiller et Punir: Naissance de la Prison* (Vintage 1995)

Furlong, CW:
  "Cayenne – The Dry Guillotine", *Harper's Magazine*
  (1913)

Heathcote JM:
> *Tennis, Lawn Tennis, Rackets, Fives* (Ashford Press Pub.; Facsimile edition 1891)

Hyndman, HM:
> *Clemenceau: The Man and his Time* (Grant Richards, 1919)

Kidd, C; Williamson D (editors):
> *Debrett's Peerage and Baronetage* (Debrett's, 1990)

Kindleberger, C; Aliber, R:
> *Manias, Panics and Crashes: A History of Financial Crisis* (Wiley Investment Classics, 2005)

Krarup Nielsen, A:
> *Hell Beyond The Seas: A convict's story of his experiences in the French penal settlement in Guiana* (Garden City Pub Co, N.Y. 1938)

Machiavelli:
> *The Prince*

Maugham, Somerset W:
> "A Man with a Conscience" (William Heinemann 1952)

O'Connor, Ulick:
> *The Fitzwilliam Story* 1877-1977 (Publisher, Fitzwilliam Lawn Tennis Club, 1977)

Renneville, Marc:
> *La Criminologie Perdue d'Alexandre Lacassagne* (1834-1924) (Crimino Corpus, 2005)

Toth, Stephen A:
> *Beyond Papillon – The French Penal Colonies 1854-1952* (University of Nebraska Press, 2006)

## Newspapers

*The Adelaide Advertiser*

*Feilding Star*

*The Grey River Argus*

*Hawera and Normanby Star*

*The Irish Times*

*The New York Daily Globe*

*The New York Times*

*The Times*

# Also published by Poolbeg

# MURDER
## at
## SHANDY HALL

## The Coachford Poisoning Case

### MICHAEL SHERIDAN

Against a tranquil rural backdrop – the sleepy County Cork village of Dripsey near Coachford – a sensational Victorian murder is played out with a potent mix of love, lust, betrayal, and ultimately naked hatred. The entry of a young and beautiful governess into Shandy Hall, the home of a retired British Army surgeon Dr Philip Cross, acts as a catalyst for an act of horror that prompts suspicion, an exhumation, an inquest, and a charged courtroom drama that grabs newspaper headlines all over the world.

The nation is transfixed by details of a murder which shatters the Victorian ideal of the home as a safe haven of privacy and comfort, and besmirches the blue-blooded reputation of an aristocratic line.

The cast of real characters includes a cruel killer, cloaked in respectability; a beautiful and naïve governess; a blameless wife; a brilliant young pathologist; a canny and clever murder detective; two accomplished courtroom adversaries; a caring and emotional judge; and a notorious hangman.

978-1-84223-473-0

Praise for

# MURDER
## *at*
## SHANDY HALL

### MICHAEL SHERIDAN

"An absolutely **extraordinary tale**" – *Pat Kenny, Today with Pat Kenny*

"This is a scholarly and **meticulous piece of historical journalism** that will be sought out by aficionados of **true crime**" – *Irish Independent*

"When Sheridan gives full rein to his imagination ... the result is **truly spine-chilling**" – *The Examiner*

"This **intriguing story** is well told by Sheridan"
                                        – *The Sunday Business Post*

 "Michael Sheridan has unearthed another **absorbing scandal** ... meticulously researched ... forensically fashioned" – *The Sunday Times*

"All the elements you need for a **compelling mystery** ... an interesting read" – *Hotpress*

"**A cracking good yarn** and [Michael] certainly knows how to tell one of those" – *Mark Cagney, Ireland AM, TV3*

"**What more could you ask for?** ... Thoroughly researched and engagingly written, this book is **sure to send a shiver up your spine**"
                                        – *Woman's Way 'Book of the Fortnight'*

 "**Beautifully** put together" – *Dublin Country Mix*

"**Fantastic** ... Recommended" – *The Tom Dunne Show, Newstalk*